Becoming Bodhisattvas

Becoming Bodhisattvas

A Guidebook for Compassionate Action

PEMA CHÖDRÖN

Edited by Helen Berliner

SHAMBHALA
Boulder
2018

Shambhala Publications, Inc.
4720 Walnut Street
Boulder, Colorado 80301
www.shambhala.com

English translation of *The Way of the Bodhisattva* (Bodhicharyavatara)
© 1997 by the Padmakara Translation Group, reprinted with permission.

This book was previously published with the title
No Time to Lose: A Timely Guide to the Way of the Bodhisattva.

9 8 7 6 5 4 3 2 1

Printed in the United States of America

∞ This edition is printed on acid-free paper that meets the
American National Standards Institute z39.48 Standard.
♻ This book is printed on 30% postconsumer recycled paper.
For more information please visit us at www.shambhala.com.
Shambhala Publications is distributed worldwide by
Penguin Random House, Inc., and its subsidiaries.

Library of Congress Cataloging-in-Publication Data
Names: Chödrön, Pema, author. | Berliner, Helen, editor.
Title: Becoming bodhisattvas: a guidebook for
compassionate action / Pema Chödrön.
Other titles: No time to lose
Description: Boulder, Colorado: Shambhala, 2018.
This book was previously published by Shambhala
under the title *No Time to Lose*.
Includes bibliographical references and index.
Identifiers: LCCN 2018015778 | ISBN 9781611806328 (paperback)
Subjects: LCSH: Śāntideva, active 7th century. Bodhicaryāvatāra. |
Mahayana Buddhism—Doctrines. | BISAC: RELIGION / Buddhism / Tibetan. |
BODY, MIND & SPIRIT / Meditation. | SELF-HELP / Meditations.
Classification: LCC BQ3147.C56 2018 | DDC 294.3/85—dc23
LC record available at https://lccn.loc.gov/2018015778

To my teacher,

Chögyam Trungpa Rinpoche,

I bow down

Contents

People Like Us Can Make a Difference

THE WAY OF THE BODHISATTVA was composed in India over twelve centuries ago, yet it remains remarkably relevant for our times. This classic text, written by the Indian sage Shantideva, gives surprisingly up-to-date instructions for people like you and me to live sanely and openheartedly, even in a very troubled world. It is the essential guidebook for fledgling *bodhisattvas*, those spiritual warriors who long to alleviate suffering, their own and that of others. Thus it belongs to the mahayana, the school of Buddhism that emphasizes all-inclusive compassion and the cultivation of our flexible, unbiased wisdom mind.

According to tradition, to write a commentary on a text such as *The Way of the Bodhisattva* (or *Bodhicharyavatara* in Sanskrit), one must have advanced spiritual realization or have been directed in a dream to compose such a treatise. Since I unfortunately have neither qualification, I simply offer this teaching with the sincere aspiration that it may help new readers to benefit from Shantideva's text as much as I have.

My own appreciation of *The Way of the Bodhisattva* came about slowly, and only after I became familiar with Patrul Rinpoche, the great wandering yogi of nineteenth-century Tibet. From his writings and the outrageous stories told about him, I came to respect and love this man dearly. He had no fixed abode, no belongings, and was very unconventional and spontaneous in his behavior. Yet he was a powerful and very wise teacher, whose spiritual realization manifested in all the situations of his life. He related to people with great compassion and tenderness, but also with ruthless honesty.

When I discovered that Patrul Rinpoche had taught this text hundreds of times, it caught my attention. He would wander around Tibet teaching anyone who would listen: rich and poor, nomads and aristocrats, scholars and people who had never studied the Buddhist teachings. Hearing this, I thought, "If this eccentric man, this dedicated yogi, loved the text so much, there must be something to it." So I began to study it in earnest.

Some people fall in love with *The Way of the Bodhisattva* the first time they read it, but I wasn't one of them. Truthfully, without my admiration for Patrul Rinpoche, I wouldn't have pursued it. Yet once I actually started grappling with its content, the text shook me out of a deep-seated complacency, and I came to appreciate the urgency and relevance of these teachings. With Shantideva's guidance, I realized that ordinary people like us can make a difference in a world desperately in need of help.

I also began to wish for a less scholarly commentary than those available, one that might reach a wide audience and be accessible even to people who know nothing of the Buddhist teachings.

For these reasons, when I was requested to teach *The Way of the Bodhisattva* at Gampo Abbey's monastic college, I was eager to give it a try. The transcripts of those talks form the basis of this book. My commentary on Shantideva's teaching is very much a student's view and a work in progress. Unquestionably, with the help of my teachers, my understanding of these verses will deepen considerably over time; nevertheless, I am truly delighted to share my enthusiasm for Shantideva's instructions.

• • •

Shantideva was born a prince in eighth-century India and, as the eldest son, was destined to inherit the throne. In one account of the story, the night before his coronation, Shantideva had a dream in which Manjushri (the bodhisattva of wisdom) appeared to him and told him to renounce worldly life and seek ultimate truth. Thus Shantideva left home immediately, giving up the throne for the spiritual path, just as the historical Buddha had done.

In another version, the night before his enthronement, Shantideva's mother gave him a ceremonial bath using scalding water. When he asked why she was intentionally burning him, she replied, "Son, this pain is nothing compared to the pain you will suffer when you're king," and on that very night, he rapidly departed.

Whatever the catalyst, Shantideva disappeared into India and began living the life of a renunciate. Eventually he arrived at Nalanda University, which was the largest, most powerful monastery in India at the time, a place of great learning that attracted students from all over the Buddhist world. At Nalanda he was ordained a monk and given the name Shantideva, which translates as "God of Peace."

Contrary to what his later reputation suggests, Shantideva was not well liked at Nalanda. Apparently he was one of those people who didn't show up for anything, never studying or coming to practice sessions. His fellow monks said that his three "realizations" were eating, sleeping, and shitting. Finally, in order to teach him a lesson, they invited him to give a talk to the entire university. Only the best students were accorded such an honor. You had to sit on a throne and, of course, have something to say. Since Shantideva was presumed to know nothing, the monks thought he would be shamed and humiliated into leaving the university. That's one story.

Another version presents a more sympathetic view of Nalanda, whereby the monks hoped that by embarrassing Shantideva, they could motivate him to study. Nevertheless, like all sentient beings who are building a case against someone, they probably derived a certain joy from the possibility of making Shantideva squirm. It's said they tried to further humiliate him by making the throne unusually high, without providing any stairs.

To their astonishment, Shantideva had no problem getting onto the throne. He then confidently asked the assembled monks if they wanted traditional teachings or something they had never heard before. When they replied that they wanted to hear something new, he proceeded to deliver the entire *Bodhicharyavatara*, or *The Way of the Bodhisattva*.

Not only were these teachings very personal, full of useful advice, and relevant to their lives, they were also poetic and fresh. The content itself was not radical. In the very first verses, Shantideva says that everything he's about to teach derives from the lineage of the Buddha. It wasn't his subject matter that was original; it was the direct and very contemporary way he expressed the teachings, and the beauty and power of his words.

Toward the end of his presentation, Shantideva began to teach on emptiness: the unconditioned, inexpressible, dreamlike nature of all experience. As he spoke, the teachings became more and more groundless. There was less and less to hold on to, and the monks' minds opened further and further. At that point, it is said that Shantideva began to float. He levitated upward until the monks could no longer see him and could only hear his voice. Perhaps this just expresses how enraptured his audience felt. We will never know for sure. What we do know is that after Shantideva's discourse on emptiness, he disappeared. By then his disappearance probably disappointed the monks, but he never returned to Nalanda and remained a wandering yogi for the rest of his life.

• • •

The Way of the Bodhisattva is divided into ten chapters. Patrul Rinpoche organized them into three main sections based on the following verse by the great Buddhist master Nagarjuna:

> May bodhichitta, precious and sublime,
> Arise where it has not yet come to be;
> And where it has arisen may it not decline,
> But grow and flourish ever more and more.

The Sanskrit term *bodhichitta* is often translated as "awakened heart," and refers to an intense desire to alleviate suffering. On the relative level, bodhichitta expresses itself as longing. Specifically, it is the heartfelt yearning to free oneself from the pain of ignorance and habitual patterns in order to help others do the same. This longing to alleviate the suffering of others is the main point. We start close to home with the wish to help those we know and love, but the underlying inspiration is global and all encompassing. Bodhichitta is a sort of "mission impossible": the desire to end the suffering of all beings, including those we'll never meet, as well as those we loathe.

On the absolute level, bodhichitta is nondual wisdom, the vast, unbiased essence of mind. Most importantly, this is your mind—yours and mine. It may seem distant but it isn't. In fact, Shantideva composed this text to remind himself that he could contact his wisdom mind and help it to flourish.

According to Patrul Rinpoche's threefold division, the first three chapters of *The Way of the Bodhisattva* elucidate the opening lines of Nagarjuna's verse—"May bodhichitta, precious and sublime/ Arise where it has not yet come to be"—and refer to our initial longing to care for others. We yearn for this transformative quality to arise in ourselves, and in all beings, even those who have never before concerned themselves with the welfare of others. Chapter 1 offers a rhapsody on the wonders of bodhichitta. Chapter 2 prepares the mind to nurture this bodhichitta longing: as if preparing soil, we prepare the mind so the seed of bodhichitta can grow. Chapter 3 introduces us to the bodhisattva's vow, the commitment to use one's life to help others.

Sadly, we're usually so preoccupied with our own comfort and security that we don't give much thought to what others might be going through. While justifying our own prejudice and anger, we fear and denounce these qualities in others. We don't want ourselves or those we care about to suffer, yet we condone revenge on our foes. Seeing the disastrous results of this "me-first" thinking in the daily news, however, we might long for bodhichitta to arise in the hearts of men and women everywhere. Then, instead of seeking revenge, we'd want even our enemies to be at peace.

Martin Luther King Jr. exemplified this kind of longing. He knew that happiness depended on healing the *whole* situation. Taking sides—black or white, abusers or abused—only perpetuates the suffering. For me to be healed, everyone has to be healed.

The people who make a positive difference in this world have big hearts. Bodhichitta is very much awake in their minds. With the skillful means to communicate to large groups of people, they can bring about enormous change, even in those who never previously looked beyond their own needs. This is the subject of the first three chapters of *The Way of the Bodhisattva*: the initial dawning of the awakened heart.

The next line of Nagarjuna's verse, "And where it has arisen, may it not decline," corresponds to the next three chapters of *The Way of the Bodhisattva* and emphasizes the need to nurture bodhichitta. If we don't encourage it, our yearning to alleviate suffering can become dormant. While it never disappears completely, the ability to love and empathize can definitely decline.

The same is true of insight. A mere glimpse of the openness of our mind might touch us deeply. It might inspire us to start reading books like this one and awaken a feeling of urgency to do something meaningful with our lives. But if we don't nurture this inspiration, it falters. Life takes over, and we forget we ever saw things from a wider perspective. Therefore, once we feel the longing of bodhichitta, we need to be told how to proceed.

In chapters 4, 5, and 6, Shantideva describes how to work skillfully with emotional reactivity and the wildness of our minds. These are essential instructions for freeing ourselves from self-absorption, the narrow-minded reference point that my teacher Chögyam Trungpa Rinpoche called "the cocoon."

In these chapters, we are also introduced to the six *paramitas*. These are six basic ways to go beyond the false security of habitual patterns and relax with the fundamental groundlessness and unpredictability of our lives. The word *paramita* literally means "going to the other shore," going beyond the usual preconceptions that blind us to our immediate experience.

In chapter 5, Shantideva presents the *paramita* of discipline; in chapter 6, the *paramita* of patience. But this is not discipline and patience in the ordinary sense of restraint and forbearance; it's the discipline and patience that awaken our heart by dissolving deep-seated habits of negativity and selfishness.

Chapters 7, 8, and 9 illuminate the last line of Nagarjuna's verse and contain teachings that encourage bodhichitta to "grow and flourish ever more and more." Chapter 7 discusses the *paramita* of enthusiasm; chapter 8, the *paramita* of meditation; and chapter 9, the wisdom of emptiness.

In this third section, Shantideva shows us how bodhichitta can become a way of life. With his support, we could eventually enter into even the most challenging situations without losing our insight or compassion. This, of course, is a gradual learning process and we may have some relapses. But as we make the journey from fear to fearlessness, Shantideva is always there with the wisdom and encouragement we need.

After some consideration, I have decided that commentary on

the ninth chapter of *The Way of the Bodhisattva* requires a book in itself. While these teachings on the *paramita* of wisdom are important to Shantideva's overall presentation, they are far more daunting than the rest of the text. They present a philosophical debate between Shantideva's "Middle-Way" view of emptiness and the views of other Buddhist and non-Buddhist schools. Because of their complexity, I feel it would be best to present them separately and at a future time. For now, I refer you to the excellent explanation in the introduction to the Padmakara translation of the *The Way of the Bodhisattva,* and to His Holiness the Dalai Lama's book *Transcendent Wisdom.*

In the tenth and final chapter Shantideva—wholeheartedly and with great passion—dedicates the benefit of his teachings to all suffering beings, whoever and wherever they may be.

• • •

I regard this text as an instruction manual for extending ourselves to others, a guidebook for compassionate action. We can read it to free ourselves from crippling habits and confusion. We can read it to encourage our wisdom and compassion to grow stronger. And we can read it with the motivation to share the benefit with everyone we meet.

This is the spirit: read *The Way of the Bodhisattva* with the intention of accepting and digesting all that rings true. Not everything will inspire you. You might find the language challenging, and you might sometimes feel provoked or offended. But remember that Shantideva's unwavering intention is to encourage us. He never doubts that we have the strength and basic goodness to help others, and he tells us everything he has learned about how to do this. Then, of course, it's up to us to use this information and make it real.

Personally, I am indebted to Shantideva for his determination to get this message across: people like you and me *can* transform our lives by awakening the longing of bodhichitta. And I am deeply grateful to him for expressing, unrelentingly, that it is urgent, very urgent, that we do so. We have no time to lose. When I look at the state of the world today, I know his message could not possibly be more timely.

> And now as long as space endures,
> As long as there are beings to be found,
> May I continue likewise to remain
> To drive away the sorrows of the world.

—*The Way of the Bodhisattva,* v. 10.55

Becoming Bodhisattvas

Developing a Clear Intention

The Excellence of Bodhichitta

T HE FIRST CHAPTER of the *Bodhicharyavatara* is an extended praise of bodhichitta. Shantideva starts on a positive note: we can connect with the very best of ourselves and help others to do the same. Bodhichitta is a basic human wisdom that can drive away the sorrows of the world.

Bodhi means "awake"; free from ordinary, confused mind, free from the illusion that we're separate from one another. *Chitta* means "heart" or "mind." According to Shantideva and the Buddha before him, the unbiased mind and good heart of bodhi hold the key to happiness and peace.

Shantideva begins his teaching with a traditional four-part opening. First, he expresses his gratitude and respect. Second, he makes a commitment to complete his presentation. Third, he expresses humility; and in verse 3, he rouses confidence. This formal beginning was very familiar to the monks of Nalanda, but its personal touch and freshness made it unique.

1.1

To those who go in bliss, the Dharma they have
mastered, and to all their heirs,
To all who merit veneration, I bow down.
According to tradition, I shall now in brief describe
The entrance to the bodhisattva discipline.

These opening lines pay homage to the "Three Jewels": the Buddha, dharma, and sangha. In the standard formula, the historical Buddha is regarded as an example or role model. The dharma refers to his teachings, and the sangha to the monastic practitioners and advanced bodhisattvas. Here however, Shantideva takes our understanding of the Three Jewels deeper.

Those who go in bliss naturally includes the buddhas, but it also refers to our own potential. We, too, can free ourselves from the hopes and fears of self-centeredness. The bliss of perceiving reality without these limitations is our birthright. Thus Shantideva doesn't bow down to something outside himself, but to his own capacity for enlightenment. He venerates those who have realized what remains possible for us all.

The Dharma they have mastered refers not only to written and oral teachings, but also to the truth of direct experience, to straightforward, unedited life as it is. Whatever happens to us— good, bad, happy, or sad—can free us from self-absorption. If we make use of these ever-present opportunities, then everything we encounter is dharma.

All their heirs refers to the mature sangha with its great sanity and compassion, but also includes aspiring bodhisattvas. All of us willing to move beyond our self-importance and find ways to care for each other are considered the Buddha's heirs.

Finally, to express his gratitude to *all who merit veneration,* he bows to the teachers and friends who have helped him along the path.

As the second step in this traditional opening, Shantideva presents his subject and commits to complete his teaching without obstacles. Moreover, he will do this *according to tradition,* presenting what he's learned and understood from the Buddha, dharma, sangha, and his other teachers as well.

We can't overestimate the power of commitment. Until we resolve unequivocally to undertake a task and see it through to the end, there is always hesitation and vacillation. Remember that Shantideva had been invited to give this talk by monks who were trying to humiliate him. Considering his audience, it's possible that he had some trepidation. Therefore, he calls on an egoless courage that is not easily threatened and goes forward.

1.2

What I have to say has all been said before,
And I am destitute of learning and of skill with words.
I therefore have no thought that this might be of benefit
    to others;
I wrote it only to sustain my understanding.

Invoking a humility that is also traditional, Shantideva expresses a clear understanding of the danger of arrogance. He knows that even if the Buddha were sitting in front of him, it would do him no good if his mind were filled with pride.

Humility, however, should not be confused with low self-esteem. When Shantideva says he is *destitute of learning and of skill with words,* he is not expressing self-contempt. The low self-esteem so common in the West rests on a fixed idea of personal inadequacy. Shantideva is committed to not getting trapped in such limiting identities. He is simply humble enough to know where he gets stuck, and intelligent enough to realize he has the tools to free himself.

In the final lines of this verse, Shantideva explains that he originally composed this narrative as a personal encouragement, never dreaming that he'd be sharing it with others.

1.3

My faith will thus be strengthened for a little while,
That I might grow accustomed to this virtuous way.
But others who now chance upon my words,
May profit also, equal to myself in fortune.

In verse 3, Shantideva completes the traditional opening by rousing confidence. To compose this text and live by its words brings him great joy. The thought that his self-reflections might now profit others makes him even happier.

In this spirit of gladness and gratitude, Shantideva begins his main presentation.

1.4

So hard to find such ease and wealth
Whereby to render meaningful this human birth!
If now I fail to turn it to my profit,
How could such a chance be mine again?

From the Buddhist point of view, human birth is very precious. Shantideva assumes that we understand this preciousness, with its relative *ease and wealth*. He urges us to contemplate our good situation and not to miss this chance to do something meaningful with our lives.

This life is, however, a brief and fading window of opportunity. None of us knows what will happen next. As I've grown older with my sangha brothers and sisters, I've seen many friends die or experience dramatic changes in their health or mental stability. Right now, even though our lives may seem far from perfect, we have excellent circumstances. We have intelligence, the availability of teachers and teachings, and at least some inclination to study and meditate. But some of us will die before the year is up; and in the next five years, some of us will be too ill or in too much pain to concentrate on a Buddhist text, let alone live by it.

Moreover, many of us will become more distracted by worldly pursuits—for two, ten, twenty years or the rest of our lives—and no longer have the leisure to free ourselves from the rigidity of self-absorption.

In the future, outer circumstances such as war or violence might become so pervasive that we won't have time for honest self-reflection. This could easily happen. Or, we might fall into the trap of too much comfort. When life feels so pleasurable, so luxurious and cozy, there is not enough pain to turn us away from worldly seductions. Lulled into complacency, we become indifferent to the suffering of our fellow beings.

The Buddha assures us that our human birth is ideal, with just the right balance of pleasure and pain. The point is not to squander this good fortune.

1.5

As when a flash of lightning rends the night,
And in its glare shows all the dark black clouds had hid,
Likewise rarely, through the buddhas' power,
Virtuous thoughts rise, brief and transient, in the
    world.

1.6

Thus behold the utter frailty of goodness!
Except for perfect bodhichitta,
There is nothing able to withstand
The great and overwhelming strength of evil.

In verses 5 and 6, the initial arising of bodhichitta is described as transient and frail. The mahayana teachings usually tell us that it's *neurosis* that is transient and insubstantial, like clouds in a clear blue sky. When we're having our emotional upheavals, the buddhas and bodhisattvas don't see us as stupid or hopeless; they see our confusion as mere troubled weather, ephemeral and fleeting, passing through our skylike mind.

But verses 5 and 6 are not from the point of view of the buddhas and bodhisattvas; they're from our point of view. We are the ones who feel stuck behind the clouds: maybe we don't have what it takes; maybe we're too weak. Even with the occasional glimpse of sky, it all seems too hard, too painful. We hear this kind of talk often, coming from our own mouths as well as from others'.

Instead of experiencing our hang-ups as solid and everlasting, rather than definitely believing they're "me," we *could* say, "This is just weather, it will pass. This is not the fundamental state." From Shantideva's perspective, these glimpses of bodhi mind have great power. Everyone knows what it's like for the clouds to part, even briefly, and to feel a sense of potential and possibility. Without this initial or ongoing flash, we'd never be inspired to investigate this path.

1.7

The mighty buddhas, pondering for many ages,
Have seen that this, and only this, will save
The boundless multitudes,
And bring them easily to supreme joy.

Shantideva knows that we can trust these glimpses of bodhichitta and that by recognizing and nurturing them, these glimpses will grow. The awakened ones, *pondering for many ages*, have seen that only this good heart of bodhi can keep us from getting hooked in the same old, self-centered ways.

At this point we might ask why bodhichitta has such power. Perhaps the simplest answer is that it lifts us out of self-centeredness and gives us a chance to leave dysfunctional habits behind. Moreover, everything we encounter becomes an opportunity to develop the outrageous courage of the bodhi heart.

When we get hit hard, we look outward and see how other people also have difficult times. When we feel lonely or angry or depressed, we let these dark moods link us with the sorrows of others.

We share the same reactivity, the same grasping and resisting. By aspiring for all beings to be free of their suffering, we free ourselves from our own cocoons and life becomes bigger than "me." No matter how dark and gloomy or joyful and uplifted our lives are, we can cultivate a sense of shared humanity.

This expands our whole perspective. Trungpa Rinpoche used to say, "The essence of the mahayana is thinking bigger." Shantideva presents that essence. His teachings are a guide to compassionate living and bigger thinking.

1.8

Those who wish to overcome the sorrows of their lives,
And put to flight the pain and suffering of beings,
Those who wish to win such great beatitude,
Should never turn their back on bodhichitta.

When Shantideva mentions *those who wish to overcome the sorrows of their lives,* he addresses the foundation teachings of Buddhism, which emphasize the cessation of personal suffering. When he talks of putting *to flight the pain and suffering of beings,* he points to the mahayana intention to free everyone without exception from pain.

Of course, he isn't saying: "I'll just look after others. It doesn't matter that I'm unhappy and constantly worried, or that I hate myself and my temper is out of control." There's no question that we want to end our own suffering. But the shift in mahayana Buddhism is this: we want to end our personal suffering so we can help others put an end to theirs. This is Shantideva's strongest message and the essence of bodhichitta.

Most of us want to share what we've understood with others. Yet in trying to do this, we see even more clearly the work that still needs to be done on ourselves. At some point, we realize that what we do for ourselves benefits others, and what we do for others benefits us. This is what Shantideva means when he says that those who wish to win great happiness *should never turn their back on bodhichitta.*

1.9

Should bodhichitta come to birth
In one who suffers in the dungeons of samsara,
In that instant he is called the buddhas' heir,
Worshipful alike to gods and men.

A pithy explanation of the Sanskrit word *samsara* is Albert Einstein's definition of insanity: "Doing the same thing over and over and thinking we'll get different results." Shantideva describes this as being caught in *the dungeons of samsara.* Nevertheless, even when we feel trapped in repetitive habits, we can feel kindness and empathy for others. When even a momentary flash of bodhichitta is born, in that instant we become a child of the buddhas and worthy of universal respect.

This verse, according to Dzongsar Khyentse Rinpoche, may be a critique of Hindu society. Shantideva is saying that we don't have to be from a certain caste to experience bodhichitta; even those considered "untouchables" are the buddhas' heirs.

Bodhichitta is not some elitist theory for sophisticated or well-educated people. It's for everyone. We don't ever have to feel we're too hopeless to call on bodhichitta; nor can we look scornfully at others and label them too frivolous or arrogant to qualify. Everyone in the dungeons of samsara is a candidate for awakening a compassionate heart.

1.10

For like the supreme substance of the alchemists,
It takes the impure form of human flesh
And makes of it the priceless body of a buddha.
Such is bodhichitta: we should grasp it firmly!

1.11

If the perfect leaders of all migrant beings
Have with boundless wisdom seen its priceless worth,
We who wish to leave our nomad wandering
Should hold well to this precious bodhichitta.

1.12

All other virtues, like the plantain tree,
Produce their fruit, but then their force is spent.
Alone the marvelous tree of bodhichitta
Will bear its fruit and grow unceasingly.

1.13

As though they pass through perils guarded by a hero,
Even those weighed down with dreadful wickedness
Will instantly be freed through having bodhichitta.
Who then would not place his trust in it?

1.14

Just as by the fires at the end of time,
Great sins are utterly consumed by bodhichitta.
Thus its benefits are boundless,
As the Wise and Loving Lord explained to Sudhana.

In this section Shantideva gives six analogies for bodhichitta.
The first, in verse 10, is alchemy. Bodhichitta can use anything—
any ordinary thought, deed, or word—to ventilate our self-
absorption. In verses 11 through 14, the analogies are a priceless
jewel, a wish-fulfilling tree, a hero, and the fire at the end of time.
The sixth analogy is a kind of etcetera, which refers to a Buddhist
scripture where many other analogies are described.

The *perfect leaders* in verse 11 are the buddhas and bodhisattvas.
Like experienced ship captains in search of gems, they know the
priceless worth of a good jewel when they see it. Sailors trust these
captains and associate them with wealth; with them, they might
make their fortunes and leave their *nomad wandering*. Shantideva
says we can have the same confidence. Like sailors who trust their
captain's knowledge, we can trust the Buddha's evaluation of *precious bodhichitta.*

In verse 12, bodhichitta is compared to a wish-fulfilling tree that
produces fruit forever. By contrast, the plantain tree bears fruit
only once before it dies. Likewise, helping someone is always a
good thing and will bear fruit in a limited way. But if our help is
motivated by the longing to free this person from confusion altogether, it will bear fruit until they attain enlightenment. A simple
act of kindness with bodhichitta intention can open us to this expansive possibility.

The analogy in verse 13 is a hero, comparable to a good friend
who keeps us out of trouble. The *perils* refer to the ripening of our
negative karmic seeds. When we use these difficult situations for

opening up instead of shutting down, it's like being accompanied by a protector.

In verse 14, the comparison is to a great fire that burns up negative tendencies. Ordinarily we buy into our negative habits, acting them out or turning them against ourselves. Either way, we make them stronger.

Bodhisattvas practice "in the middle of the fire." This means they enter into the suffering of the world; it also means they stay steady with the fire of their own painful emotions. They neither act them out nor repress them. They are willing to stay "on the dot" and explore an emotion's ungraspable qualities and fluid energies—and to let that experience link them to the pain and courage of others.

The sixth analogy refers to a Buddhist scripture in which a future buddha, called Maitreya, gave 230 other examples of bodhichitta to his disciple Sudhana.

1.15

Bodhichitta, the awakening mind,
In brief is said to have two aspects:
First, aspiring, *bodhichitta in intention;*
Then, *active bodhichitta,* practical engagement.

1.16

Wishing to depart and setting out upon the road,
This is how the difference is conceived.
The wise and learned thus should understand
This difference, which is ordered and progressive.

Here Shantideva presents the two aspects of relative bodhichitta: aspiration and action. Aspiring, or intentional, bodhichitta is like wishing to take a trip; active bodhichitta is actually setting out on the journey. We first aspire to attain enlightenment and benefit others, then we do whatever it takes to make this a reality.

To give a mundane example: let's say you're stuck in grasping or craving; you know that you collect and hoard, that you panic when something's taken from you or you have to let it go. How do you work with unreasonable attachment, for your own sake and the happiness of others?

One way would be to cultivate generosity. At the level of aspiration bodhichitta, you might look around your room for something you love. Then, visualize giving it away: your beautiful red sweater, that special book, or the chocolate you're hoarding under your bed. You don't have to literally give it away, just visualize this. Then expand the offering to include millions of sweaters, books, or chocolates. Send these out to particular individuals or into the universe for anyone to receive.

In this way, aspiration bodhichitta accomplishes two things: it fulfills our wish to lessen the pain of self-absorption and our wish to benefit others. Moreover, if we aspire for others to experience not only our gifts but also the joys of an unfettered mind, our intention becomes vaster still.

Intention bodhichitta is a powerful way to work with situations we don't feel ready to handle. For example, by simply aspiring to give away something we're attached to, we train our fearful mind to let go. Then active bodhichitta—in this case, the ability to literally *give*—will come about in time.

If we equate "giving" with "freedom from craving," then we become more eager to act, even if it causes some pain.

1.17

Bodhichitta in intention bears rich fruit
For those still wandering in samsara.

And yet a ceaseless stream of merit does not flow
    from it;
For this will rise alone from *active bodhichitta.*

1.18

For when, with irreversible intent,
The mind embraces bodhichitta,
Willing to set free the endless multitudes of beings,
At that instant, from that moment on,

1.19

A great and unremitting stream,
A strength of wholesome merit,
Even during sleep and inattention,
Rises equal to the vastness of the sky.

Aspiration bodhichitta brings enormous benefit. For those of us wandering in samsara, it *bears rich fruit.* We can see why this would follow. At the level of intention, we begin with what's manageable and let our understanding evolve. By the time we're able to act on our intention, we have realized something profound: we've understood that selfless action liberates *us* from fear and sorrow.

In verses 18 and 19, Shantideva explains that our intention to free all beings from suffering can become irreversible, bringing benefit *equal to the vastness of the sky.* This happens when we no longer question the wisdom of thinking of others; we truly know this to be the source of indestructible happiness. Something shifts at the core of our being, and when it does, we experience a ceaseless flow of benefit *even during sleep and inattention.*

This is the happiness of egolessness. It's the joy of realizing there is no prison; there are only very strong habits, and no sane reason for strengthening them further. In essence these habits are insubstantial. Moreover, there is no solid self-identity or separateness. We've invented it all. It is this realization that we want for *the endless multitudes of beings.*

1.20

> This the Tathagata,
> In the sutra Subahu requested,
> Said with reasoned demonstration,
> Teaching those inclined to lesser paths.

Here, Shantideva tells us that the Buddha gave this teaching on the merits of bodhichitta to people *inclined to lesser paths,* those primarily seeking freedom from their personal pain. In this sutra, requested by his disciple Subahu, the Buddha was inspiring them to take the next step and awaken bodhichitta.

His reasoning goes like this: sentient beings are as countless as grains of sand in the Ganges. Because there are more than the mind can grasp, the wish to save them all is equally inconceivable. By making such an aspiration, our ordinary, confused mind stretches far beyond its normal capacity; it stretches limitlessly. When we expand our personal longing for liberation to include immeasurable numbers of beings, the benefit we receive is equally immeasurable.

In short, the more we connect with the inconceivable, indescribable vastness of mind, the more joyful we will be.

1.21

> If with kindly generosity
> One merely has the wish to soothe
> The aching heads of other beings,
> Such merit knows no bounds.

1.22

No need to speak, then, of the wish
To drive away the endless pain
Of each and every living being,
Bringing them unbounded virtues.

This is the logic of the mahayana. If it's wonderful for one person's headache to be soothed, then even better if everyone's headaches could be relieved.

Of course, when our wish becomes immeasurable, it could create a dilemma. Would-be bodhisattvas who take the teachings too literally might say: "There's no way to eliminate the headaches of all beings! What are we going to do? Send everyone in the world an aspirin?"

On the other hand, there is the response of Bernard Glassman Roshi, who worked with the homeless in Yonkers, New York. He said that he knew there was no way to end homelessness, yet he would devote his life to trying. This is the aspiration of a bodhisattva. Don't worry about results; just open your heart in an inconceivably big way, in that limitless way that benefits everyone you encounter. Don't worry whether or not it's doable. The intention is vast: may everyone's physical pain be relieved and, even more to the point, may everyone attain enlightenment.

1.23

Could our fathers or our mothers
Ever have so generous a wish?
Do the very gods, the rishis, even Brahma
Harbor such benevolence as this?

1.24

For in the past they never,
Even in their dreams, conceived
Such profit even for themselves.
How could they have such aims for others' sake?

Our mothers and fathers may be very kind. But even though they raise us and want what's best for us, can they free us from our habitual patterns? More importantly, do they aspire for all beings without exception to be equally free? In verse 23, Shantideva makes another reference to the Hindu religion by asking if even the *rishis* (venerated sages) or Brahma (the creator of the universe) would have such an aspiration as this.

In these verses, Shantideva refers indirectly to the caste system in which some people are worthy of awakening and others, because of their bad karma, are not. If even the gods and *rishis* think like this, how could they wish for others to be free from biased mind?

1.25

For beings do not wish their own true good,
So how could they intend such good for others' sake?
This state of mind so precious and so rare
Arises truly wondrous, never seen before.

When Shantideva talks about those who *do not wish their own true good,* he's referring to most of us. Working with habitual patterns is not usually our priority. Most of us are not impassioned about deescalating our emotions and prejudices or awakening bodhichitta. This *true good* is not our main focus. We'd simply like to get through the day without mishap, and we definitely don't want to be bothered with those who give us grief. Yet without the aspiration for freedom, how could we want this for others? We can only wish for them what we value for ourselves.

This opportunity to awaken bodhichitta is *so precious and so rare.* To experience something that liberates us from the narrow-mindedness of our biases and preconceptions is, as Shantideva says, *truly wondrous.* What's more, there is no one who cannot experience this, if they're willing to give it a try.

1.26

The pain-dispelling draft,
This cause of joy for those who wander through the
    world—
This precious attitude, this jewel of mind,
How shall it be gauged or quantified?

What is comparable to this *pain-dispelling draft*? This excellent medicine of bodhichitta frees us from self-centeredness, bringing us relief and a loving heart.

This cause of joy is found by *those who wander through the world.* Even we baby bodhisattvas don't design our lives to escape the chaos of the world; we go into the thick of things and work with whatever we find. Samsara becomes our practice ground, our boot camp, so to speak. If we find we continually get hooked into the drama, we temporarily retreat to work on ourselves. But our passion is to alleviate ever greater depths of suffering and meet ever greater challenges with equanimity.

1.27

For if the simple thought to be of help to others
Exceeds in worth the worship of the buddhas,
What need is there to speak of actual deeds
That bring about the weal and benefit of beings?

1.28

For beings long to free themselves from misery,
But misery itself they follow and pursue.
They long for joy, but in their ignorance
Destroy it, as they would a hated enemy.

Again Shantideva praises the benefits of an ordinary, altruistic thought, while adding how much greater it is to actually follow through. To help others at the most meaningful level, however, we first address our own confusion.

As Shantideva points out, although we long to free ourselves from misery, it is *misery itself we follow and pursue.* We may assume we do crazy things intentionally, but in truth these actions aren't always volitional. Our conditioning is sometimes so deep that we cause harm without even realizing it. We long for joy and do the very things that destroy our peace of mind. Again and again, we unwittingly make matters worse. If we're going to help other people get free, we have to work compassionately with our own unfortunate tendencies. Shantideva, we will find, is an expert on dismantling these repeating patterns.

1.29

But those who fill with bliss
All beings destitute of joy,
Who cut all pain and suffering away
From those weighed down with misery,

1.30

Who drive away the darkness of their ignorance—
What virtue could be matched with theirs?
What friend could be compared to them?
What merit is there similar to this?

Verses 29 and 30 refer indirectly to the *paramita* of generosity, the generosity that frees us from stress and selfishness. According to the teachings, there are three types of generosity, three ways of helping others by giving of ourselves.

The first kind of generosity is the giving of material things, such as food and shelter.

The second is "giving the gift of fearlessness." We help those who are afraid. If someone is scared of the dark, we give them a flashlight; if they're going through a fearful time, we comfort them; if they're having night terrors, we sleep next to them. This may sound easy, but it takes time and effort and care.

The third kind of generosity drives away the darkness of ignorance. This is "the gift of dharma" and is considered the most profound. Although no one can eliminate our ignorance but ourselves, nevertheless, through example and through teachings, we can inspire and support one another.

The inconceivable wish to help all sentient beings always begins with oneself. Our own experience is the only thing we have to share. Other than that, we can't pretend to be more awake or more compassionate than we actually are. Much of our realization comes from the honest recognition of our foibles. The inability to measure up to our own standards is decidedly humbling. It allows us to empathize with other people's difficulties and mistakes.

In short, the best friend is one who realizes our sameness and is skilled in helping us help ourselves.

1.31

If they who do some good, in thanks
For favors once received, are praised,
Why need we speak of bodhisattvas—
Those who freely benefit the world?

1.32

Those who, scornfully with condescension,
Give, just once, a single meal to others—
Feeding them for only half a day—
Are honored by the world as virtuous.

1.33

What need is there to speak of those
Who constantly bestow on boundless multitudes
The peerless joy of blissful buddhahood,
The ultimate fulfillment of their hopes?

Verse 32 refers to the Indian custom of formalized giving. If once a day, week, or month one gives meals to beggars, one is seen as a virtuous member of society. Thus Shantideva addresses giving with an agenda.

Most of us living in cities with homeless people do this. We come up with a plan—like giving to the first person who asks us—in hope of relieving our guilt for the rest of the day. Of course, giving in this way is beneficial, but we could definitely stretch further. When we give money to homeless men and women, we could aspire for them to be free of all their pain. We could aspire to extend our own comfort and happiness to them and to homeless people everywhere. Even more to the point, we could recognize how much we have in common and give freely without resentment or condescension.

Even in the very early stages of practicing aspiration bodhichitta, we can include all beings. If *bestowing on boundless multitudes the peerless joy of blissful buddhahood* seems a bit beyond you, just keep it real. When we get sick, for example, we don't usually think of the sickness of others. But that shift can happen: when you fall ill, you could think of others in the same boat. Even getting into a soothing bath could bring you out of your cocoon. Count-less people don't have such comfort: people who are freezing and longing for warmth, people who are exhausted and have no way to relax. We can aspire for all beings to be free of their suffering and to enjoy the pleasures we ourselves enjoy.

The last three verses address the proper treatment of a bodhi-sattva.

1.34

And those who harbor evil in their minds
Against such lords of generosity, the Buddha's heirs,
Will stay in hell, the Mighty One has said,
For ages equal to the moments of their malice.

1.35

By contrast, good and virtuous thoughts
Will yield abundant fruits in greater measure.
Even in adversity, the bodhisattvas
Never bring forth evil—only an increasing stream of
    goodness.

1.36

To them in whom this precious sacred mind
Is born—to them I bow!
I go for refuge in that source of happiness
That brings its very enemies to perfect bliss.

In verse 34, we have the first mention of hell. As a child, I was taught that hell was the ultimate punishment. This is where you were sent when you died if you were really, really bad. I'm glad to report this isn't the view here. To understand this reference from a Buddhist perspective, we look to cause and effect and the way we continually imprint our minds. We sow the seeds of our future hells or happiness by the way we open or close our minds right now.

The all-consuming hells described graphically in many Tibetan texts do not exist apart from the minds of the beings who experience them. For instance, in his final dedication, Shantideva refers to *those whose hell it is to fight and wound.* The idea here is that when we intentionally harm another, particularly someone dedicated to benefiting others, the long-term consequences of our cruelty will be experienced as hellish outer circumstances. It is our own aggression that hurts us. It's not that we're punished and sent to hell; hell is the manifestation of a vindictive mind.

It is also important to understand what Shantideva means by *those who harbor evil in their minds.* The key word here is "harbor." Harboring hatred toward anyone produces an anguished frame of mind. We remain in this hellish state *for ages equal to the moments of our wrath*—in other words, for as long as we hold on to our hatred, instead of letting it go.

Virtuous thoughts, on the other hand, bring us happiness. Instead of separating us and making us feel more cut off and afraid, they bring us closer to others.

In verse 35, Shantideva says that *even in adversity* bodhisattvas bring forth only goodness. Frequently, in times of adversity we become afraid, striking out in anger or indulging in various addictions, in hope of escaping our pain. Shantideva says that bodhisattvas let the suffering of adversity soften them and make them kinder, and that we could aspire to do the same.

This bodhisattva path takes some work. Our habitual patterns are very entrenched. Nevertheless, when hard times make us more selfish and withdrawn, we could see this as our moment of truth. Transformation can occur right in this painful place. Instead of the *evil* of more neurosis and harshness, adversity can bring about humility and empathy. By bringing us to our knees, so to speak, it can tenderize us and make us more capable of reaching out to others.

In the last verse, Shantideva bows to all of us who are willing to awaken bodhichitta; and he bows to bodhichitta itself, *the source of happiness that brings its very enemies to perfect bliss.*

These closing words may seem to contradict verse 34, with its hellish consequences for those who act aggressively. But from the point of view of the awakened ones, happiness can come even to those who *harbor evil in their minds.* As a result of our compassionate intentions, even our "enemies" can be liberated from self-absorption and thus attain enlightenment.

Knowing where the root of happiness lies saves us from escalating pain. If someone insults you, for instance, you may long to retaliate, but you know this won't benefit anyone. Instead, in the very grip of wanting to get even, you can say to yourself, "May the rage that I feel toward this person cause both of us to be liberated."

This is the aspiration of a young bodhisattva, one in the process of learning to let go. Even if we don't genuinely *feel* it, we're able to say, "May this seemingly negative connection be our link to waking up."

Preparing the Ground

Confession

I HAVE OFTEN WONDERED how the first glimmers of bodhichitta come about. How do any of us go from being completely self-absorbed in the "dungeons of samsara" to connecting with even a glimpse of the longing and vast perspective of bodhichitta?

In chapter 2 of *The Way of the Bodhisattva*, Shantideva introduces the "sevenfold offerings," seven practices that prepare the mind and heart for awakening. These are traditional methods for gathering merit. Shantideva begins in verse 1 with the practice of making offerings.

2.1

To the buddhas, those thus gone,
And to the sacred Law, immaculate, supreme, and rare,
And to the Buddha's offspring, oceans of good qualities,
That I might gain this precious attitude, I make a perfect
offering.

This practice consists of three parts: the special object of offering, the special intention, and the special offerings themselves.

The special object is the Three Jewels: the buddhas; the dharma, or *sacred Law;* and the sangha, or community of the *Buddha's offspring.* The point here is the resonance of wakefulness: the wakefulness that is seemingly "out there" resonating with the wakefulness that is seemingly "in here." Thus, veneration of *any* example of wisdom summons our own openness and brings out our best.

The special intention of making offerings is to *gain the precious attitude* of bodhichitta. We do this practice with the clear intention of awakening the bodhi heart. For example, when we're feeling inadequate or closed-hearted, we could uplift ourselves with the simple but potent gesture of mentally offering the most pleasing and beautiful things in our lives. Shantideva, as we'll soon see, is passionate about this practice. He enthusiastically offers all the beauty he perceives in the world; he offers himself; and he offers elaborate visualizations of the best gifts imaginable.

When we make offerings of real value, the act of giving so runs against the grain of our habitual selfishness that the effect is liberating. Giving enables us to let go of those attachments that increase our vulnerability and fear. In this way, the practice ventilates the claustrophobia of self-absorption and moves us closer to the generous mind of bodhichitta.

By making offerings to the buddhas, bodhisattvas, and other objects of veneration, we connect not only with our expansiveness but also with the warmth of devotion and love. By making offerings to those who are suffering and in need of help, we gain access to our tenderness and compassion. So this seemingly simple practice of giving—opening up and letting go—can be profoundly transformative.

Whatever moves us beyond self-centeredness sows positive seeds in our mind-stream. With the right causes and conditions, these seeds will blossom into fortunate circumstances. This good fortune is called "merit" and manifests as supportive outer conditions and mental states. The ultimate merit comes from connecting with the unbiased clarity of our mind.

When we side with our sanity instead of the small-mindedness of self-absorption, we gather merit. This is a heartfelt way of making friends with one's self. Trungpa Rinpoche once said, "The person who collects the most merit has to be humble and willing to give, rather than willing to collect." In this spirit, with the intention to gather merit and with the longing to experience bodhichitta, Shantideva performs these seven practices.

2.2

I offer every fruit and flower
And every kind of healing medicine;
And all the precious things the world affords,
With all pure waters of refreshment;

2.3

Every mountain, rich and filled with jewels;
All sweet and lonely forest groves;
The trees of heaven, garlanded with blossom,
And branches heavy, laden with their fruit;

2.4

The perfumed fragrance of the realms of gods
    and men;
All incense, wishing trees, and trees of gems;
All crops that grow without the tiller's care
And every sumptuous object worthy to be offered;

2.5

Lakes and meres adorned with lotuses,
All plaintive with the sweet-voiced cries of water birds
And lovely to the eyes, and all things wild and free,
Stretching to the boundless limits of the sky;

2.6

I hold them all before my mind, and to the supreme
    buddhas
And their heirs will make a perfect gift of them.
O, think of me with love, compassionate lords;
Sacred objects of my prayers, accept these offerings.

2.7

For I am empty-handed, destitute of merit,
I have no other wealth. But you, protectors,
You whose thoughts are for the good of others,
In your great power, accept this for my sake.

These first offerings of nature's bounty—fruits and flowers, water, mountains, trees—can't be "owned." They could be made by the poorest of the poor. We could offer the sky, the sound of birdsong, or the pleasure of seeing a sunrise. Like Shantideva, we could joyfully make vast and wondrous offerings of everything we see, hear, taste, and smell, and *every sumptuous object* we enjoy.

By seizing those moments of delight, we always have a precious gift on hand. Even if we're living in the streets—*empty-handed, destitute of merit, and with no other wealth*—we are rich with priceless gifts. Because we appreciate the world and perceive its available abundance, we can offer this to others. Instead of desirable things becoming objects of greed, we turn them into vehicles of liberation by using them to make the best of offerings.

2.8

The buddhas and their bodhisattva children—
I offer them myself throughout my lives.
Supreme courageous ones, accept me totally.
For with devotion I will be your servant.

2.9

For if you will accept me, I will be
A benefit to all, and freed from fear.
I'll go beyond the evils of my past,
And ever after turn my face from them.

In verses 8 and 9, Shantideva offers himself. His reasoning is practical: anything that lures us out of self-centeredness bodes well. At the everyday level, we can literally offer ourselves. In a meeting, for instance, someone might say, "We need an extra person to work late." When we feel the familiar tug of resistance, we could offer ourselves, even though it takes a leap. Once we determine to free ourselves from our fear-based habits, opportunities to practice will arise everywhere.

Of course, Shantideva is not addressing coworkers or friends; he's addressing the buddhas and bodhisattvas. Yet in truth, we're not doing this for the buddhas. When Shantideva offers himself to those who embody wisdom and compassion, *he* is the one who will benefit. The buddhas don't need us to be their servants. On the other hand, who wouldn't rejoice to see us lightening up and becoming less stingy and possessive?

Making offerings frees us from the pain of self-absorption. Are we willing to offer something as precious as our time, energy, and anything else we're hanging onto? Are we willing to loosen up habits of selfishness, fear, and small-mindedness? If so, we can benefit greatly from this practice.

2.10

A bathing chamber excellently fragrant,
With floors of crystal, radiant and clear,
With graceful pillars shimmering with gems,
All hung about with gleaming canopies of pearls—

2.11

There the blissful buddhas and their heirs
I'll bathe with many a precious vase,
Abrim with water, sweet and pleasant,
All to frequent strains of melody and song.

2.12

With cloths of unexampled quality,
With peerless, perfumed towels I will dry them
And offer splendid scented clothes,
Well dyed and of surpassing excellence.

2.13

With different garments, light and supple,
And a hundred beautiful adornments,
I will grace sublime Samantabhadra,
Manjughosha, Lokeshvara, and their kin.

Shantideva visualizes magnificent offerings and shows us how enjoyable this practice can be. We can luxuriate in wonderful fantasies and visualize sumptuous offerings, not only for ourselves but also for the buddhas, bodhisattvas, and all sentient beings.

In verses 10 and 11, he describes an exquisite bathing chamber. In verses 12 and 13, he offers excellent cloth—the softest, most luxurious towels; beautiful, scented garments—all those things we covet in the catalogs. We can delight in our daydreams, and then give it all away!

These gifts are offered to three of the eight main bodhisattvas: *Samantabhadra, Manjughosha, Lokeshvara.* Samantabhadra is associated with boundless generosity. This is a quality we, too, possess: a mind of generosity with infinite potential to grow.

Manjughosha manifests the unconditional wisdom that is available to us all. Lokeshvara embodies compassion. We venerate him knowing that our own compassion can develop and expand.

2.14

And with a sumptuous fragrance that
Pervades a thousand million worlds,
I will anoint the bodies of the buddhas,
Light and gleaming bright, like pure and burnished
    gold.

2.15

I will place before the Buddha, perfect object of my
    worship,
Flowers like the lotus and the mandarava,
Utpala, and other scented blossoms,
Worked and twined in lovely scented garlands.

2.16

I will offer swelling clouds of incense,
Whose ambient perfume ravishes the mind,
And various foods and every kind of drink,
All delicacies worthy of the gods.

2.17

I will offer precious lamps,
All perfectly contrived as golden lotuses,
A bed of flower petals scattering
Upon the level, incense-sprinkled ground.

Shantideva seems to be enjoying himself thoroughly. He offers
fragrant oils with which to *anoint the bodies of the buddhas* and
flowers gathered in garlands like Hawaiian leis. When he offers a
lamp, it's not just a little candle; it's an exquisite lamp in the form
of a golden lotus, on a bed of flower petals scattered on incense-
sprinkled ground.

Starting with verse 15, the offerings take on special significance.
Traditionally, each offering is understood to cultivate a specific
quality. The offering of flowers, for example, increases our ability
to feel love and compassion; the offering of incense, in verse 16, increases the capacity for discipline.

Anything we offer uncovers our inherent good qualities. It's like
removing a lid: as a result, we might feel immersed in richness and
find ourselves being less possessive and more generous. In this way,
making offerings is said to overcome miserliness. Cultivating this
practice is a very straightforward, nonconceptual way to uncover
our basic goodness.

2.18

I will offer palaces immense and resonant
    with song,
All decked with precious pearls and pendant gems,
Gleaming treasures fit to ornament the amplitude
    of space:
All this I offer to the loving bodhisattvas.

2.19

Precious parasols adorned with golden shafts
And bordered all around with jeweled fringes,
Upright, well-proportioned, pleasing to the eye,
Again, all this I give to all the buddhas.

2.20

May a multitude of other offerings,
Accompanied by music sweet to hear,
Be made in great successive clouds,
To soothe the sufferings of living beings.

2.21

May rains of flowers, every precious thing,
Fall down in an unceasing stream
Upon the jewels of sacred Dharma,
The Triple Gem and all supports for offering.

In verse 18, the offering of beautiful palaces *resonant with song* symbolizes creating harmonious, uplifted communities. The traditional offering of ceremonial parasols, in verse 19, is associated with the ability to benefit beings. In verse 20, the offering of music increases our capacity to communicate the dharma, so that people can hear the sweetness of truth.

In verse 21, the offering is the aspiration for a continual rain of flowers and precious jewels to descend upon the sacred texts, the Three Jewels, and anything else that supports our practice.

Finally, in verses 22 and 23, he will make the most sublime offering: the offering of following the example of our teachers and practicing what we've been taught.

2.22

Just as Manjughosha, gentle and melodious,
Made offerings to all the conquerors,
Likewise I will make oblation
To the buddhas and their bodhisattva children.

2.23

I will offer prayers by every way and means
To these vast oceans of good qualities.
May clouds of tuneful praise
Ascend unceasingly before them.

The next of the seven practices is prostrations. By offering prostrations, we prepare the ground further for the seed of bodhichitta
to take root. In verses 24 through 26, Shantideva again accumulates
merit by giving of himself.

2.24

To buddhas of the past, the present, and all future time,
And to the Doctrine and Sublime Assembly,
With bodies many as the grains of dust
Upon the ground, I will prostrate and bow.

2.25

To shrines and all supports
Of bodhichitta I bow down:
All abbots who transmit the vows, all learned masters,
And all noble ones who practice Dharma.

2.26

Until the essence of enlightenment is reached,
I go for refuge to the buddhas.
Also I take refuge in the Doctrine
And all the host of bodhisattvas.

Any offering can be expanded. For instance, when we visualize giving away our cherished belongings, we don't imagine just one book or sweater; we expand that offering into countless books or sweaters. Similarly, in verse 24, Shantideva visualizes countless images of his body making prostrations.

There are many benefits to this practice. First and foremost, prostrations overcome arrogance. Trungpa Rinpoche used to say that because we have basic goodness, we can take pride in surrendering. We don't have to hang on to our accomplishments or good fortune. We can afford to be humble and bow down to those who embody wisdom, those courageous ones who worked hard so that the teachings still remain alive today.

Second, prostrations connect us with our own sanity. In the presence of an extremely open and compassionate person, we can feel these qualities unfold in ourselves. Some seemingly separate person or object of veneration can awaken the clarity and freshness of our mind. As a gesture of respect, love, and gratitude to those who show us our basic goodness, we bow down and prostrate.

Third, prostrations serve as a way to overcome resistance and surrender our deeply entrenched neuroses and habits. Each time we bow, we offer ourselves: our confusion, our inability to love, our hardness and selfish ways. It's like opening our hands and saying: "With this gesture I willingly acknowledge how stuck I am. I surrender it all to the vast and compassionate heart of bodhichitta. Until attaining the essence of enlightenment, I take refuge in awakened mind."

Doing prostrations with any of these three intentions will prepare us to experience the heart of bodhi.

From verse 27 until the end of this chapter, Shantideva presents the practice of confession or, as Trungpa Rinpoche translated it, "laying aside our neurotic crimes." Whenever we do something we wish we hadn't, we give it our full, compassionate attention. Rather than hiding our mistakes from ourselves and others, we forthrightly declare them. By acknowledging them to *ourselves,* we avoid self-deception. In certain circumstances, we may also declare them to someone else, as witness to our wise intention.

To see clearly how we strengthen or weaken crippling patterns, we have to bring them to light. It's like getting ready for bed at night: we easily remove our clothes in a room by ourselves, but the presence of another person heightens our awareness. The role of others, whether it's *the great protectors* or our friends, is simply to hear us out, without judging or needing to fix us. In this way confession overcomes ignorance, or lack of self-reflection.

You may ask, "Isn't it enough to acknowledge my regrets to myself?" It does help a lot, but not enough to completely dissolve self-deception. When we express our regrets to the buddhas or another human being, we can't kid ourselves. As an act of self-compassion and self-respect, we use a witness to expose ourselves to ourselves. Thus instead of carrying around a burden of shame, we're free to make a fresh start. The benefit of laying aside our "neurotic crimes" is being able to go forward without guilt.

The practice of confession is an excellent way to move beyond guilt and self-deception. It relies on the view that neurosis, while it may *feel* monolithic or immutable, is essentially transitory and insubstantial. It is just very strong energy that we mistakenly identify as a solid and permanent "me." Confessing, like making offerings and prostrations, helps us let go of this fixed version of who we are.

When we do something we wish we hadn't, we don't remain oblivious; we acknowledge it with what Dzigar Kongtrul Rinpoche calls "positive sadness." Instead of condemning ourselves, we can connect with the openhearted tenderness of regret. Thus the habits of self-deception and guilt have a chance to wither away. This is the essential point of the practice of confession.

2.27

To perfect buddhas and bodhisattvas,
In all directions, where they may reside,
To them who are the sovereigns of great mercy,
I press my palms together, praying thus:

2.28

"In this and all my other lifetimes,
Wandering in the round without beginning,
Blindly I have brought forth wickedness,
Inciting others to commit the same.

2.29

"I have taken pleasure in such evil,
Tricked and overmastered by my ignorance.
Now I see the blame of it, and in my heart,
O great protectors, I declare it!"

In these verses, Shantideva introduces the traditional Tibetan practice of the "four powers of confession," four methods for laying aside neurotic deeds. These are: (1) recognition of misdeeds with "positive sadness," (2) reliance on basic wisdom, (3) remedial action, and (4) the resolve to do our best to not keep making the same mistakes.

Verse 27 presents "reliance" on basic wisdom. In the presence of the unbiased, nonjudgmental wisdom of *the sovereigns of great mercy,* Shantideva declares, in verses 28 and 29, that he has caused harm. With honesty and trust in his basic goodness, he acknowledges that he has missed the mark.

This healing acknowledgement is the power of recognition with positive sadness. When he says *Blindly I have brought forth wickedness, inciting others to commit the same,* he applies the kind of compassionate self-reflection that brings freedom. As Dzigar Kongtrul says, "We can admit to ourselves that out of ignorance we've done harm, without getting caught in story lines about 'bad me.'"

The third of the four powers is called "remedial action," or "opposing power." Having recognized the unfortunate things we do, this action allows us to resolve the past, thus freeing us to move beyond repression and guilt.

Examples of remedial action range from classical to contemporary practices. The Vietnamese master Thich Nhat Hanh, for instance, worked with an American veteran of the Vietnam War who could not shake his overwhelming guilt for having killed innocent bystanders. For him, the healing action was to return to Vietnam and spend time helping people in distress. In the same spirit, if we've killed animals in the past, perhaps now we could protect them.

Another method is the "life review." At least once a year, I imagine that I am about to die. Looking back as truthfully as I can at my entire life, I give full attention to the things I wish hadn't occurred. Recognizing these mistakes honestly but without self-recrimination, I try to rejoice in the innate wisdom that allows me to see so bravely, and I feel compassion for how I so frequently messed up. Then I can go forward. The future is wide open, and what I do with it is up to me.

Shantideva's remedial action is the declaration *In my heart, O great protectors, I declare it.* By openly expressing his regrets, he performs the healing, remedial action.

The fourth power, resolve, comes in the last verse of this chapter, verse 65. Shantideva vows to do his best not to repeat the same mistakes and to go forward without the unnecessary baggage of guilt.

These four powers of confession generate a more openhearted relationship with the world. We can transform the regret that we're basically bad and wish we weren't into the understanding that we're basically good and don't want to keep covering that over.

2.30

"Whatever I have done against the Triple Gem,
Against my parents, teachers, and the rest,
Through force of my defilements,
By the faculties of body, speech, and mind;

2.31

"All the evil I, a sinner, have committed,
The sin that clings to me through many evil deeds;
All frightful things that I have caused to be,
I openly declare to you, the teachers of the world."

This translation *I, a sinner* may be misleading. Buddhism stresses going beyond any fixed identity: good, bad, or in-between. Basically, with the right methods for working with our minds and the willingness to use them, we all have the ability to turn anything around. We can get beyond the solid opinions and prejudices that cause us to act unwisely; and we can uncover our basic openness and goodness. In verses 30 and 31, Shantideva declares everything that keeps him from living a compassionate life, without any sense of badness or guilt.

One positive view of words like "sin" and "sinner" is that they get our attention and remind us this is not a subject to be taken lightly. I prefer to avoid words that are culturally loaded, so we don't infuse Buddhist teachings with misleading projections.

Trungpa Rinpoche, for instance, translated the Tibetan word *dikpa* as "neurotic crimes" rather than "sin," choosing a psychological rather than an ethical interpretation. Words that identify us as fundamentally marred don't seem helpful. Without them, we're more likely to feel inspired to connect with our inherent strength and goodness.

2.32

"Before my evil has been cleansed away,
It may be that my death will come to me.
And so that, come what may, I might be freed,
I pray you, quickly grant me your protection!"

2.33

The wanton Lord of Death we can't predict,
And life's tasks done or still to do, we cannot stay.
And whether ill or well, we cannot trust
Our lives, our fleeting, momentary lives.

2.34

And we must pass away, forsaking all.
But I, devoid of understanding,
Have, for sake of friend and foe alike,
Provoked and brought about so many evils.

2.35

My enemies at length will cease to be;
My friends, and I myself
Will cease to be;
And all is likewise destined for destruction.

In verses 32 through 46, Shantideva introduces impermanence and death. His intention is to point out the need for self-reflection before it's too late. Any of us could suddenly pass away. This produces a strong motivation for reviewing our lives with an attitude of self-forgiveness. Then we can die with no regrets.

In verse 32 Shantideva says *grant me your protection,* and in other Buddhist liturgies we read "grant your blessings." But from *whom* are we asking help and blessings? How can we understand this nondualistically? Trungpa Rinpoche explained that it's not so much the notion of someone protecting or blessing us; it's more an attitude of "let it be so." May I be protected and blessed by the inspiration of wisdom mind. Let this be so!

Verse 34 discusses a provocative topic: long after our friends and foes are gone, we still carry the imprints of our positive and negative reactions. Our habitual patterns remain in place long after the objects of our attachment and aversion cease. The problem is not our friends and foes, per se; the problem is the way we relate to them, or to any external circumstance. What habits are we strengthening when we get enmeshed in our attachments and aversions? How will we experience the world a month, a year, or five years from now? Will we be even angrier, more grasping and fearful, or will some shift have occurred? This depends entirely on the tendencies we reinforce today.

Shantideva tells us it's futile to get worked up about those who, just like us, live *fleeting, momentary lives.*

2.36

All that I possess and use
Is like the fleeting vision of a dream.
It fades into the realms of memory;
And fading, will be seen no more.

2.37

And even in the brief course of this present life,
So many friends and foes have passed away,
Because of whom, the evils I have done
Still lie, unbearable, before me.

2.38

The thought came never to my mind
That I too am a brief and passing thing.
And so, through hatred, lust, and ignorance,
I've been the cause of many evils.

2.39

Never halting, night or day,
My life is slipping, slipping by.
And nothing that has passed can be regained—
And what but death could be my destiny?

Verse 36 evokes the insubstantial quality of our lives. It is Shantideva's first reference to the illusory, dreamlike nature of reality. Whenever we feel ourselves getting hooked, just recalling these words can be a powerful support. They can help us cut through emotional entanglements and tune into a bigger view.

These verses address the essential groundlessness of our experience. If we are trying to ignore the truth of death, we might find ourselves in the kind of panic Shantideva describes. Any degree of attention to our experience will easily convince us that life is *slipping, slipping by*. In my own experience, getting older is a good motivator for not wasting this precious human life.

2.40

There I'll be, prostrate upon my bed,
And all around, the ones I know and love—
But I alone shall be the one to feel
The cutting of the thread of life.

2.41

And when the vanguard of the Deadly King has gripped
    me,
What help to me will be my friends or kin?
For only goodness gained in life will help me:
This, alas, is what I shrugged away.

We die alone. Friends, family, or material abundance can do
nothing to change this simple fact. When my children were
teenagers, I took them to meet the Sixteenth Karmapa. As they
weren't Buddhists, I asked His Holiness to say something that
didn't require any understanding of the dharma. Without hesitat-
ing, he told them: "You are going to die; and when you do, you will
take nothing with you but your state of mind." In verse 41, Shantideva reiterates this and then talks graphically about the horrors
of death.

2.42

O protectors! I, so little heeding,
Had hardly guessed at horror such as this—
And all for this brief, transient existence,
Have gathered so much evil to myself.

2.43

The day they take him to the scaffold,
Where his body will be torn and butchered,
A man is changed, transfigured by his fear:
His mouth is dry, his eyes start from his brow.

2.44

If so it is, then how will be my misery
When stricken down, beside myself with fear,
I see the fiend, the messenger of Death,
Who turns on me his fell and dreadful gaze?

2.45

Who can save me, who can now protect me
From this horror, from this frightful dread?
And then I'll search the four directions,
Seeking help, with panic-stricken eyes.

2.46

Nowhere help or refuge will be found.
And sunk beneath the weight of sorrow,
Naked, helpless, unprotected—
What, when this befalls me, shall I do?

Shantideva uses two traditional teaching techniques. One proclaims the beauty and benefits of connecting with bodhichitta. The other employs fear tactics to shake us loose from our neurotic habits and frighten us into wakefulness.

The latter style doesn't work very well in the West; without trust in our basic goodness, its message is easily misunderstood. The point is to understand that everything we do has consequences, and they won't always be comfortable. Each day, we're either strengthening or weakening negative patterns. But as Trungpa Rinpoche once said, "Karma is not punishment; it's the consequences that we're temporarily stuck with. We can undo it by following the path."

While death can indeed be terrifying, it also presents an opportunity for enlightenment. This depends on what we cultivate during our lifetimes. In preparing for death, it's extremely helpful to cultivate familiarity with bodhichitta and the unconditional openness of our mind.

In bodhichitta training, we learn to use whatever pain or fear we experience to open our hearts to other people's distress. In this way, our personal misery doesn't close us down; it becomes a stepping-stone toward a bigger perspective. By training this way during life, dying will awaken compassion. Even the discomfort of physical pain, breathing difficulties, or fear will automatically awaken bodhichitta.

The best possible preparation for dying is to recognize the nature of mind. In watching people die, I've observed that death can be a strong support for waking up. Everything is naturally falling apart: our body is falling apart, our way of perceiving reality is falling apart, everything we've clung to is dissolving. The letting go that we cultivated during our life is happening naturally; this is what we've wanted, and now it's occurring on its own.

For those who spend their lives learning to relax with groundlessness, death is liberating. But if we live our lives trying to hold on to this brief and transient existence, we're going to be scared, very scared, when we die. Death is the ultimate unknown that we are forever avoiding; it's the ultimate groundlessness that we try to escape. But if we learn to relax with uncertainty and insecurity, then death is a support for joy.

If we spend our lives searching for outside help—through looking good, shopping therapy, addictions, and so on—we will look for something solid to hold on to when we die. When we find our-selves *seeking help, with panic-stricken eyes,* we'll discover too late that this habitual response will not help. This is Shantideva's sobering message.

We have to ask ourselves, "In what do I seek refuge?" When I'm feeling scared, unhappy, or lonely, in what do I personally seek refuge? Shantideva infers that seeking refuge in the ungraspable, inconceivable heart and mind of bodhichitta will pay off at the time of our deaths.

2.47

Thus from this day forth I go for refuge
To buddhas, guardians of wandering beings,
Who labor for the good of all that lives,
Those mighty ones who scatter every fear.

2.48

In the Dharma that resides within their hearts,
That scatters all the terrors of samsara,
And in the multitude of bodhisattvas,
Likewise I will perfectly take refuge.

If we take refuge in awakened mind itself—courageous and lim-itless—instead of seemingly solid ground, it will *scatter every fear* at the time we need this most.

2.49

Gripped by dread, beside myself with terror,
To Samantabhadra I will give myself;
And to Manjushri, the melodious and gentle,
I will give myself entirely.

2.50

To him whose loving deeds are steadfast,
O my guardian, Avalokita,
I cry out from depths of misery,
"Protect me now, the sinner that I am!"

2.51

Now to the noble one, Akashagarbha,
And to Kshitigarbha, from my heart I call.
And all protectors, great, compassionate,
To them I go in search of refuge.

2.52

And to Vajrapani, holder of the diamond,
The very sight of whom will rout
All dangers like the deadly host of Yama;
To him indeed I fly for safety.

2.53

Formerly your words I have transgressed,
But now I see these terrors all around.
To you indeed I come for help,
And pray you, swiftly save me from this fear.

In verse 53, Shantideva infers that when he didn't understand the workings of cause and effect, he continued strengthening negative propensities. Now, however, he comprehends that he is the one creating the causes of his future happiness or unhappiness. He is therefore inspired to follow the example of the master bodhisattvas mentioned here, and to put their teachings into practice. In this way, they will always be with him, protecting him from fear.

2.54

For if, alarmed by common ills,
I act according to the doctor's words,
What need to speak of when I'm constantly brought low
By lust and all the hundred other torments?

2.55

And if, by one of these alone,
The dwellers in the world are all thrown down,
And if no other remedy exists,
No other healing elsewhere to be found

2.56

Than words of the omniscient physician,
Uprooting every ill and suffering,
The thought to turn on him deaf ears
Is raving folly, wretched and contemptible.

The analogy here is a very familiar one in Buddhist teachings: we suffer from an illness; the Buddha is a physician and master diagnostician; and the teachings are medicine. In order for the medicine to work, we have to take it as prescribed; we can't just read the prescription. To be cured, we have to *act according to the doctor's words.*

When people discover that they or a loved one has a terrible illness, they're inspired to do whatever they can to find a cure. This helps not only the sick person, but everyone else with the same disease. In this case, however, we all have the same disease. While an illness like AIDS or cancer may affect millions of people, the disease of ignorance and self-absorption affects us all. To be given a healing remedy from *the omniscient physician* and not even try it—not even give it a good one or two years—is not just folly, it is *raving folly, wretched and contemptible.*

2.57

If along a small and ordinary cliff
I need to pick my way with special care,
What need to speak of the immense crevasse
That plunges down, unnumbered fathoms deep?

This *immense crevasse* refers to the samsaric mindset of continually seeking comfort and trying to avoid pain. Shantideva asks why, if we're so attentive walking along a *small and ordinary cliff*, we aren't at least that heedful about the dangerous crevasse of samsara? For endless lifetimes, we've been falling into this crevasse. Let's finally get smart and not fall in anymore. And should we stumble now and then, let's catch ourselves and climb back out. That's the message.

2.58

"Today, at least, I shall not die,"
So rash to lull myself with words like these!
My dissolution and my hour of death
Will come upon me ineluctably.

2.59

So why am I so unafraid,
For what escape is there for me?
Death, my death will certainly come round,
So how can I relax in careless ease?

Whether we practice or not, death will come, *So how can I relax in careless ease?* In fact, we *can* relax if we regularly apply the four powers of confession. By reviewing what has gone before and bringing everything into the light, we will be able to relax and let go at the time of our deaths. Having looked honestly at the past and present, we can die with a clear conscience.

2.60

Of life's experience, all seasons past,
What's left to me, what now remains?
By clinging to what now is here no more,
My teacher's precepts I have disobeyed.

Even though we can't possibly hold on to anything, clinging remains one of our strongest habits. Useless though it may be, we devote much of our energy to grasping at that which is elusive and impermanent.

In this present moment, there is nothing left of the past but memories. Our nostalgia for the good times, our fear of the bad times: that's all that's really left. Instead of getting hooked further by nostalgia and fear, we can simply acknowledge these tendencies and question the intelligence of continuing to harm ourselves for the sake of such transient concerns.

2.61

This span of life and all that it contains,
My kith and kin are all to be abandoned!
I must leave them, setting out alone,
What grounds are there for telling friend from foe?

What are our criteria *for telling friend from foe?* A friend might be the cause of emotional upheavals and negative habits, while a

so-called foe might profit us immensely. It's often when someone
hurts us that we have a breakthrough in understanding. The teachings often penetrate when things fall apart. "Friend" and "enemy"
are common concepts; but it's hard to say who will help or hinder
the process of awakening.

2.62

And therefore how can I make sure
To rid myself of evil, only cause of sorrow?
This should be my one concern,
My only thought both night and day.

2.63

Therefore, all the sins I have committed,
Blinded in the dark of ignorance:
Actions evil by their nature
Or the faults of broken vows,

2.64

Mindful of the suffering to come,
I join my palms and ceaselessly prostrate,
And all my evils I will now confess
Directly in the presence of the buddhas.

2.65

I pray you, guides and guardians of the world,
To take me as I am, a sinful man.
And all these actions, evil as they are,
I promise I will never do again.

Shantideva ends with a summary of the four powers of confession and a passionate vow to free himself from the causes of sorrow.

It's extremely difficult to resist the seduction of habits, even knowing how unsatisfying the end results will be. We persist in the same old patterns, which illogically hold out the promise of comfort. To rid ourselves of inevitable suffering, it's crucial to acknowledge on the spot how we repeatedly get hooked. Dzigar Kongtrul calls this process developing "heartbreak with samsara." Trungpa Rinpoche refers to it as "nausea with samsara": nausea with the tendency to act on unwise impulses, over and over again.

This is a tricky practice for Westerners. We tend to regard our shortcomings as proof not of our humanity but of our unworthiness. The four powers of confession, however, place emphasis on pragmatic intelligence. We face the facts compassionately and get smart about promoting our best interests.

Being *mindful of the suffering to come* provides strong motivation to resist the undertow of harmful urges. In chapters 5 and 6, Shantideva will give detailed instructions for working creatively with the seduction of old habits. But first, we have to intelligently and compassionately acknowledge that we're hooked.

So, in the presence of the *guides and guardians of the world*, Shantideva holds back nothing. Relying on the inspiration of awakened mind, he presents an unabridged version of his previous deeds and says *Take me as I am*. Having fully acknowledged past and present actions, he wholeheartedly aspires never again to be deceived by the false promises of addictions and rote responses. By cleaning the slate, he creates the opportunity for his basic sanity to emerge.

Transcending Hesitation

Commitment

CHAPTER 3 OF *The Way of the Bodhisattva* is the final chapter on preparing the ground for bodhichitta. Here Shantideva concludes his presentation of the sevenfold offerings with the final four practices: rejoicing, requesting the teachers to present the dharma, asking them to remain with us, and dedicating the merit.

Rejoicing in the good fortune of others is a practice that can help us when we feel emotionally shut down and unable to connect with others.

Rejoicing generates good will. The next time you go out in the world, you might try this practice: directing your attention to people—in their cars, on the sidewalk, talking on their cell phones—just wish for them all to be happy and well. Without knowing anything about them, they can become very real, by regarding each of them personally and rejoicing in the comforts and pleasures that come their way. Each of us has this soft spot: a capacity for love and tenderness. But if we don't encourage it, we can get pretty stubborn about remaining sour.

I have a friend who, when he begins getting depressed and with-drawn, goes to a nearby park and does this practice for everyone who walks by. He finds this pulls him out of the slump before it's too late. The tricky part is getting out of the house, instead of giv-ing in to the seduction of gloom.

When you begin the practice of rejoicing in others' good for-tune, you can expect to encounter your soft spot—as well as your competitiveness and envy. Sitting on a park bench feeling warmth for strangers is relatively easy to do; but when good fortune comes to those we know better, especially those we dislike, it can give us an up-close look at our jealousy.

This has certainly been the case for me. Until I began to prac-tice rejoicing, I wasn't aware of how much envy I had. I remember hearing that a colleague's book was rapidly becoming a best seller, and being pained that my first reaction was resentment. Likewise, when I practice generosity, I see my holding back more vividly than ever before. By practicing patience my anger is harder to deny. For someone on the spiritual path, seeing this can be em-barrassing.

Who would have thought that the practice of rejoicing would be a setup for seeing our neurosis? Our usual response would be to feel that we've blown it; but for aspiring bodhisattvas this isn't the case. Because our intention is to wake up so we can help others do the same, we rejoice as much in seeing where we're stuck as we rejoice in our loving-kindness.

This is the only way for true compassion to emerge: this is our opportunity to understand what others are up against. Like us, they aspire to open up, only to see themselves close down; like us, they have the capacity for joy, and out of ignorance they block it. For their sake and ours, we can let the story lines go and stay present with an open heart, and we can rejoice that we're even in-terested in such a fresh alternative.

3.1

With joy I celebrate
The virtue that relieves all beings
From the sorrows of the states of loss,
And places those who languish in the realms of bliss.

To introduce the practice of rejoicing, Shantideva expresses his happiness that beings can move from lower to higher realms. According to tradition, beings in samsara are born into six different realms. The three lower realms are the *states of loss* referred to in verse 1. They are characterized by suffering so intense that, even though it's dreamlike and impermanent, it seems eternal and inescapable. The *realms of bliss* refer to the three higher states, including the human realm. Here one has less suffering and therefore a far greater chance of freeing oneself from samsara.

Whether we believe these realms exist as actual places or simply as psychological states is not the point. Either way, it is our state of mind that determines whether we live in misery or bliss. Fortunately we have an inborn ability to free ourselves from confusion. It is this ever-present possibility of freedom that Shantideva rejoices in here.

We might wonder about this *virtue* that allows us to move from greater to lesser suffering. According to the Buddhist teachings, this shift occurs once we understand karma. When we fully accept that the actions of our body, speech, and mind have pleasant or unpleasant consequences, we're motivated to act, speak, and think in ways that benefit rather than harm us.

I have a Buddhist friend who's an inmate at San Quentin Prison in California. One day he was being harassed by a guard, but he did not retaliate. The other men saw this and asked him how he kept his cool. He told them that if he made the guard madder, he might go home and beat his children. This is the kind of virtuous and compassionate understanding Shantideva refers to in his opening stanza.

3.2

And I rejoice in virtue that creates the cause
Of gaining the enlightened state,
And celebrate the freedom won
By living beings from the round of pain.

3.3

And in the buddhahood of the protectors I delight
And in the stages of the buddhas' offspring.

Shantideva rejoices in the possibility of *gaining the enlightened state*. In verse 2, this refers to the *arhats* and their experience of personal liberation. What joy, that beings can release themselves from *the round of pain*. Freedom is possible and we have role models to prove it. If they can do it, so can we. He rejoices in the arhats and in our own enlightened potential.

In verse 3, he delights in the full *buddhahood of the protectors,* as well as the partial enlightenment of bodhisattvas. How marvelous that they attain liberation for the benefit of themselves and others.

3.4

The intention, ocean of great good,
That seeks to place all beings in the state of bliss,
And every action for the benefit of all:
Such is my delight and all my joy.

The *ocean of great good* refers to aspiration bodhichitta. Once the intention to awaken for the benefit of others becomes our guiding principle, even emotional upheavals won't lead us astray. People who are clear about their commitment become like mountains, remaining steady even when the weather gets wild. It is important to keep this in mind, and not to think we can't go forward until the storms completely subside.

Shantideva rejoices in those who long *to place all beings in the state of bliss* and in those of us who even glimpse such an expansive aspiration and commit to training our minds. Likewise he rejoices in those actively engaged in relieving suffering *for the benefit of all.*

Now the reference to *all beings* may sound unreasonably vast; but really it's just a way of looking out at the world to see if there's anyone we detest, anyone we fear or can't stop resenting. To include all beings seriously challenges our usual tendency to choose whom we like and dislike, whom we wish to see prosper or fail. These old habits die hard. So, while holding the intention to benefit all beings excluding none, we take it one step at a time.

I read a series of articles about a woman whose main practice was to stop hating political leaders. By day thirty-five, she reported "not doing too good but still not caving in." That's definitely the bodhisattva spirit. Allow ample time for change to occur, so you don't lose heart just because the process goes slowly.

The practice of rejoicing overcomes jealousy and competitiveness. This is accomplished by heightening our unbiased awareness of those very qualities we wish to deny.

3.5

And so I join my hands and pray
The buddhas who reside in every quarter:
Kindle now the Dharma's light
For those who grope, bewildered, in the dark of
    suffering!

Here Shantideva presents the fifth of the sevenfold offerings: the practice of requesting teachers to clarify our understanding of the dharma. Asking the wise to illuminate our confusion overcomes "wrong views," such as believing that people are basically bad or that karma is a punishment bestowed on us by outer forces.

3.6

I join my hands, beseeching the enlightened ones
Who wish to pass beyond the bonds of sorrow:
Do not leave us in our ignorance;
Remain among us for unnumbered ages!

In verse 6, Shantideva introduces the sixth practice: asking the teachers to stay with us and not dwell permanently in nirvana. Without these examples of wisdom, it is difficult to connect with our own potential.

Wisdom and compassion are always accessible to us. Yet, without some example of what's possible, we rarely tap into our inner strength. Great teachers often provide our first glimpses of the expansiveness of our mind. If they remain with us, we have living examples to remind us of our wisdom. Thus tradition says this practice overcomes the fear of remaining in ignorance and confusion forever.

3.7

And through these actions now performed,
By all the virtue I have just amassed,
May all the pain of every living being
Be wholly scattered and destroyed!

Here Shantideva presents the final practice: the practice of dedicating our merit. This practice overcomes self-absorption. Instead of hoarding our good fortunes, we give it all away—to specific people or to sentient beings everywhere. We do this with the aspiration that their pain *be wholly scattered and destroyed.*

The word *merit* is problematic for some Western Buddhists. To say that doing virtuous acts will make everything go smoothly for us in the future just isn't that convincing for some of us. Some may find Trungpa Rinpoche's ultimate view more accessible. Accumulating merit, he says, depends on letting go of our possessiveness altogether. This can't be done with a business-deal mentality; it's not like putting money into a savings account for our retirement years. Merit can only be accumulated by letting go.

From this point of view, sharing the merit means surrendering completely, with an attitude of letting whatever happens happen: if it's better for me to have pleasure, let me have pleasure; if it's better to have pain, let me have pain. We aren't collecting anything for ego to hold on to; it's quite the opposite.

In verses 8, 9, and 10, merit is dedicated with specific intentions. First, Shantideva dedicates his merit to the sick. If someone you love is ill and suffering greatly, for example, you're willing to give away all that you hold dear, with the aspiration that they benefit from your sacrifice. You could express this intention in words similar to Shantideva's.

3.8

For all those ailing in the world,
Until their every sickness has been healed,
May I myself become for them
The doctor, nurse, the medicine itself.

3.9

Raining down a flood of food and drink,
May I dispel the ills of thirst and famine.
And in the ages marked by scarcity and want,
May I myself appear as drink and sustenance.

In verse 8, he gives three examples of how a bodhisattva might manifest: as a doctor, a nurse, and as medicine itself. His aspiration is not only to help people who are physically ill, but also to help those suffering from the sicknesses of craving, aggression, and ignorance. Thus he longs to help with material things such as medicine, food, and drink, and to bring benefit at the deeper level of spiritual nourishment. The main point is to not hold back for fear of ending up with nothing yourself.

3.10

For sentient beings, poor and destitute,
May I become a treasure ever plentiful,
And lie before them closely in their reach,
A varied source of all that they might need.

Here Shantideva dedicates his merit to the *poor and destitute,* again on both the material and spiritual levels. A bodhisattva might appear as *a treasure,* as shelter, a nurse, or anything that relieves our pain and opens our eyes to a bigger picture.

In the story of the great Indian Buddhist master Naropa, his teacher Tilopa appeared to him in the form of a maggot-ridden dog. Feeling disgust, Naropa tried to jump over the poor creature and run away. Immediately the dog changed into Tilopa, who said, "If you have aversion for sentient beings, how do you ever expect to awaken from samsaric mind?"

Anything that awakens our compassion or wisdom serves as a bodhisattva.

3.11

My body, thus, and all my goods besides,
And all my merits gained and to be gained,
I give them all away withholding nothing
To bring about the benefit of beings.

This is Shantideva's instruction for developing a refreshingly generous mind: a mind with the power to overcome clinging and the "I want, I need" of self-absorption. It's as close as we can come to giving up *everything* that's "me" or "mine."

The journey to enlightenment involves shedding, not collecting. It's a continual process of opening and surrender, like taking off layer after layer of clothes, until we're completely naked with nothing to hide. But we can't just pretend, making a big display of disrobing, then putting everything back on when no one's looking. Our surrender has to be genuine.

After training with Tilopa for many years, Naropa began to teach his own students. The most famous of these was the Tibetan teacher known as Marpa the translator. Marpa, who had gone to study with Naropa in India, had a large amount of gold dust to present to his teacher as a parting gift. When he was about to return home, he offered this ceremoniously. But Naropa saw he was holding some back for his journey. He demanded that Marpa give him everything, saying, "Do you think you can buy my teaching with your deception?" Reluctantly, Marpa surrendered all his gold dust, which Naropa then casually threw into the air.

This was a moment of shock and disbelief for Marpa, but also a moment of great opening. Finally, he became an empty vessel and could receive Naropa's blessings without any reservations. Until he gave up everything, self-importance blocked his way.

In this verse Shantideva vows to surrender the three main bases of self-importance: attachment to possessions, body, and merit. The Tibetan word for attachment is *shenpa*. Dzigar Kongtrul describes it as the "charge" behind emotions: the charge behind "I like and don't like," the charge behind self-importance itself.

Shenpa is the feeling of getting "hooked," a nonverbal tightening or shutting down. Suppose you are talking to someone and suddenly you see her jaw clench; she stiffens or her eyes glaze over. What you're seeing is *shenpa*: the outer manifestation of an inner tug, the subtlest form of aversion or attraction. We can see this in each other; more importantly we can feel this charge in ourselves.

Possessions evoke *shenpa* all the time: we're afraid of losing them, breaking them, or never getting enough. It doesn't have to do with the things themselves. It's the *charge* behind wanting them or being afraid they'll be taken away. To get hooked in this way is completely unreasonable, as if the objects of our desire could provide security and lasting happiness. Nevertheless, *shenpa* happens. It's that sticky feeling that arises when we want things to go our way.

Our bodies also provoke *shenpa*. This manifests in various ways. It's the anxious feeling that's triggered by our health, our appearance, our desire to avoid physical pain. Personally, despite my sincere aspiration to alleviate the suffering of others, my willingness sometimes falls apart at the slightest discomfort. This summer, for instance, I hesitated to help a bird caught in a rose bush, for fear of being pricked by thorns.

This body is a precious vessel, our ship for reaching enlightenment. But if we spend all of our time painting the decks, we'll never leave port and this brief opportunity will be lost. Moreover, our body, like everything else, is impermanent and prone to death and decay. Perhaps it's time to see it for what it is and stop strengthening our *shenpa*.

According to Patrul Rinpoche, the easiest thing to relinquish is our possessions, and we know how hard that can be. Giving up attachment to our bodies, he says, is even more challenging; yet the most difficult to give up is our merit. Can you imagine willingly letting go of all your good fortune? Would you be able to relinquish your good qualities, pleasing circumstances, comforts, and prestige so that others may be happy?

You would think that the *shenpa* triggered by our merit would be easier to let go of than attachment to our bodies or possessions. Buddhist practitioners pretend to do it all the time. But relinquishing attachment to merit means letting go on the most profound and difficult level; even our clutching to security and the illusion of certainty would go. Giving away merit is equivalent to shedding everything. It is the ultimate way to become *shenpa*-free.

3.12

Nirvana is attained by giving all,
Nirvana the objective of my striving.
Everything therefore must be abandoned,
And it is best to give it all to others.

With these words Shantideva summarizes the essence of verse 11: if liberation is what we want, we'll need to let go of everything. No holding something back for a rainy day. This is probably the hardest message for any of us to hear.

3.13

This body I have given up
To serve the pleasure of all living beings.
Let them kill and beat and slander it,
And do to it whatever they desire.

3.14

And though they treat it like a toy,
Or make of it the butt of every mockery,
My body has been given up to them—
There's no use, now, to make so much of it.

When I first read these verses I was appalled. I didn't want to consider going this far, nor did I feel it was wise to do so. From a Western perspective, this advice seems to feed right into the self-loathing so prevalent in our culture. But knowing that Shantideva's intention is always to support and encourage us, I looked past my initial aversion and discovered the wisdom of his words.

This, I realized, was the approach of the civil rights workers. In order to benefit not only African Americans but also their oppressors, they were willing to put their bodies and feelings on the line. For the greater good, they entered into dangerous situations. Being *the butt of every mockery* was the least of it; they knew they would be beaten, insulted, and perhaps killed. This is an example of bodhisattva wisdom and courage. Yet these were just ordinary people—ordinary people who had given birth to the bodhi heart.

These verses describe what many famous bodhisattvas were willing to go through: people like Nelson Mandela, Mother Teresa, Aung San Suu Kyi, and Gandhi. It also describes the bravery of countless unsung heroes and heroines.

3.15

And so let beings do to me
Whatever does not bring them injury.
Whenever they catch sight of me,
Let this not fail to bring them benefit.

When someone beats or mocks us, they're not exactly strengthening healthy patterns. From a bodhisattva's point of view, they are harming themselves more than us. Therefore Shantideva says that sentient beings can do anything to him, as long as it doesn't result in their own injury.

There is a story of a Tibetan monk who wept when he remembered how the Chinese had tortured him in prison. His listeners, of course, assumed that the reason for his tears was the memory of his personal trauma. However, he wasn't crying for himself; he was crying for the Chinese who, as a result of their cruelty, would reap such intense suffering in the future.

If we could maintain this long-range perspective, it wouldn't be so difficult to wish for our oppressors to stop creating their own pain. This approach takes some cultivating; but if we work with it, we will sow seeds of happiness for all concerned.

3.16

If those who see me entertain
A thought of anger or devotion,
May these states supply the cause
Whereby their good and wishes are fulfilled.

3.17

All those who slight me to my face,
Or do me any other evil,
Even if they blame or slander me,
May they attain the fortune of enlightenment!

All of the thoughts and actions of others toward me, even negative ones, can create a positive connection between us, one that will bring both of us benefit now and in the future.

As I read verse 17, I was thinking of Shantideva's audience at Nalanda. By now he probably had the monks in the palm of his hand, but originally they wanted to humiliate him. Here he's telling them indirectly, "Whatever your original intention, may it be the cause for your attaining enlightenment." This is a form of forgiveness on the spot. Beyond forgiveness, he is actually wishing them well—the ultimate wellness of enlightenment.

3.18

May I be a guard for those who are protectorless,
A guide for those who journey on the road.
For those who wish to go across the water,
May I be a boat, a raft, a bridge.

3.19

May I be an isle for those who yearn for landfall,
And a lamp for those who long for light;
For those who need a resting place, a bed;
For all who need a servant, may I be their slave.

3.20

May I be the wishing jewel, the vase of plenty,
A word of power and the supreme healing;
May I be the tree of miracles,
And for every being the abundant cow.

In verses 18 through 20, Shantideva takes his intention further. He aspires to benefit sentient beings in any form that works. In fact, you never know how a bodhisattva might manifest in your life.

When the Mormons originally settled in Utah, their first crops were being devastated by locusts. When they prayed for help, thousands of seagulls appeared and gobbled up all the locusts: seagull bodhisattvas came to the rescue of people who were about to starve.

The image of an *isle* represents a safe resting place. We can provide this for a friend who's depressed and in need of support and encouragement. To lift someone's spirits, we might take him out for a cup of coffee or join him on a walk. In these simple ways, we become like an island where people can relax and find the strength to go forward.

Becoming *a servant* means doing whatever will help. At Gampo Abbey part of our monastic training is learning to serve each other without arrogance or complaint. The *wishing jewel* and the *vase of plenty* are examples of providing whatever is needed effortlessly and in great abundance.

The remaining fourteen verses are known as the "bodhisattva vow." Generations of bodhisattvas have repeated these words daily, in order to maintain their intention to help others.

3.21

Like the earth and the pervading elements
Enduring as the sky itself endures,
For boundless multitudes of living beings,
May I be their ground and sustenance.

3.22

Thus for every thing that lives,
As far as are the limits of the sky,
May I provide their livelihood and nourishment
Until they pass beyond the bonds of suffering.

Without hesitation, Shantideva makes the commitment to enter the bodhisattva path. He begins with the aspiration to provide steadfastness and sustenance for all beings until they attain enlightenment.

The next two verses are the heart of the bodhisattva vow. By saying them three times, we can renew our commitment at any time. In essence, we're vowing to do on-the-job training forever.

3.23

Just as all the buddhas of the past
Embraced the awakened attitude of mind,
And in the precepts of the bodhisattvas
Step by step abode and trained,

3.24

Just so, and for the benefit of beings,
I will also have this attitude of mind,
And in those precepts, step by step,
I will abide and train myself.

The words *step by step* are important here. Even the fully awakened ones trained step by step, and we follow their example. Since this vow can be broken by one harsh word or flash of anger, we would obviously be wise to be patient with ourselves and give up hope of always getting it right. We can renew our intention to stay open again and again and again. Every morning before I get out of bed, I recite these two verses three times, and then I start my day.

There are three approaches to working with the bodhisattva vow. Our commitment can be made with the attitude of a king or queen, a ferryman, or a shepherd. These images represent ways to go forward realistically, step by step, given our current capabilities.

At the level of a king or queen, we work on ourselves first. Although our specific intention is to benefit others, we know this is only possible if we ourselves wake up. Anyone who works in the helping professions knows how easy it is to lose one's patience or feel aversion. It soon becomes obvious that we can't do the work of benefiting others until we've put our own kingdom in good working order.

The next level is the aspiration of the ferryman. Here we find ourselves in the same boat with all sentient beings, crossing the water together. The analogy has a sense of "just like me." Like me, all beings experience themselves as the central character in life's drama. Like me, they're enslaved by attachments and aversions, hopes and fears. No one wants to experience physical or emotional pain any more than I do. We all want to feel safe and free from fear.

With this as the basis of our bodhisattva training, we reach out beyond our self-centered version of reality and bring others into our lives. When our own depression or resentment arises, it becomes a stepping-stone to understanding the darkness felt by others. If we have insomnia, a toothache, a burn, or cancer, instead of making us retreat into our own little world, it becomes the basis for empathy and loving-kindness.

This approach also works when things are going well. When we feel relaxed and happy, we can remember that others also enjoy these states of mind. They, too, want to feel comfortable and at home with themselves and their world. May all of us be happy and at our ease; and may we all experience the clarity and freshness of our mind.

The next image, the shepherd, represents what we generally think of as "real" compassion. Just as shepherds put the welfare of their sheep before their own, we aspire to put others before ourselves. This is how most of us think we should work with our bodhisattva commitment, but truthfully, not many of us feel we can do it. Of course, we have all been in situations where we've spontaneously put others first: we've given our bus seat to an elderly person, or stayed up all night with a troubled friend. Parents do it all the time; they'll even run into traffic to pull their toddler to safety. But to hold this as our only model would definitely be misleading. Instead, we can proceed at any of these three levels: a king or queen, ferryman, or shepherd.

To awaken bodhichitta, we start where we are and go forward step by step.

3.25

That this most pure and spotless state of mind
Might be embraced and constantly increase,
The prudent who have cultivated it
Should praise it highly in such words as these:

3.26

"Today my life has given fruit.
This human state has now been well assumed.
Today I take my birth in Buddha's line,
And have become the buddhas' child and heir."

Having recited the two key verses of the vow, Shantideva then rejoices. From his point of view, once we make the commitment and begin to practice mind training, we are already bodhisattvas. This is an encouraging way to look at our spiritual journey. In some schools of thought, this doesn't occur until sometime in the distant future; but Shantideva says that having taken the vow, we're already *the buddhas' child and heir.* What's more, we have this book as our training guide.

3.27

"In every way, then, I will undertake
Activities befitting such a rank.
And I will do no act to mar
Or compromise this high and faultless lineage."

Shantideva joyfully proclaims his intention to act in ways that befit a bodhisattva. This kind of confidence doesn't crumble each time we stumble and fall. When we say that we will do nothing to *compromise this high and faultless lineage,* we say it knowing we won't always succeed. Nevertheless, our aspiration to awaken bodhichitta is very strong. Without trying to measure up to some unrealistic ideal, we aspire to move in the direction of further sanity. We don't want to squander this precious human birth strengthening negative habits that weaken our capacity for enlightenment.

3.28

"For I am like a blind man who has found
A precious gem within a mound of filth.
Exactly so, as if by some strange chance,
The enlightened mind has come to birth in me."

Right in the middle of our foulest emotions, we find this *precious gem;* there in the midst of confusion and reactivity, we find the jewel of bodhichitta. The most negative emotions can serve as the basis for compassion. When we're enraged at some "enemy," for example, we could own that negativity and wish for everyone to be free of aggression, including our foe. No matter what arises, we can always find the soft spot of the bodhi heart.

In verses 29 through 33, Shantideva gives eight more analogies for bodhichitta: an elixir that slays not only death but, more importantly, dualistic thinking; the inexhaustible treasure of non-dual, nonconceptual awareness that heals the poverty of ignorance; a medicine that cures our most basic obscurations of dualistic perception and negative emotions; a wish-fulfilling tree that grants all our spiritual aspirations; a universal bridge for passing safely over the lower realms; the full moon of compassion; the sun whose light illuminates the darkness; and the best of butters, representing the richness of our bodhi mind.

3.29

"This is the draft of immortality,
That slays the Lord of Death, the slaughterer of
     beings,
The rich unfailing treasure-mine
To heal the poverty of wanderers.

3.30

"It is the sovereign remedy,
That perfectly allays all maladies.
It is the wishing tree bestowing rest
On those who wander wearily the pathways of existence.

3.31

"It is the universal vehicle that saves
All wandering beings from the states of loss—
The rising moon of the enlightened mind
That soothes the sorrows born of the afflictions.

3.32

"It is a mighty sun that utterly dispels
The gloom and ignorance of wandering beings,
The creamy butter, rich and full,
All churned from milk of holy Teaching."

With the following verses Shantideva concludes this chapter on making the commitment to attain enlightenment, in order to help all beings do the same.

3.33

"Living beings! Wayfarers upon life's paths,
Who wish to taste the riches of contentment,
Here before you is the supreme bliss—
Here, O ceaseless wanderers, is your fulfillment!"

I can imagine Shantideva rising up in his seat with enthusiasm, saying, "Come along, come along. Please don't close your ears to

what I'm saying. This is your chance. Please take it!" Our fulfillment is so close at hand; we can awaken bodhichitta with our every
thought, word, and action. We have a wealth of instructions, more
than we could ever use, for finding this *supreme bliss* that's right in
front of our noses.

3.34

"And so, within the sight of all protectors,
I summon every being, calling them to buddhahood—
And till that state is reached, to every earthly joy!
May gods and demigods, and all the rest, rejoice!"

In this last line, Shantideva exhorts us to fulfill our birthright.
Until then, he wishes us *every earthly joy:* all the helpful circumstances we need to relax and enjoy our journey to enlightenment.

Using Our Intelligence

Awareness

ROUSING THE BODHI HEART means connecting
with our longing for enlightenment, with the clear
desire to alleviate the escalating suffering we see in the world
today. Most people do not give much thought to enlightenment.
But most of us do long for a better world situation, and we long to
be free of neurotic habits and mental anguish. This is the ideal
state of mind for awakening bodhichitta. We know we want to be
part of making things better, and that we need to get saner to do
this effectively. It's the perfect place to start.

If we can commit to pursuing this goal, we're on the same page
as Shantideva. Like us, he had to work with a wild mind, overpow-
ering emotions, and entrenched habitual patterns. Like us, he was
able to use his life, just as it was, to work intelligently with his reactivity. The yearning to do this is "aspiration bodhichitta." Although
we may not always be able to stop ourselves from bringing pain to
others, our intention to sort out our confusion and be of service
remains unwavering.

In chapters 1–3 of *The Way of the Bodhisattva,* Shantideva shares his aspiration to make waking up and benefiting others his top priority. In these next three chapters, he will provide methods for insuring that this bodhichitta passion doesn't decline.

This is a very important topic. When we're young, we have a natural curiosity about the world around us. There's a natural spark that energizes us and motivates us to learn, as well as a fear of becoming like some of the older people we see: stuck in their ways, with closed minds and no more spirit of adventure.

It's true that as some people get older, they begin spending more time in pursuit of comfort and security. But Shantideva is passionately determined to keep his youthful curiosity alive. He aspires to continually stretch his heart beyond its current preconceptions and biases. Instead of staying stuck in his cocoon, he wants to grow in flexibility and enthusiasm.

The bodhisattva path is not about being a "good" person or accepting the status quo. It requires courage and a willingness to keep growing.

In chapter 4, Shantideva addresses two topics essential to keeping one's passion alive. The first is attentiveness; the second is working skillfully with emotions. The title of this chapter in Tibetan is *pag-yü*, which has been translated many different ways. Here it is translated as "awareness"; elsewhere it is called "conscientiousness," "heedfulness," and "carefulness." I feel the most descriptive translation is "attentiveness": paying attention with intelligent awareness of what's happening. A traditional analogy is walking along the edge of a deep crevasse: we're attentive and keenly aware of the consequences of carelessness.

Attentiveness is a significant component of self-reflection. By paying attention when we feel the tug of *shenpa,* we get smarter about not getting hooked.

In the following verses, Shantideva gives five examples of when to apply attentiveness: when bodhichitta arises; before we make a commitment; after we've made a commitment; when relating with the cause and effect of karma, or consequences of our actions; and finally, when we are seduced by our *kleshas.*

The Sanskrit word *klesha* refers to a strong emotion that reliably leads to suffering. It's sometimes translated as "neurosis" and, in this text, as "afflictions" and "defiled emotions." In essence, *kleshas* are dynamic, ineffable energy, yet it's energy that easily enslaves us and causes us to act and speak in unintelligent ways.

Kleshas arise with the subtle tension inherent in dualistic perception. If we don't catch this tension, it sets off a chain reaction of "for" or "against." These reactions quickly escalate, resulting in full-blown aggression, craving, ignorance, jealousy, envy, and pride—in other words, full-blown misery for ourselves and others. Kleshas survive on ignorance—ignorance of their insubstantial nature and the way we reinforce them—and they are fueled by thoughts. That their power can be diffused by attentiveness is the main theme of chapter 4.

In verse 1, Shantideva begins his presentation of the five times to apply attentiveness.

4.1

The children of the Conqueror who thus
Have firmly grasped this bodhichitta
Should never turn aside from it
But always strive to keep its disciplines.

Once bodhichitta has arisen—and knowing that, with carelessness, it could decline—we use attentiveness to keep its *disciplines.* This refers specifically to the six *paramitas,* which Shantideva will discuss at some length in future chapters.

4.2

Whatever was begun without due heed,
And all that was not properly conceived,
Although a promise and a pledge were given,
It is right to hesitate—to press on or draw back.

Before making any commitment, we should ponder it from every angle and be attentive to the possible consequences. If we've jumped into something blindly, it's wise to hesitate and ask, "Should I press on or draw back?" But having thought about our decision intelligently, why have any doubts? Make a well-considered choice and don't look back. This is the wisest approach.

4.3

> Yet all the buddhas and their heirs
> Have thought of this in their great wisdom;
> I myself have weighed and pondered it,
> So why should I now doubt and hesitate?

Being attentive before we act is not just advice for beginners. Even the buddhas and bodhisattvas are attentive before they make commitments. Shantideva himself weighed whether or not to take the bodhisattva vow. Having done so, he could relax. There would be no more reason for vacillation.

When we aren't sure what to do, we can seek inspiration from the teachers we trust. Based on their words and example, we may decide to take a leap. Here Shantideva says that he, like *the buddhas and their heirs,* has reflected carefully on his decision and sees no cause to draw back.

4.4

> For if I bind myself with promises,
> But fail to carry out my words in deed,
> Then every being will have been betrayed.
> What destiny must lie in store for me?

[handwritten margin note: Wow. Devotion for the benefit of others]

The stakes are too high for Shantideva to turn his back on sentient beings. Thus, in this and the following verses, he considers the consequences of being inattentive or careless after making a commitment as vast as the bodhisattva vow.

4.5

If in the teachings it is said
That one who in his thought intends
To give away a little thing but then draws back
Will take rebirth among the hungry ghosts,

4.6

How can I expect a happy destiny
If from my heart I summon
Wandering beings to the highest bliss,
But then deceive and let them down?

These verses address waffling. If you've ever had the impulse to be generous and then changed your mind, chances are you were influenced by greed or attachment. You had a chance to stretch; instead you strengthened the causes of poverty mentality, of "hungry ghosts," the mentality of insatiable neediness and "never enough."

If this is the case, Shantideva asks himself, what would be the outcome of taking a vow to benefit all beings and then failing to maintain it?

Reneging on the bodhisattva vow doesn't mean sometimes not feeling up to the task; it means opting for our own comfort and security on a permanent basis. Having made the commitment, there is no question we will sometimes feel inadequate and doubt our ability to be of benefit. These temporary lapses should be expected. But if we decide to let the bodhichitta spark go out, if we repress our appetite for challenge and growth, the consequences will be very sad indeed. We'll become examples of the old adage "you can't teach old dogs new tricks." The gravest sorrow comes from closing our minds to the suffering of others and feeling justified in doing so.

4.7

And as for those who, losing bodhichitta,
Nonetheless attain to liberation,
This is through the inconceivable effect of karma,
Only understood by the Omniscient.

This verse refers to the *arhat* Shariputra, one of the Buddha's closest disciples. He exemplifies the rare case of someone who became enlightened *despite* having lost heart and given up on his vow to forsake his own enlightenment until all beings were free of suffering.

According to legend, in a previous life Shariputra met a starving ogre who begged Shariputra to cut off his own arm. This, the ogre said, was the only food that would satisfy his hunger. Without any hesitation, Shariputra severed his right arm and offered it. The ogre was quite unhappy and complained, "I don't want your right arm; I want your left." Apparently this was the last straw for Shariputra. He became so discouraged with the unreasonableness of sentient beings, he gave up on his bodhisattva vow.

When bodhisattvas pledge themselves to work with increasingly difficult situations, they are, in fact, just asking for trouble. We have to face the fact that this includes working with the unreasonableness of sentient beings like you and me.

4.8

This failure is indeed the gravest
Of all bodhisattva downfalls.
For should it ever come to pass,
The good of every being is cast down.

Shantideva reiterates this point: the gravest mistake for any bodhisattva is to turn away permanently from the challenges of the world. Some discouragement is unavoidable; but if we completely give up on our longing and passion to extend ourselves, our results will probably not be as good as Shariputra's!

Fortunately, the bodhisattva vow is said to be like a golden vase: very valuable, yet easy to mend when broken. We can renew our bodhichitta commitments at any time. Inherent in the vow is kindness for our human frailty and the encouragement that it's never too late to start fresh.

4.9

And anyone who, for a single instant,
Halts the merit of a bodhisattva
Will wander endlessly in states of misery,
Because the welfare of all beings is brought low.

The second gravest mistake is anything that *halts the merit of a bodhisattva*. This is not so hard to do. When we hurt or insult people we dislike, who knows? We might be obstructing the merit of a bodhisattva. The best advice therefore is to treat everyone with care.

4.10

Destroy a single being's joy
And you will work the ruin of yourself.
But if the happiness of all is brought to nothing ...
What need is there to speak of this?

When we deliberately destroy even one being's joy, we also hurt ourselves. Being mean may bring short-term gratification, but in the end we just feel worse. If this is so, *what need is there to speak* of the outcome of forsaking our longing to alleviate suffering?

Shantideva advises us to be attentive to the cause and effect of karma and become intelligent about the consequences of our actions. He continues to address this subject in verses 11 through 25.

4.11

And one who wanders in samsara,
Who time and time again embraces bodhichitta,
Only to destroy it through his faults,
Will long be barred from bodhisattva grounds.

If we continually renew and break our commitments, we will *long be barred* from progressing along the bodhisattva path. We won't, however, be barred forever; despite the wording of verse 9, we will not *wander endlessly* in misery. The notion of eternal damnation is foreign to Buddhist thinking. Some states of mind may *seem* endless, but even the worst suffering is impermanent and there is always a way out.

 Nevertheless, by reinforcing old habits and obstructing the yearning to grow, we slow down our progress considerably. The habit of vacillating has consequences. We feel increasingly restless and dissatisfied; and we begin to regard ourselves as procrastinators, losers, people who never get anything done.

On the other hand, through attentiveness to the way karma unfolds, we can act intelligently and use this precious human life as a path to enlightenment, rather than a path to hell.

4.12

Therefore I will act devotedly
According to the promise I have made.
For if I fail thus to apply myself,
I'll fall from low to even lower states.

Moment by moment, depending on the way we work with our minds, we either wake up or fall deeper and deeper into sleep. Thus, we either become more flexible and adventurous or more set in our ways. May we therefore act according to our promise.

4.13

Striving for the benefit of all that lives,
Unnumbered buddhas have already lived and passed,
But I, by virtue of my sins, have failed
To come within the compass of their healing works.

The Buddha's blessings shine upon all of us without bias. But if we're living our lives in a north-facing cave, we won't receive the benefit of what's offered.

Three attitudes prevent us from receiving a continual flow of blessings. They are compared to three "pots": a full pot, a pot with poison in it, and a pot with a hole in the bottom.

The pot that's filled to the brim is like a mind full of opinions and preconceptions. We already know it all. We have so many fixed ideas that nothing new can affect us or cause us to question our assumptions.

The pot containing poison is like a mind that's so cynical, critical, and judgmental that everything is poisoned by this harshness. It allows for no openness and no willingness to explore the teachings or anything else that challenges our righteous stance.

The pot with a hole is like a distracted mind: our body is present but we're lost in thought. We're so busy thinking about our dream vacation or what's for dinner that we're completely deaf to what's being said.

Knowing how sad it is to receive blessings and not be able to benefit, Shantideva wants to save himself grief by remaining open and attentive. Nothing will improve, he says, unless we become more intelligent about cause and effect. This is a message worth considering seriously.

4.14

And this will always be my lot
If I continue to behave like this,
And I will suffer pains and bondage,
Wounds and laceration in the lower realms.

There is a repeating pattern to our behavior that we somehow seem to miss. When we're challenged, our habitual reactions are especially predictable: we strike out or withdraw, scream or weep, become arrogant or feel inadequate. These strategies for seeking security and avoiding discomfort only increase our uneasiness. But alas, they seem addictive; even though the results are unsatisfactory, we use them again and again.

Attentiveness functions like a guardian who protects us from repeating the same mistakes and strengthening the same patterns. We can catch ourselves getting hooked and avoid being swept away by *shenpa*.

4.15

The appearance of the buddhas in the world,
True faith and the attainment of the human form,
An aptitude for good: all these are rare.
And when will all this come to me again?

There are a few recurrent themes in Shantideva's teachings. One of them is the advantage of a precious human birth. We have too much going for us to waste this life, especially since we can't know when our good fortune might be lost. In verses 16 through 26, he says more on this important subject.

4.16

Today, indeed, I'm hale and hearty,
Have enough to eat, and am without affliction.
And yet this life is fleeting and deceptive.
This body is but briefly lent to me.

This precious life is like a dream. Even when it's a very pleasant dream, it's fleeting and uncertain. We will waste our good fortune if we take it for granted.

Too often, we're complacent about our favorable circumstances, particularly here in the West. But what happens to our state of mind when our modern conveniences break down? When the power goes off and our food starts to rot? The point is to let our present comforts support—not hinder—the bodhisattva way of life.

4.17

And yet the way I act is such
That I shall not regain a human life!
And losing this, my precious human form,
My evils will be many, virtues none.

Being attentive to the consequences of our actions is still the subject here. We can use our intelligence to act wisely instead of habitually.

In verse 18, Shantideva emphasizes being attentive to what we sow. Again, he says, our future well-being depends on sowing wholesome seeds rather than seeds of suffering.

4.18

Here is now the chance for wholesome deeds,
But if I fail now to accomplish virtue,

What will be my lot, what shall I do,
When trapped in lower realms, enmeshed in misery?

4.19

Never, there, performing any virtue,
Only ever perpetrating evil,
Thus for a hundred million aeons,
Happy states will never come to me.

When we're comfortable, it's relatively easy to open our hearts to another's suffering. But in states of intense misery, it's very difficult. If we're starving and someone gives us a bowl of rice, do we share it with someone else in the same boat? Because of our fear of starvation and death, we might find this extremely difficult. When we're *enmeshed in misery,* we just want relief from our pain. For one moment of not starving, we might easily turn our backs on someone else. That's the message: when suffering is intense, it's harder to think of others and harder to access bodhichitta.

Right now, because of our good birth, we have a chance to create the causes and conditions of happiness rather than misery, of inner strength and generosity rather than fearfulness and greed. This might not be so easy later on.

4.20

This is why Lord Buddha has declared
That like a turtle that perchance can place
Its head within a yoke adrift upon a shoreless sea,
This human birth is difficult to find!

Here we have the classic analogy for the difficulty of gaining a precious human birth: it's as rare as a sea turtle surfacing every hundred years to put its head through the hole of a floating yoke.

We might easily be born as an insect, a fish, or a human with no chance of hearing the dharma; our present good circumstances are rare.

4.21

If evil acts of but a single instant
Lead to deepest hell for many ages,
The evils I have done from time without beginning—
No need to say that they will keep me from the states
    of bliss!

If one intentional act of harm, even if it's over in an instant, reinforces hellish states of mind, then there's *no need to say* what will come of the harm we've intentionally caused, not just in this life but from beginningless time.

When we do a life review, we inevitably find we have some regrets. We've all said or done things that we wish we hadn't. Yet this doesn't mean we're doomed. By simply acknowledging what we've done, we interrupt the ignorance that sustains habitual patterns. Thus, instead of sabotaging our future happiness, we cultivate a relaxed and flexible mind.

The essential point is that we can at any time choose the path of suffering or happiness.

4.22

And mere experience of such pain
Does not result in being freed from it.
For in the very suffering of such states,
More evil will occur, and then in great abundance.

Shantideva reminds us, again, that intense pain usually hardens us and makes us more fearful and self-centered.

In the *Dharmapada,* a compilation of the Buddha's teachings, it says that great suffering can awaken great compassion. This is the bodhisattva ideal. The bodhichitta teachings explain how pain can make us kinder instead of more neurotic; how it can link us with others and awaken bodhichitta instead of causing greater harm. Without these teachings, however, suffering doesn't free us; it increases our tendency to stay stuck.

4.23

Thus, having found reprieve from all these
      things,
If I now fail to train myself in virtue,
What greater folly could there ever be?
How more could I betray myself?

Having found this precious situation, *how more could I betray myself?* Shantideva is saying that by letting down sentient beings, we're simultaneously betraying ourselves. As Booker T. Washington put it, "Don't let any person bring you so low as to hate them." Who really suffers most when we are filled with hatred? The key here is that we betray ourselves more than anyone else.

4.24

And though all this I understand,
But later waste my time in foolish idleness,
Then when my time to die comes round,
My sorrows will be black indeed.

Knowing that we are now in a situation where we can help ourselves, if we don't let this understanding inform our lives, what will be our state of mind when we die?

4.25

And when my body burns so long
In fires of hell so unendurable,
My mind likewise will also be tormented—
Burned in flames of infinite regret.

This verse makes the same point: if we keep strengthening the wrong habits, our minds will be tormented with *infinite regret*. But how should we understand this? If thinking of karma as punishment is a wrong view, and if there is no great avenger in the sky, what is being said here?

Shantideva is talking about the destructive power of negative emotions and the way they enslave us when we strengthen them. From here until the end of the chapter, having talked about attentiveness to cause and effect, he discusses the need to be attentive to the kleshas: aggression, craving, ignorance, jealousy, arrogance, pride, and all their offspring.

4.26

For it's as if by chance that I have gained
This state so hard to find, wherein to help myself.
And now, when freedom—power of choice—is mine,
If once again I'm led away to hell,

4.27

I am as if benumbed by sorcery,
My mind reduced to total impotence
With no perception of the madness overwhelming
    me.
O what is it that has me in its grip?

From moment to moment, we can choose how we relate to our emotions. This power of choice gives us freedom, and it would be crazy not to take advantage of it.

On the other hand, when habitual reactions are strong and long-standing, it's difficult to choose intelligently. We don't intentionally choose pain; we just do what's familiar, which isn't always the best idea. I think we can all relate with feeling *benumbed by sorcery, reduced to total impotence,* or overwhelmed by *madness.* But what actually has us in its grip? The answer is our kleshas: *limbless and devoid of faculties*—with, in essence, no substance or solidity at all!

[margin note: Fascinating but Neuroscience *]*

4.28

Anger, lust—these enemies of mine—
Are limbless and devoid of faculties.
They have no bravery, no cleverness;
How then have they reduced me to such slavery?

[margin note: Wow *]*

This is the sixty-four-thousand-dollar question. How can this powerful but completely ungraspable, ineffable energy do us so much harm? In the following verses Shantideva begins to answer this question by presenting the five faults of the kleshas, the five problematic aspects of our confused emotions.

The first fault, presented in verse 28, is that we become enslaved by the kleshas. This insight alone would undercut their power, if we were attentive to it. But as Shantideva says, it's as if we're under a spell.

Emotional reactivity starts as a slight tightening. There's the familiar tug of *shenpa* and before we know it, we're pulled along. In just a few seconds, we go from being slightly miffed to completely out of control.

Nevertheless, we have the inherent wisdom and ability to halt this chain reaction early on. To the degree that we're attentive, we can nip the addictive urge while it's still manageable. Just as we're about to step into the trap, we can at least pause and take some deep breaths before proceeding.

4.29

I it is who welcome them within my heart,
Allowing them to harm me at their pleasure!
I who suffer all without resentment—
Thus my abject patience, all displaced!

The second fault of the kleshas is that we welcome them. They're familiar. They give us something to hold on to, and they set off a predictable chain reaction that we find irresistible. This insight can be especially helpful.

When we realize that we *like* our kleshas, we begin to understand why they have such power over us. Hatred, for example, can make us feel strong and in charge. Rage makes us feel even more powerful and invulnerable. Craving and wanting can feel soothing, romantic, and nostalgic: we weep over lost loves or unfulfilled dreams. It's painfully and deliciously bittersweet. Therefore, we don't even consider interrupting the flow. Ignorance is oddly comforting: we don't have to do anything; we just lay back and don't relate to what's happening around us.

Each of us has our own personal way of welcoming and encouraging the kleshas. Being attentive to this is the first and crucial step. We can't be naïve. If we like our kleshas, we will never be motivated to interrupt their seductiveness; we'll always be too complacent and accommodating.

A good analogy for the kleshas is a drug pusher. When we want drugs, the pusher is our friend. We welcome him because our addiction is so strong. But when we want to get clean, we associate the pusher with misery, and he becomes someone to avoid. Shantideva's advice is to treat our crippling emotions like drug pushers.

If we don't want to stay addicted for life, we have to see that our negative emotions weaken us and cause us harm.

It is just as difficult to detox from emotions as it is to recover from heavy drugs or alcohol. However, when we see that this addiction is clearly ruining our life, we become highly motivated. Even if we find ourselves saying, "I don't want to give up my kleshas," at least we're being honest, and this stubborn declaration might begin to haunt us.

But I'll tell you this about klesha addiction: without the intelligence to see that it harms us and the clear intention to turn it around, that familiar urge will be very hard to interrupt before it's going strong.

Do not, however, underestimate the healing power of self-reflection. For example, when you're about to say a mean word or indulge in self-righteousness or criticism, just reflect on the spot: "If I strengthen this habit, will it bring suffering or relief?"

Of course, you need to be completely honest with yourself and not blindly buy into what the Buddha and Shantideva have to say. Maybe your habits give you pleasure as well as pain; maybe you'll conclude that they really don't cause you to suffer, even though the teachings say they should. Based on your own personal experience and wisdom, you have to answer these questions for yourself.

Verses 30 and 31 say more about the futility of habitual responses to kleshas, and the danger of welcoming that which causes suffering.

4.30

If all the gods and demigods besides
Together came against me as my foes,
Their mighty strength—all this would not avail
To fling me in the fires of deepest hell.

Shantideva says that nothing outside of us has the power to hurt us like the kleshas. We need to contemplate this and find out if it's true.

wow

4.31

And yet, the mighty fiend of my afflictions,
Flings me in an instant headlong down
To where the mighty lord of mountains
Would be burned, its very ashes all consumed.

Here he reflects that getting emotionally worked up has consequences so painful and intense they could reduce the mightiest of mountains to dust. But, again, the Buddhist teachings encourage us to reflect on our own experience to see if what's being taught rings true.

In verse 32, we have the third fault of the kleshas: if we're not attentive, the kleshas will continue harming us for a very long time.

4.32

No other enemy indeed
Has lived so long as my defiled emotions—
O my enemy, afflictive passion,
Endless and beginningless companion!

Long after those we despise have moved away or died, the hatred habit remains with us. The more we run our habitual patterns, the stronger they become—and, of course, the stronger they get, the more we run them. As this chain reaction becomes harder to interrupt, our experience of imprisonment becomes more intense until we feel hopelessly trapped with a monstrous companion. No outer foe will ever plague us as much as our own kleshas.

Verse 33 presents the fourth fault: give the kleshas an inch and they'll take a mile.

4.33

All other foes that I appease and wait upon
Will show me favors, give me every aid,
But should I serve my dark defiled emotions,
They will only harm me, draw me down to grief.

Shantideva warns us not to be naïve about the pusher; we have to know his strategies and seductive ways. Likewise, we simply can't afford to be ignorant about the power of emotions. We can neither welcome nor indulge them in hopes they'll bring us happiness or security.

When the teachings tell us to "make friends with our emotions," they mean to become more attentive and get to know them better. Being ignorant about emotions only makes matters worse; feeling guilty or ashamed of them does the same. Struggling against them is equally nonproductive. The only way to dissolve their power is with our wholehearted, intelligent attention.

Only then is it possible to stay steady, connect with the underlying energy, and discover their insubstantial nature. We can't be stupid about this process. There's no way to abide with our dynamic, ungraspable emotions if we keep fueling them with thoughts. It's like trying to put out a fire with kerosene.

4.34

Therefore, if these long-lived, ancient enemies of mine,
The wellspring only of increasing woe,
Can find their lodging safe within my heart,
What joy or peace in this world can be found?

In verse 34, Shantideva presents the fifth and final problematic aspect of the kleshas: as long as we are enslaved by them, there will never be world peace. We will have no peace of mind personally, and the suffering of beings everywhere will continue unabated. War will continue; and violence, neglect, addiction, and greed will continue endlessly. By steadying ourselves *before* we're taken over by our emotions, we create the causes of peace and joy for us all.

4.35

And if the jail guards of the prisons of samsara,
The butchers and tormentors of infernal realms,
All lurk within me in the web of craving,
What joy can ever be my destiny?

Typically we blame others for our misery. But Shantideva says we create our own *infernal realms:* our personal hells are interdependent with our klesha-ridden minds. In his view, we must take responsibility for what happens to us. If we give safe lodging to neurosis, then how can we expect it to result in joy?

Just before the Buddha attained enlightenment, his kleshas arose in full force. He was tempted by anger, desire, and all the rest; but unlike most of us, he didn't take the bait. He is always pictured as wide awake: fully present—on the dot—relaxed and undistracted by the powerful energy of the kleshas.

In one of the Harry Potter books, the budding bodhisattva, Harry, is put under a curse that creates an extremely strong urge to give in to the kleshas and do harm. The power of Harry's intelligence and kindness, however, is even stronger. He doesn't believe the voices of the kleshas or get seduced by their promises of comfort, and so the curse doesn't work.

4.36

I will not leave the fight until, before my eyes,
These enemies of mine are all destroyed.
For if, aroused to fury by the merest slight,
Incapable of sleep until the scores are settled,

4.37

Foolish rivals, both to suffer when they die,
Will draw the battle lines and do their best to win,
And careless of the pain of cut and thrust,
Will stand their ground, refusing to give way,

4.38

No need to say that I will not lose heart,
Regardless of the hardships of the fray.
These natural foes today I'll strive to crush—
These enemies, the source of all my pain.

Because Shantideva was a prince in the warrior tradition, it's natural for him to use images of war. His words, however, are not meant to convey aggression. The courage of the samsaric warrior is used as an analogy for the compassionate courage of the bodhisattva. We need bravery to nonaggressively stand our ground against the kleshas. With the weapons of clear determination, intelligent awareness, and compassion, we can short-circuit their seductiveness and power.

Of course, we may experience discomfort in the process, the same discomfort and restlessness we go through with any withdrawal. According to tradition, giving in to the lure of kleshas is easy in the beginning, but makes our lives increasingly more difficult in the end. In contrast, withdrawing from habitual responses is difficult in the beginning, but our lives become increasingly more relaxed and free in the end.

When we're going through klesha withdrawal, it helps to know we're on the right track. Shantideva remarks that—just as *foolish rivals* endure physical pain, sleeplessness, and even death—he will go through the anguish of detox to cease being a slave to his kleshas. He will not lose heart and give up because of pain or fear.

4.39

The wounds inflicted by the enemy in futile wars
Are flaunted by the soldier as a trophy.
So in the high endeavor for so great a prize,
Why should hurt and injury dismay me?

Wow

In the wars fought because of greed or hatred, soldiers proudly display their wounds: their injuries are like trophies for bravery. We can also expect "wounds" when we interrupt the momentum of the kleshas. In such a worthy endeavor as liberation from samsara, we could take pride in the suffering we go through. Instead of complaining, let's regard these wounds as trophies.

4.40

When fishers, butchers, farmers, and the like,
Intending just to gain their livelihood,
Will suffer all the miseries of heat and cold,
How can I not bear the same to gain the happiness of
    beings?

People go through hell for their livelihood. Fishermen go out on icy waters in the bitter cold. Farmers lose everything when there's an untimely frost. Athletes endure incredible pain to win the prize. We're willing to go through almost anything if we think it will pay off. What if we were that willing to do what it takes to nurture the bodhi heart? With this kind of intention, we could achieve the greatest satisfaction for ourselves and others—far greater than the benefits of any other pursuit.

4.41

When I pledged myself to free from their affliction
Beings who abide in every region,
Stretching to the limits of the sky,
I myself was subject to the same afflictions.

4.42

Thus I did not have the measure of my strength—
To speak like this was clear insanity.
More reason, then, for never drawing back,
Abandoning the fight against defiled confusion.

This is what distinguishes a mature bodhisattva, such as Shanti-deva, from bodhisattvas-in-training. When he says that taking the bodhisattva vow *was clear insanity,* he's not expressing feelings of despondency or inadequacy. He's saying it as an incentive to get busy, to do whatever it takes to live his life as attentively and wakefully as possible. Instead of indulging in guilt and other variations on the theme of failure, he spurs himself on.

The next time you are feeling hopeless because you can't make a dent in your confusion, you can encourage yourself with Shanti-deva's words: *More reason, then, for never drawing back.*

Every courageous gesture we make, whether or not we think it's successful, definitely imprints our mind in a positive way. The slightest willingness to interrupt our old habits predisposes us to greater bravery, greater strength, and greater empathy for others. No matter how trapped we feel, we can always be of benefit. How? By interrupting our defeatist story lines and working intelligently and wisely with our kleshas.

4.43

This shall be my all-consuming passion;
Filled with rancor I will wage my war!
Though this emotion seems to be defiled,
It halts defilement and shall not be spurned.

In verse 43, *this emotion* is anger. Although it is usually seen as a problem, Shantideva takes a homeopathic approach and vows to use anger to cure anger. Rousing his passionate enthusiasm for the task, he proceeds with all-consuming warriorship and joy.

4.44

Better if I perish in the fire,
Better that my head be severed from my body
Than ever I should serve or reverence
My mortal foes, defiled emotions.

As the years go by, I understand this kind of passionate determination and confidence more and more. The choice is mine. I can spend my life strengthening my kleshas or I can weaken them. I can continue to be their slave; or, realizing they're not solid, I can simply accept them as my own powerful yet ineffable energy. It's increasingly clear which choice leads to further pain and which one leads to relaxation and delight.

4.45

Common enemies, when driven from the state,
Retreat and base themselves in other lands,
And muster all their strength the better to return.
But our afflictions are without such stratagems.

4.46

Defiled emotions, scattered by the eye of wisdom!
Where will you now run, when driven from my mind?
Whence would you return to do me harm?
But oh—my mind is feeble. I am indolent!

Now Shantideva presents the bright side. He is joyful that he can
free himself from the kleshas and expresses this joy from verse 45
to the end.

Happiness comes with knowing that once they're uprooted by
the eye of wisdom, the kleshas can never return. Their power evap-
orates once we see their empty, ephemeral nature. Dzigar Kongtrul
recalls how terrified the youngest monks in his monastery would
be by the annual snow lion dance. When they got older and realized the snow lion wasn't real, that it was only a costume, they
automatically lost their fear. This is an apt analogy for the essential
emptiness of the kleshas.

4.47

And yet defilements are not in the object,
Nor yet within the faculties, nor somewhere in
      between.
And if not elsewhere, where is their abode
Whence they might wreak their havoc on the world?
They are simple mirages, and so—take heart!

Banish all your fear and strive to know their nature.
Why suffer needlessly the pains of hell?

Despite all this war imagery, Shantideva is not really encouraging us to do battle with the kleshas. He is asking us to examine them carefully and discover their illusory nature.

The next time you start to get angry, ask yourself, "Where does this klesha abide?" Does it abide in the person I'm angry with? Does it abide in my sense perceptions? Or somewhere in between? What is the nature of this anger? And who is it that's angry?

Look closely, too, at how you fuel the kleshas with your thoughts. Just look at any thought and ask: Where did this thought come from? Where is it right now? And then, "Where did it go?" If you can find anything solid to hold on to when you look at the arising, dwelling, and passing of a thought, I'd like to be the first to know.

We build up fantasy worlds in our minds, causing the kleshas to escalate. Then, like awakening from a dream, we discover this fantasy has no substance and the kleshas have no basis.

My friend's father has Alzheimer's disease. Previously he was a very angry man. But since he lost his memory, he's changed. Because he can't remember what he was angry about, he can't fuel his bitterness. When he becomes irritated, he just can't make it stick. Without his story lines, the causes for anger dissolve.

Of course we don't always feel up to working so attentively with our kleshas. As Shantideva says, our minds sometimes seem feeble and lazy. But take heart: we don't have to gear up for a big struggle. The enemy is a mirage!

4.48

This is how I should reflect and labor,
Taking up the precepts just set forth.
What invalid in need of medicine
Ignored his doctor's words and gained his health?

Just as a sick person won't get well without following her doctor's advice, we won't be helped by these teachings unless we put them into practice. This is not academic study; we could study the *Bodhicharyavatara* daily, and still keep strengthening our kleshas. These teachings are a way of life. To awaken bodhichitta, nurture it, and have it flourish, take Shantideva's words very personally and use them whenever you find yourself getting hooked and carried away.

Taming the Mind

Vigilance, Part One

I N CHAPTER 5 of *The Way of the Bodhisattva*, Shanti-deva gives instruction on the *paramita* of discipline. The theme of discipline generally emphasizes conduct, the way we speak and act. The main theme here, however, is taming the mind. In order for any outer discipline to transform us—and for bodhichitta to not diminish—it's essential to tame the wildness of our minds.

5.1

Those who wish to keep a rule of life
Must guard their minds in perfect self-possession.
Without this guard upon the mind,
No discipline can ever be maintained.

The method for taming the mind is *shamatha* meditation. *Shamatha* is a Sanskrit word meaning "calm abiding," or "the development of peace." In this practice, we generally work with the breath as our object of meditation. But whatever object we use, the instruction is always the same: when we see that our mind is wandering, we gently bring it back. In this way, we come back to the present, back to the immediacy of our experience. This is done without harshness or judgment, and it's done over and over again.

When the mind is wild, we have no foundation for maintaining discipline: specifically, the three disciplines of not causing harm, gathering virtue, and benefiting others. How can we work with the kleshas, or act and speak with kindness, or reach out to others, if our mind is crazed? Without the stability and alertness of a tamed mind, how can we be present? Therefore, mindfully, gently, and repeatedly, we train in coming back.

Taming the mind takes time. Through good and bad moods, through periods of peacefulness and klesha attacks, we train in being present. Day by day, month by month, year by year, we become better able to *keep a rule of life,* better able to lead the life of a bodhisattva who can hear the cries of the world and extend a hand.

5.2

Wandering where it will, the elephant of mind,
Will bring us down to pains of deepest hell.
No worldly beast, however wild,
Could bring upon us such calamities.

In Buddhist literature there are many animal analogies for the wildness of mind: monkey mind, for example, or the out-of-control nature of an untamed horse. Here Shantideva magnifies the image by choosing the most powerful of all tamable beasts: an elephant. If a wild horse or monkey can wreak havoc, imagine the destruction that could result from a crazed elephant!

If I were delivering verse 2, it might read like this: "If our mind remains untamed and distracted, we will have constant emotional upheavals, and our anger and addictions will get stronger." But Shantideva is not one to mince words. A scattered mind, he says, *will bring us down to pains of deepest hell.*

Here "hell" is a synonym for the dire consequences of a distracted mind. Shantideva uses bold language to make sure we get this point. Until we start taming the mind, we're constantly pushed around by our emotions. Nothing in this world—no beasts, muggers, or outer threats—cause us as much unhappiness as our own wild elephant mind.

5.3

If, with mindfulness' rope,
The elephant of the mind is tethered all around,
Our fears will come to nothing,
Every virtue drop into our hands.

Cultivating mind's inherent capacity to stay put is called mindfulness training. Mindfulness is like the rope that keeps the wild elephant from destroying everything in sight. The rope of mindfulness brings us back to our immediate experience: to our breath, to our walking, to the book in our hands.

This point is essential: mindfulness tethers the mind to the present. Initially this takes effort, but this effort is applied with a very light touch. It's like brushing your teeth: you brush, you get distracted, and you just naturally come back. No big deal. And so it goes with mindfulness training: mind is present, mind wanders, and mind comes back. No big deal. By gently returning to the present, gradually all *our fears will come to nothing, every virtue drop into our hands.* When mind calms down, everything seems workable.

Now Shantideva's words might give us the idea that this will be quick: "I'll work with my mind and by this time next month my problems may be over." But in truth, our mental habits are ancient and take awhile to unwind. So we need to train with patience, intelligence, and gentleness. These supportive qualities will then increase; at times they may seem to magically drop into our hands.

When the mind is settled, virtuous qualities come to us more naturally. We have fresh insights and more kindness, relaxation, and steadiness.

5.4

Tigers, lions, elephants, and bears,
Snakes and every hostile beast,
Those who guard the prisoners in hell,
All ghosts and ghouls and every evil phantom,

5.5

By simple binding of this mind alone,
All these things are likewise bound.
By simple taming of this mind alone,
All these things are likewise tamed.

5.6

For all anxiety and fear,
All sufferings in boundless measure,
Their source and wellspring is the mind itself,
Thus the Truthful One has said.

Here Shantideva is saying something revolutionary: all anxiety, fear, and suffering disappear when we tame our mind. Even if we come upon a tiger or a ghost, we'll stay cool. When we are present and awake, emotions have a short life span, but when we're unconscious, they can last for years.

5.7

The hellish whips to torture living beings—
Who has made them and to what intent?
Who has forged this burning iron ground;
Whence have all these demon women sprung?

5.8

All are but the offspring of the sinful mind,
Thus the Mighty One has said.
Thus throughout the triple world
There is no greater bane than mind itself.

Here Shantideva says explicitly that hellish circumstances, such as whips and other horrors, come only from a hellish state of mind. This view helps us to understand the *demon women* in verse 7. In traditional teachings on the hell realms, they represent objects of insatiable lust and could just as easily be called "demon men." In the description of one particularly torturous state, we are continually seduced up a hill made of razor-sharp swords to reach our lover. Although we're cut to shreds, we keep climbing to the top, only to have this sexy apparition turn into a devouring demon. This happens over and over again. Such suffering results from the out-of-control craving of an extremely lustful mind; it starts as an ember, but quickly ignites into a full-blown hell of insatiable desire.

As much as the monks in Shantideva's audience might have liked to blame their horniness on women, and as much as any of us would like to look outside of ourselves for the cause of our misery, *there is no greater bane than mind itself.* An unobserved, wild mind can keep us trapped in some very uncomfortable places.

5.9

If transcendent giving is
To dissipate the poverty of beings,
In what way, since the poor are always with us,
Have former buddhas practiced perfect generosity?

5.10

The true intention to bestow on every being
All possessions—and the fruits of such a gift:
By such, the teachings say, is generosity perfected.
And this, as we may see, is but the mind itself.

In verses 9 through 17, Shantideva presents a helpful approach to understanding the six *paramitas*: generosity, discipline, patience, enthusiasm, meditation, and wisdom. He explains how they are transformed into enlightened activity by taming the mind. Until we work with the mind, the *paramitas* can't really liberate us. This is because the *paramitas* and letting go of self-clinging are the same.

So it is with all of our actions: they either undercut our attachments or strengthen them; they bring us into the present or distract us. Whenever any action takes us beyond self-absorption, it becomes a *paramita*, but this only happens when we're willing to tame our minds.

For example, bodhisattvas practice the first *paramita*, generosity, with the wish to end the *poverty* of beings. Now, a skeptic might say, "The aspiration is noble, but I notice nothing much has changed; material poverty still runs rampant." To which Shantideva might reply, "Until we deal with poverty *mind*, the redistribution of all the wealth in the world won't change the outer situation."

A beggar woman once asked the Buddha for food. Seeing her

immense craving, he wished to alleviate her suffering at the core. So, when she held out her bowl, he promised to give food to her and her family every day for the rest of their lives, on one condition. She had to say "No, I do not need this," and then wait a few minutes before taking her food. Sadly, the poor woman couldn't bring herself to say these words. The Buddha gave her that day's food anyway, but she never appeared again.

With insatiable craving, whether we're rich or poor, we will always find ourselves living in a world of never enough. This is Shantideva's point.

5.11

Where, indeed, could beings, fishes, and the rest
Be placed, to shield them totally from suffering?
Deciding to refrain from harming them
Is said to be perfection of morality.

The same logic applies to the *paramita* of discipline, in verse 11. Until we decide never to harm others, how can beings find a place of permanent safety? To the degree that we refrain from hurting one another, to that degree the world is a kinder place. Without this clear intention, no conventional disciplined conduct, however ethical it seems, will ever free us from the unconscious actions of a self-centered mind.

5.12

The hostile multitudes are vast as space—
What chance is there that all should be subdued?
Let but this angry mind be overthrown
And every foe is then and there destroyed.

This verse refers to the primary antidote to aggression: the *paramita* of patience. Again, Shantideva points to the interdependence of our states of mind and our perceptions of the world around us. Thus, without anger, there is no enemy. By calming our enraged mind, *every foe is then and there destroyed.* Certainly we know danger when we see it, but this doesn't mean we hate the person holding the gun. When hatred consumes us, we perceive enemies everywhere.

5.13

To cover all the earth with sheets of hide—
Where could such amounts of skin be found?
But simply wrap some leather round your feet,
And it's as if the whole earth had been covered!

Verse 13 is probably the most famous verse in the *Bodhicharya-vatara*. The analogy suggests we've been walking barefoot over blazing hot sands, thorns, and stones, and our feet are bruised and bleeding. Suddenly, we come up with a way to end our suffering: we'll cover the surface of the whole world with leather! This is, of course, impossible. But what if we wrapped leather around our feet? Then we could walk anywhere without a problem.

Our problems can't be solved by eliminating each and every outer cause. Nevertheless, people everywhere take this approach: "It's the world's fault; it's too rough, too sharp, too alien. If I could get rid of these outer woes, I'd be happy."

Shantideva says: If you want to protect your feet, wear shoes; and if you want to protect yourself from the world's provocations, tame your mind. The antidote to misery is to stay present.

5.14

Likewise, we can never take
And turn aside the outer course of things.

But only seize and discipline the mind itself,
And what is there remaining to be curbed?

Sometimes we *can* change or *turn aside* the course of outer events. Just look at the work of Gandhi and Martin Luther King Jr. But we can see from our planet's history that injustices never seem to end. The only way to make real change in the world, Shantideva says, is to discipline the mind. Imagine how the world would change if everyone were taming their mind.

5.15

A clear intent can fructify
And bring us birth in lofty Brahma's realm.
The acts of body and of speech are less—
They do not generate a like result.

From the Buddhist point of view, a clear and concentrated mind can bring us the bliss of *lofty Brahma's realm*. Mere actions and words can't generate *a like result*. A clear, stable mind, in fact, brings the even greater benefit of eliminating our own and others' suffering where it originates. To attain that kind of settled mind we need the *paramita* of enthusiasm to keep us motivated.

5.16

Recitations and austerities,
Long though they may prove to be,
If practiced with distracted mind,
Are futile, so the Knower of the Truth has said.

Even years and years of meditation, *if practiced with distracted mind,* won't free us from habitual patterns. The *paramita* of meditation is about taming the mind, not just sitting in an upright posture, thinking about life's joys and sorrows.

5.17

All who fail to know and penetrate
This secret of the mind, the Dharma's peak,
Although they wish for joy and sorrow's end,
Will wander uselessly in misery.

Ultimately the key to happiness and freedom from suffering is a direct experience of the emptiness or suchness of all experience. This is *the Dharma's peak,* the subject of Shantideva's ninth chapter. Since this book does not include teachings on the ninth, or "wisdom," chapter, let me say a few words here about its importance.

None of us wants to be miserable; we all want to be happy. But we can't achieve this aim if we stay stuck in biased, narrow-minded thinking. No matter how much we long for joy, it will elude us if we continue buying into concepts of right and wrong, good and bad, acceptance and rejection. What ultimately frees us from these constricting patterns is to stop reifying our experience, and to connect with the ineffable, groundless nature of all phenomena.

This nature cannot be said to exist or not exist—or anything in between. As Shantideva says in the wisdom chapter:

9.34

When real and nonreal both
Are absent from before the mind,
Nothing else remains for mind to do
But rest in perfect peace, from concepts free.

There is no better use of a human life than to realize the unfabricated nonconceptual freshness of our mind. This is the source of all wisdom and all compassion.

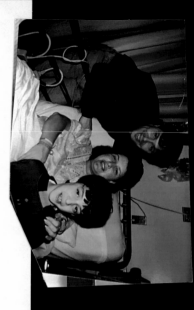

5.18

This is so, and therefore I will seize
This mind of mine and guard it well.
What use to me so many harsh austerities?
But let me only discipline and guard my mind!

Just as harshness doesn't work to tame a wild animal, it also doesn't work to tame the wildness of our minds. Rather than the austerities of some traditions, Shantideva encourages us to use gentleness to train the mind.

5.19

When in wild, unruly crowds
We move with care to shield our broken limbs,
Likewise when we live in evil company,
Our wounded minds we should not fail to guard.

5.20

For if I carefully protect my wounds
Because I fear the hurt of cuts and bruises,
Why should I not guard my wounded mind,
For fear of being crushed beneath the cliffs of hell?

If we have a broken limb, we're quick to protect it. We pay attention, for instance, when we pass through a *wild, unruly crowd.* We can use this same natural response to guard our distracted, impulsive mind. In situations that could easily trigger this overreactive mind, we'd be wise to be especially alert and attentive to what's happening.

In certain places or with certain people, we might easily get swept into aggression or addictions. It's not that those people or places are inherently "evil"; our mind is just still too vulnerable not to get into trouble. When we are in recovery, for example, we do not risk hanging out with our old drinking or drug-using buddies.

The consequences of being taken over by addictions—or jealousy, hatred, or ignorance—are both painful and predictable: it can feel like *being crushed beneath the cliffs of hell.*

5.21

If this is how I act and live,
Then even in the midst of evil folk,
Or even with fair women, all is well.
My diligent observance of the vows will not
    decline.

Shantideva was addressing an assembly of celibate monks, for whom women were generally regarded as temptation and trouble. Here he addresses their prejudiced and fearful minds. He's saying, in effect: You may think the problem is *fair women,* but the problem is your mind. If you monks tame your minds, you can go anywhere and be with anyone; you could hang out with Playboy bunnies without any difficulty. There'd be no such thing as *evil folk.* Without a steady mind, how can you speak of wanting to help all beings? You'll always be caught by attraction and aversion.

5.22

Let my property and honor all grow less,
And likewise all my health and livelihood,
And even other virtues—all can go!
But never will I disregard my mind.

5.23

All you who would protect your minds,
Maintain awareness and your mental vigilance.
Guard them both, at cost of life and limb—
Thus I join my hands, beseeching you.

Having made an irrefutable case for taming the mind, Shantideva now discusses more precisely how it's done. The primary instruction is to nurture mindfulness and alertness, translated here
as *awareness* and *mental vigilance*. In Tibetan these are *trenpa* and
sheshin: trenpa, or "mindfulness," is the mind's natural ability to
stay present; *sheshin* is "alertness," the mind's ability to know
what's happening. These qualities may be dormant at present, but
they can be revived through *shamatha* meditation.

Shantideva is *beseeching you* to cultivate mindfulness and alertness and maintain these two qualities. "Please listen to me," he says.
"You will never regret it."

5.24

Those disabled by ill health
Are helpless, powerless to act.
The mind, when likewise cramped by ignorance,
Is impotent and cannot do its work.

The ignorance referred to here is twofold. The deepest ignorance is our misperception of reality, our dualistic perception. This
is the illusion of subject and object, self and other. The translator
Herbert Guenther calls this "primitive views about reality."

This ignorance is so ingrained, we take it for granted. Yet this
misperception of separateness sets off an unfortunate chain reaction: it creates a tension between you and me that leads to concepts

of "for and against," "like and dislike," "want and don't want," and all the rest of our misery.

This generates the second kind of ignorance: the ignorance of the kleshas. Once born, our emotions quickly intensify, and suffering increases. Thus the ignorance of dualistic perception leads predictably to turmoil.

Just as ill health incapacitates the body, ignorance covers the freshness of our pristine, naked mind. The inability to see without bias and preconceptions clouds our natural mindfulness and alertness. Without a clear, stable mind, we live a fear-based life so controlled by our emotions that we don't really know what's going on. Just as physical therapy can restore the body to basic health, *shamatha* meditation is the mental therapy that can restore our basic sanity.

5.25

And those who have no mental vigilance,
Though they may hear the teachings, ponder them
    or meditate,
With minds like water seeping from a leaking jug,
Their learning will not settle in their memories.

When we are distracted, we can't remember anything we've studied or read. Our mind is like a *leaking jug* or a pot with a hole in the bottom. If we continue cultivating distractedness instead of the alertness of *sheshin*, we will become even more proficient at mental wandering than we already are.

5.26

Many have devotion, perseverance,
Are learned also and endowed with faith,
But through the fault of lacking mental vigilance,
Will not escape the stain of sin and downfall.

Kleshas and distractedness go together. Even with the excellent qualities of devotion, perseverance, learning, and faith, the kleshas will continue to capture us. Unless our mind is present and re-laxed, we will find ourselves frequently worked up, which, as we know, has unpleasant consequences.

5.27

Lack of vigilance is like a thief
Who slinks behind when mindfulness abates.
And all the merit we have gathered in
He steals, and down we go to lower realms.

5.28

Defilements are a band of robbers
Waiting for their chance to bring us injury.
They steal our virtue, when their moment comes,
And batter out the life of happy destinies.

These verses repeat the main instruction: the kleshas overtake us when we're distracted. Like a *band of robbers,* they wait until we're unconscious: it's when we're not paying attention that we get mugged, and all our good fortune and happiness is lost.

Emotional chaos can do us more harm than any ordinary bandits. With mindfulness, however, we can catch the klesha urges while they're small and disarm them before they harm us.

5.29

Therefore, from the gateway of awareness
Mindfulness shall not have leave to stray.
And if it wanders, it shall be recalled,
By thoughts of anguish in the lower worlds.

The *gateway of awareness* refers to our growing understanding of what truly helps and harms us. This intelligence is traditionally called "knowing what to cultivate and what to refrain from." It isn't based on some preconceived list; it's knowing for ourselves what opens our minds and what increases our misery. When we see the mind get stuck in notions of "for and against" or some seductive fantasy, we recall how much pain was caused by getting swept away in the past and we gently return to the present. As soon as we see we're hooked, we let go of the story line and return to the immediacy of our experience.

5.30

In those endowed with fortune and devotion,
Mindfulness is cultivated easily—
Through fear, and by the counsels of their abbots,
And staying ever in their teacher's company.

In verses 30 through 32, Shantideva talks about devotion. This is the gratitude and love we have for our teachers. In mahayana Buddhism the teacher is called the *kalyanamitra*, or "spiritual friend." But this friend does not extend to us what Trungpa Rinpoche called "idiot compassion," continually feeding our neuroses or bailing us out so we can get in trouble again. This friend teaches us to help ourselves.

Earlier Shantideva said that devotion won't help us if we have a wandering mind. Here he goes further: with the openheartedness of devotion, it is much easier to cultivate mindfulness.

Why is this so? If we have the good fortune, or merit, to meet a man or woman who's awake, just being in his or her presence, or encountering their teachings, we experience the clarity of our own mind. Sometimes when my habitual patterns seem overwhelming, just imagining the face of Trungpa Rinpoche inspires me to come back to being present. When nothing else works, the thought or words of our teachers can motivate us to stay alert and not be seduced by old patterns.

Devotion, gratitude, and love for our teachers bring us back to the vastness and warmth of bodhichitta. Whether or not they're physically present, we are always in their company. When we combine their wise counsel with a healthy fear of continuing to make the same mistakes, we find we have all the support we need to cultivate mindfulness and alertness.

5.31

The buddhas and the bodhisattvas both
Possess unclouded vision, seeing everything:
Everything lies open to their gaze,
And likewise I am always in their presence.

5.32

One who has such thoughts as these
Will gain devotion and a sense of fear and shame.
For such a one, the memory of Buddha
Rises frequently before the mind.

The *buddhas and the bodhisattvas* embody awakened mind. To say that *everything lies open to their gaze* means that the clarity and warmth of that mind is always available. In that sense, we are always in the presence of awakened mind and can tune in to it at any time. Realizing this brings both inspiration and the support of what here is called *fear and shame.*

"Fear" refers to understanding the consequences of giving in to the habitual tug of the kleshas. It is not a fear of anything external; it is the fear of causing our own suffering. We know we don't want to keep going in that direction, that we want to stop.

"Shame" is a loaded word for westerners. Like most things, it can be seen in a positive or negative light. Negative shame is accompanied by guilt and self-denigration. It is pointless and doesn't help us even slightly.

Positive shame, on the other hand, is recognizing when we've harmed ourselves or anyone else and feeling sorry for having done so. It allows us to grow wiser from our mistakes. Eventually it dawns on us that we can regret causing harm without becoming weighed down by negative shame. Just seeing the hurt and heartbreak clearly motivates us to move on. By acknowledging what we did cleanly and compassionately, we go forward.

Beautiful

5.33

When mindfulness is stationed as a sentinel,
A guard upon the threshold of the mind,
Mental scrutiny is likewise present,
Returning when forgotten or dispersed.

When we do *shamatha* meditation practice, we are choosing to be awake. Mindfulness is the *sentinel* that notices when we wander off. It's not a harsh or judgmental guard, but more like a protector. *Mental scrutiny,* or alertness, is also present as the impetus to come back. Again and again, the mind will wander away or get *forgotten or dispersed,* and again and again we gently bring it back.

5.34

If at the outset, when I check my mind,
I find within some fault or insufficiency,
I'll stay unmoving, like a log,
In self-possession and determination.

Here *fault or insufficiency* refers to the dullness *or* wildness of our minds.

When we first sit down in meditation, we can check our state of mind to see what's going on. If we see dullness or wildness, instead of fueling it with our thoughts, we simply stay awake to whatever is happening, without condemning or succumbing to it. This brings a sense of workability to our practice and makes us feel more self-possessed.

The traditional instruction for working with drowsiness is to perk ourselves up by breathing more deeply and looking slightly upward. When the mind is wild, the instruction suggests remaining in the meditation posture but dropping the technique altogether, along with any sense of struggle. Whatever is happening with our mind, we can see it and make the necessary adjustment. Thus we become our own meditation instructor.

5.35

I shall never, vacantly,
Allow my gaze to wander all about,
But rather with a focused mind
Will always go with eyes cast down.

These are instructions for taming the mind when we're out and about. If you've ever been to Thailand or Burma, you know that the monks there train this way. When they go out for alms, they walk *with eyes cast down* and never look around. This is mindfulness practice in action: lowering the gaze and making no eye contact. It was probably a standard instruction for the monks at Nalanda. The idea is to lessen distractions and heighten awareness of habitual tendencies.

It can be helpful to create certain times to practice mindfulness in this very undistracted way, being alert to any tendency to get too tight or too loose.

5.36

> But that I might relax my gaze,
> I'll sometimes raise my eyes and look around.
> And if some person stands within my sight,
> I'll greet him with a friendly word of welcome.

There are times for tight practice; but there is also the need for warmth and awareness of one's environment. Shantideva instructs the monks not to be aloof. When it's appropriate to look around and be friendly, one should do just that.

Our guideline is "not too distracted, not too uptight." If someone along the way is wounded, you don't just walk by with downcast eyes. If a little child tickles you, you're not so serious that you can't laugh. Being awake means acting appropriately.

5.37

> And yet, to spy the dangers on the road,
> I'll scrutinize the four directions one by one.
> And when I stop to rest, I'll turn my head
> And look behind me, back along my path.

5.38

> And so, I'll spy the land, in front, behind,
> To see if I should go or else return.
> And thus in every situation,
> I shall know my needs and act accordingly.

The point of this training is to not be distracted by our conditioned responses. In this way, we can see clearly what needs to be done and *act accordingly.* As is said, we care for whatever needs our care and destroy whatever needs to be destroyed. Not blinded by likes and dislikes, enemies and friends, we can see very clearly how to proceed.

5.39

Deciding on a given course,
Determining the actions of my body,
From time to time I'll verify
My body's actions, by repeated scrutiny.

Verse 39 refers to training in mindfulness of body. *From time to time* we take a fresh look at what's going on with our body and our actions. Without being critical or proud about what we observe, we simply pay attention to what we're doing.

5.40

This mind of mine, a wild and rampant elephant,
I'll tether to that sturdy post: reflection on the
    Teaching.
And I shall narrowly stand guard
That it might never slip its bonds and flee.

The subject of this and the following verses is training in mindfulness of mind. The confused wild elephant of the mind is tethered with the rope of mindfulness and held fast with the hook of alertness.

The *sturdy post* to which we tether our minds is *reflection on the Teaching*. We might reflect on cause and effect, on the misery produced by the kleshas, or on the benefit of taming the mind. The point is, when we realize we're hooked, it is very helpful to teach ourselves the dharma.

5.41

Those who strive to master concentration
Should never for an instant be distracted.
They should constantly investigate themselves,
Examining the movements of their minds.

This verse describes a very tight practice. Traditionally such an approach is compared to walking a plank over a steep ravine: this is how present we try to be. It is balanced by the practice described in verse 42.

5.42

In fearful situations, times of celebration,
One may desist, when self-survey becomes impossible.
For it is taught that in the times of generosity,
The rules of discipline may be suspended.

This is practical advice for the overzealous: a fledgling bodhisattva, for example, who goes to a party and tries to practice tight mindfulness instead of just relaxing and having fun. Such rigid self-observance is too harsh and, in terms of rousing the good heart of bodhichitta, counterproductive.

The best advice for a new bodhisattva is to tame your mind without losing your sense of humor.

5.43

When something has been planned and started on,
Attention should not drift to other things.
With thoughts fixed on the chosen target,
That and that alone should be pursued.

Many of us have the tendency to start things and then get distracted. Like three-year-old children, our minds jump from one thing to another, and our bodies follow.

To tame the wild mind, Shantideva suggests that when you start something, you pursue it to the end. In this age of multitasking, his instruction is radical: calm the mind by doing one thing at a time!

5.44

Behaving in this way, all tasks are well performed,
And nothing is achieved by doing otherwise.
Afflictions, the reverse of vigilance,
Can never multiply if this is how you act.

Afflictions will not multiply if you are fully present. You can test this for yourself. When you're more awake, do kleshas and confusion deescalate? If the answer is yes, this is a very useful piece of information indeed.

5.45

And if by chance you must take part
In lengthy conversations worthlessly,
Or if you come upon sensational events,
Then cast aside delight and taste for them.

There's a story in the biography of Trungpa Rinpoche that describes the first time he rode in a car. He was a teenager traveling in Tibet with his teacher, Khenpo Gangshar. The Chinese Communists had begun occupying the country, and the situation was very dangerous. Some people had already been put in prison. Nevertheless, the young Rinpoche was very excited at the prospect of this new adventure.

Khenpo Gangshar, however, took this opportunity to remind him of the power of material forces. If Rinpoche lost himself now and got carried away, he warned him, he would never know what they were up against. This is the kind of wakefulness Shantideva is suggesting here—not some kind of somber rigidity.

Moreover, Shantideva says, we can waste a lot of time distracting ourselves with mindless chatter. I'm reminded of a Native American man from the Taos Pueblo called Little Joe Gomez. In the early seventies, he met some people who were practicing complete silence. They were wearing chalkboards around their necks in case they needed to communicate. This got Little Joe laughing. When someone asked him what was so funny, he said, "Very easy to not talk; very difficult to talk mindfully." As far as he was concerned, the better practice was to converse consciously.

5.46

If you find you're grubbing in the soil,
Or pulling up the grass or tracing idle patterns on the
    ground,
Remembering the teachings of the Blissful One,
In fear, restrain yourself at once.

Tracing idle patterns on the ground refers to doodling. One time during a meeting, I was making little drawings and squiggles on the side of my notebook. Trungpa Rinpoche saw what I was doing and asked, "Did you know monks and nuns aren't supposed to doodle?" This was, in fact, the first I'd heard of it! Nevertheless, it became obvious to me why we doodle: we aren't very interested in being present.

This is basic mindfulness training. It may seem a bit extreme to be afraid of doodling or *pulling up the grass*. But life is short. Instead of strengthening the habits of a wandering mind, let's train in staying present. In Tibetan the word for meaningless distraction is *dunzi*. We can waste a whole life with *dunzi*. This is Shantideva's point here.

5·47

When you feel the wish to walk about,
Or even to express yourself in speech,
First examine what is in your mind.
For they will act correctly who have stable minds.

You've decided to meditate for forty-five minutes, and you're fifteen minutes into your sitting. Suddenly, you remember something important that you must do. *Dunzi* has entered the picture. If you fail to acknowledge that tug as just a tug or the thought as just thinking, you'll find yourself watering the plants or checking your e-mail.

Instead, the initial urge to *walk about* or phone someone can simply be acknowledged. Without praise or blame, you can touch these thoughts, let them go, and come back to taming your mind.

The Three Disciplines

Vigilance, Part Two

CHAPTER 5 OF *The Way of the Bodhisattva* continues with a section on the "three disciplines": not causing harm, gathering virtue, and benefiting others. The first discipline, not causing harm, is introduced in verses 48 through 54. This is the most fundamental instruction for not making a mess of things: the instruction for deescalating the kleshas by "remaining like a log."

5.48

When the urge arises in the mind
To feelings of desire or wrathful hate,
Do not act! Be silent, do not speak!
And like a log of wood be sure to stay.

5.49

When the mind is wild with mockery
And filled with pride and haughty arrogance,

And when you want to show the hidden faults of
    others,
To bring up old dissensions or to act deceitfully,

5.50

And when you want to fish for praise,
Or criticize and spoil another's name,
Or use harsh language, sparring for a fight,
It's then that like a log you should remain.

Here Shantideva describes being on the verge of getting carried away. There are four places we can interrupt this powerful urge: at the preverbal level; when thoughts are still small; when they've already ensnared us; and just before we act out.

Emotional turmoil begins with an initial perception—a sight, sound, thought—which gives rise to a feeling of comfort or discomfort. This is the subtlest level of *shenpa*, the subtlest stage of getting hooked. Energetically there is a perceptible pull; it's like wanting to scratch an itch. We don't have to be advanced meditators to catch this.

This initial tug of "for" or "against" is the first place we can remain as steady as a log. Just experience the tug and relax into the restlessness of the energy, without fanning this ember with thoughts. If we stay present with the rawness of our direct experience, emotional energy can move through us without getting stuck. Of course, this isn't easy and takes practice.

The second opportunity for staying steady and alert is when our thoughts are underway but haven't gained momentum. By interrupting thoughts before we get worked up, we diffuse the intensity of emotions. Emotional intensity can't survive without our thoughts, so this is a pivotal instruction.

If we don't catch these subtle thoughts, our emotions escalate. Nevertheless, this is the third place we can remain like a log; we can let the story line go even *after* the emotional heat has started to rise. It's never too late to interrupt the escalation of the kleshas.

The fourth place we can hold our seats is just before we take the fatal step of speaking or acting out. Shantideva addresses this stage in verse 48: his advice is, "Do not act! Be silent, do not speak!"

The sooner we interrupt this predictable chain reaction the better. At the preverbal stage of getting hooked, emotions are less enticing. They are still quite workable at the early stage of the thought process. By dissolving thought here, the klesha urge has no fuel and can't expand or become explosive.

When you feel the sting of an insult, for example, you don't have to magnify it with your thoughts or buy into a story line that works you into a rage. Just acknowledge the thoughts and let them fade away. Then abide with the sharpness and bite of your experience.

If you *do* get stirred up and the drama gets well under way, you can still interrupt the process. It's definitely more difficult, but it's possible.

The final instruction—to refrain from words or actions—points to the easiest place to notice the urge, but the hardest time to refrain. Now the *shenpa* pull is so strong, it feels irresistible. Nevertheless, the instruction remains the same: let go of the thoughts and relax with the underlying energy.

The practice of "remaining like a log" is based on refraining, not repressing. When you realize you're thinking, just acknowledge that. Then turn your attention to your breath flowing in and out, to your body, to the immediacy of your experience. Doing this allows you to be present and alert, and thoughts have a chance to calm down.

With this practice, it can be helpful to gently breathe in and out with the restlessness of the energy. This is a major support for learning to stay present. Basic wakefulness is right *here*, if we can just relax. Our situation is fundamentally fluid, unbiased, and free, and we can tune into this at any time. When we practice "remaining like a log," we allow for this opportunity.

The basic message is this: instead of turning up the heat and bringing your emotions to a boil, add some cool refreshing water to the mix and the *shenpa* charge will subside.

5.51

And when you yearn for wealth, attention, fame,
A circle of admirers serving you,
And when you look for honors, recognition—
It's then that like a log you should remain.

5.52

And when you want to do another down
And cultivate advantage for yourself,
And when the wish to gossip comes to you,
It's then that like a log you should remain.

5.53

Impatience, indolence, faint heartedness,
And likewise haughty speech and insolence,
Attachment to your side—when these arise,
It's then that like a log you should remain.

Here we have all our strategies for trying to escape the underlying discomfort of *shenpa*. This agitated energy is painful. We feel the need to do something with it: brag, gossip, cower—anything to get away. With a steady mind, we can see these strategies more clearly and stop supporting them with our thoughts, emotions, and actions.

"Remaining like a log" is a powerful and useful practice for all of us. The more we tame our minds, the sooner we can acknowledge thoughts of for and against and attachment to having it our way.

Even when things have gotten out of control, we can still pause and refrain from pouring kerosene on the fire.

5.54

Examine thus yourself from every side.
Note harmful thoughts and every futile striving.
Thus it is that heroes in the bodhisattva path
Apply the remedies to keep a steady mind.

Shantideva summarizes the preceding verses by telling us to note all our urges, thoughts, and futile strategies and remain steady, as steady as a log. This completes the section on the first discipline, not causing harm. Starting with verse 55, Shantideva gives teachings on the second discipline, gathering virtue. Then, in verses 83 through 107, he will describe the third discipline, benefiting others.

Practicing discipline according to these guidelines can liberate us from suffering.

5.55

With perfect and unyielding faith,
With steadfastness, respect, and courtesy,
With modesty and conscientiousness,
Work calmly for the happiness of others.

These are the general instructions for gathering virtue. I notice that Western students sometimes wince at the word virtue. Virtue, here, means cultivating qualities that resonate with, rather than block, enlightened mind. Even in conventional thinking, basic warmth and open-mindedness are considered virtues. They are qualities that connect us with others rather than push us apart. Although they're always available to us, we can help the process along by cultivating them. Sadly, we're already quite skilled at cultivating qualities that block our basic goodness. Nevertheless we can easily become accomplished in gathering virtue.

The Tibetan word for virtue is *gewa*. Some common examples of *gewa* are nonaggression, love, and compassion. Shantideva also lists the qualities of faith, steadfastness, respect, courtesy, modesty, conscientiousness, and calmness. Some of these qualities require some explanation.

In Buddhism there are many kinds of faith. One example is "eager faith." We all want to deescalate our suffering. When we see that we can create the causes for contentment instead of misery, we become extremely eager to do so.

Another example is "confident faith," which is based on confidence in bodhichitta. We have faith that basic goodness is within us. This jewel may be buried, but it is always present and available to all of us. We feel confident that we can find it, nurture it, and bring it out. Confidence and eagerness work together. This is the faith, or *gewa,* that Shantideva refers to: the faith that we can do it.

Steadfastness is another virtue that Shantideva mentions. This is cultivated in our meditation practice. No matter what—sick or well, tired or alert, in good or bad weather—we train in being present and awake to whatever occurs. With faith and steadfastness, we stick with ourselves through all kinds of moods and states of mind.

We also develop respect and courtesy for ourselves and others. These virtuous qualities are gentle and unbiased: everything and everyone is included.

The quality of modesty, or humility, comes naturally when we're attentive. When we see how reactive and unkind we can be, this humbles us considerably. Instead of causing despair, however, this painful realization can connect us with the tenderness of bodhichitta. Modesty, or humbleness, is the opposite of armoring ourselves: it allows us to be receptive and hear what others have to say.

Conscientiousness denotes diligence and honesty. With this virtuous quality we can *work calmly for the happiness of others.* Instead of working frantically, we pace ourselves and relax.

5.56

Let us not be downcast by the warring wants
Of childish persons quarreling.
Their thoughts are bred from conflict and emotion.
Let us understand and treat them lovingly.

Verse 56 makes it clear why we need to gather virtue. Virtue makes it possible for us to deal compassionately with one another. The word childish, here, is not used in a derogatory way. It conveys loving concern for those who, out of ignorance, continue to strengthen habits of suffering.

We tend to get provoked by *childish persons quarreling.* The energy of negativity is very seductive and draws us in. Shantideva's instruction is to diffuse the charge by reflecting on *why* people do what they do. People who quarrel are slaves to their emotions. They don't choose to get angry and yell, but, like all of us, they get overwhelmed by their kleshas and carried away. If we too get caught in the negative undertow, doesn't that put us in the same boat? Instead of getting provoked by strife or scorn, wouldn't it be better to break the cycle of aggression and treat people with understanding?

As we stabilize our minds, we'll see more honestly how we get incited and how difficult it is to remain like a log. Thus when others get snared, we *treat them lovingly,* just as we'd want to be treated in this same predicament. Without being condescending or disapproving, we realize our sameness and communicate from the heart.

5.57

When doing virtuous acts, beyond reproach,
To help ourselves, or for the sake of others,
Let us always bear in mind the thought
That we are self-less, like an apparition.

We can also make too big a deal about doing things right. Identifying oneself as the "virtuous one" can be a problem for the bodhisattva. We might question the solidity of this identity and contemplate the Buddha's teaching *that we are self-less, like an apparition.* Then, *when doing virtuous acts,* we could apply the instruction called "threefold purity": make no big deal about the doer, no big deal about what's being done, and no big deal about the result.

5.58

This supreme treasure of a human life,
So long awaited, now at last attained!
Reflecting always thus, maintain your mind
As steady as Sumeru, king of mountains.

Once again, Shantideva refers to the good fortune of a human birth. We have the advantage of hearing and understanding these teachings that can transform our lives. Having attained this *supreme treasure,* we're being urged not to waste it. Use this precious opportunity, Shantideva says, to maintain mindfulness and alertness. Train in being *as steady as Sumeru, king of mountains.*

In verses 59 through 70, Shantideva says many things about the body, some of which may be more helpful than others.

5.59

When vultures with their love of flesh
Are tugging at this body all around,
Small will be the joy you get from it, O mind!
Why *are* you so besotted with it now?

Being overly attached to the body is an obstacle to gathering virtue. It is also an obstacle to not causing harm and to benefiting others. Why is this so? Obsessing about our body makes us so self-absorbed that we can't see beyond our own needs.

No matter how much time and energy we put into caring for our bodies, we can't stop the process of dying. We might try to slow it down by eating well and exercising; but death can come without warning. The real question is this: since our time is limited, how do we want to spend it?

5.60

Why, O mind, do you protect this body,
Claiming it as though it were yourself?
You and it are each a separate entity,
How ever can it be of use to you?

When you die, you leave your body behind. You might ask, "If my body is 'me,' how could this possibly be?" The answer is that *you and it are each a separate entity.* Therefore, regard the body as a short-term rental: take care of it and keep it clean, but not to the point of absurdity. Treat your body with respect, but not with a sense of ownership.

5.61

Why not cling, O foolish mind, to something clean,
A figure carved in wood, or some such thing?

Why do you protect and guard
An unclean engine for the making of impurity?

Here Shantideva emphasizes the impurity of the human body: it's a very efficient *engine* for creating shit, piss, blood, and gore. When it's not cleaned, it reeks and its breath smells bad. Why be so attached to this; why not be attached to something fresh and clean, like *a figure carved in wood*?

This was a standard meditation during Shantideva's time. It is still used in some Buddhist countries, but it's a difficult one for many Westerners. Too often, we already view our physical bodies with distaste. For this reason, Trungpa Rinpoche once said he didn't think this traditional meditation on the impurity of the body—with its feces, urine, mucus, and blood—worked very well in the West. But Shantideva's intention is not to fill us with self-loathing; it's to free us from obsession.

5.62

First, with mind's imagination,
Shed the covering of skin,
And with the blade of wisdom, strip
The flesh from off the bony frame.

5.63

And when you have divided all the bones,
And searched right down amid the very marrow,
You should look and ask the question:
Where is "thingness" to be found?

When we look at the body in finer and finer detail, can we find what we're protecting? If we visualize searching *right down amid the very marrow* for the *thingness* of our body, can we find it?

Attachment to one's physical form is based on the body being a reliable, continuous entity. But can we pinpoint what we're clinging to when we probe it to its depths?

5.64

If, persisting in the search,
You find no underlying object,
Why still cherish—and with such desire—
The fleshly form you now possess?

Finding *no underlying object* doesn't mean not finding a fingernail or earlobe. What we can't locate is something tangible to hold on to. Which raises the question: What are we so attached to anyway? Here's a contemplation I've found helpful. Sitting in meditation, visualize yourself as an infant, and then as a little child just learning to walk. Then visualize this outer form getting older, up to your present age. Reflect on whether or not this is the same body. Then go into the future. Your skin is becoming slack and wrinkled, your hair is thinning and turning gray, your teeth are falling out, and your hearing is starting to go. Visualize this continual change of the body all the way up to death.

Unless we die young, this is exactly what will happen—no matter how much health food or vitamins we consume. Old age and death are inevitable. Contemplating the body in this way can shake up our attachments considerably.

5.65

Its filth you cannot eat, O mind;
Its blood likewise is not for you to drink;
Its innards, too, unsuitable to suck—
This body, what then will you make of it?

5.66

As second best, it may indeed be kept
As food to feed the vulture and the fox.
The value of this human form
Lies only in the way that it is used.

In verse 65, we have a taste of Shantideva's humor, an eighth-century Buddhist joke. Why indeed do we not see the foolishness of being overly attached to the body?

The value of this human form is in the way we use it. Without our bodies, we can't attain enlightenment. But if we live in hope and fear about its condition, it won't be a useful vehicle for getting to the other shore.

5.67

Whatever you may do to guard and keep it,
What will you do when
The Lord of Death, the ruthless, unrelenting,
Steals and throws it to the birds and dogs?

Shantideva addresses another recurring theme: the certainty of our deaths—and, in this case, the futility of pampering that which is destined to leave us.

5.68

Slaves unsuitable for work
Are not rewarded with supplies and clothing.
This body, though you pamper it, will leave you—
Why exhaust yourself with such great labor?

When servants don't do their work, they're not rewarded with food and clothing. So why continue pampering our bodies, when we know they will surely stop functioning? The real problem here is self-importance. Obsessing about how we look and feel wastes precious time and causes us to lose touch with the difficulties of others.

5.69

So pay this body due remuneration,
But then be sure to make it work for you.
But do not lavish everything
On what will not bring perfect benefit.

If you're able to do so, you should *pay this body due remuneration:* nourishing foods, medicines, and whatever else it needs—but draw a line about how much time you spend at the gym. It would also be wise to recognize "negative attachment." Denigrating the body is as futile and as much a distraction as pampering.

5.70

Regard your body as a vessel,
A simple boat for going here and there.
Make of it a wish-fulfilling gem
To bring about the benefit of beings.

This is, without question, the main point. Trungpa Rinpoche often spoke about the importance of respecting the body and paying attention to all the details of our lives. In his Shambhala teachings, eating and dressing well are ways of perking ourselves up and developing confidence in our basic goodness. It's a fine line, however, between taking pride in our appearance and being obsessed with it. Upliftedness is a way of expressing our human dignity; obsession is a way of wasting our life. Gradually, we get clear about this difference.

The next section, still in the general category of gathering virtue, discusses mindfulness in daily life.

5.71

Thus with free, untrammeled mind,
Put on an ever-smiling countenance.
Rid yourself of scowling, wrathful frowns,
And be a true and honest friend to all.

Our facial expressions have quite an impact. When someone has a wrathful expression, it affects us. Even if it has nothing to do with us, we feel threatened. We take the scowl or frown very personally. Although no words are spoken and we may not even know this scowling person, we may feel deeply threatened, wounded, or scorned. This may be ridiculous, but it happens.

While an *ever-smiling countenance* may seem a bit extreme, a friendly expression makes people feel more comfortable than *scowling, wrathful frowns*.

5.72

Do not, acting inconsiderately,
Move furniture and chairs so noisily around.
Likewise do not open doors with violence.
Take pleasure in the practice of humility.

If we live with other people, these are important guidelines. We gather virtue when we're considerate about how our actions affect the environment. At retreats with Zen teacher Toni Packer, for example, there are very few rules; but participants *are* asked to keep silence and to be mindful of opening and closing doors.

5.73

Herons, cats, and burglars
Go silently and carefully;
This is how they gain what they intend.
And one who practices this path behaves likewise.

Burglars, cats, and herons are not your usual role models. But they are perfect examples for moving attentively and patiently in order to accomplish a goal. When herons move too rapidly they can't catch any fish. Likewise, when we're mindless we can't accomplish our worldly goals, let alone live the life of a bodhisattva.

5.74

When useful admonitions come unasked
To those with skill in counseling their fellows,
Let them welcome them with humble gratitude,
And always strive to learn from everyone.

Getting feedback is sometimes the only way to discover our blind spots, especially when that feedback stings. Whether it's meant to be mean or helpful, feedback has a way of getting us to look at things we don't want to see. If we resent it or close our ears, our blind spots will never be revealed.

So *always strive to learn from everyone,* but know that, ultimately, you are the only one who really knows when you're stuck.

5.75

Praise all who speak the truth,
And say, "Your words are excellent."
And when you notice others acting well,
Encourage them in terms of warm approval.

This is good child-rearing instruction and good advice for adults as well. Too often the only thing people hear from us is criticism. Shantideva encourages us to give approval when it is due and to express our warmth and appreciation.

5.76

Extol them even in their absence;
When they're praised by others, do the same.
But when the qualities they praise are yours,
Appreciate their skill in knowing qualities.

Rejoicing in the good qualities of others takes us out of self-centeredness and expands our view of the world. This is a way to gather virtue, which helps us as much as others.

Here Shantideva addresses the difficulty we often have accepting compliments. We gather virtue when we can accept praise straightforwardly, without either getting all puffed up or refusing to believe it. We gather virtue by letting ourselves be touched by someone else's appreciation of our good qualities.

5.77

The goal of every act is happiness itself,
Though even with great wealth, it's rarely found.
So take your pleasure in the qualities of others.
Let them be a heartfelt joy to you.

5.78

By acting thus, in this life you'll lose nothing;
In future lives, great bliss will come to you.
The sin of envy brings not joy but pain,
And in the future, dreadful suffering.

We all want to be happy. Yet our desire for happiness is frequently not in sync with our actions: we overindulge in various substances; we tell people off because it feels good to set them straight. Instead of increasing our well-being, we strengthen the very qualities that cause suffering. So, even though we all want it, happiness is rarely found.

One way to guarantee happiness, Shantideva says, is to rejoice in the good qualities of others. Not only is this an antidote for envy, it also generates warmth and brings us *heartfelt joy*. When we begin to appreciate the kindness and courage of others, we find pleasure everywhere. Dzigar Kongtrul calls this "rejoicement therapy."

5.79

Speak with honest words, coherently,
With candor, in a clear, harmonious voice.
Abandon partiality, rejection, and attraction,
And speak with moderation, gently.

This is easier said than done. Mindful speech can be one of the more difficult practices. To speak honestly and coherently is hard enough, but to speak with moderation is an even greater challenge. Trungpa Rinpoche put great effort into having his students speak slowly, mindfully, and clearly. This was a rewarding and illuminating practice. Slowing down our speech can have a remarkably calming effect. It can also make us nervous. We're so used to mindlessness and speed that slowing down can feel threatening.

Shantideva encourages us to speak gently and without bias. It can be embarrassing to see how much prejudice we convey with our words. Acknowledging biased mind before it turns into speech can spare us a lot of pain. Without justification or guilt, praise or blame, we can recognize we're getting caught and keep silent.

5.80

And catching sight of others, think
That it will be through them
That you will come to buddhahood.
So look on them with open, loving hearts.

This will become a prevalent theme: sentient beings are the cause of our enlightenment. When they bother us, we learn patience; when they're suffering, we learn loving-kindness and compassion. No matter what reaction they evoke, we can relate to them in a way that leads to buddhahood. Instead of buying into aversion, we become tolerant. Instead of staying stuck in selfishness, we extend a hand to someone in distress. Instead of letting jealousy sabotage us, we train in rejoicement therapy.

5.81

Always fired by highest aspiration,
Laboring to implement the antidotes,
You will gather virtues in the fields
Of qualities, of benefits, of sorrow.

When we're passionate about our bodhisattva aspirations, we make an effort to implement the antidotes to the kleshas. Traditionally the antidote to the klesha of anger is said to be patience; the antidote to envy is rejoicing; and the antidote to lust is recognizing the impurity of the body. Using these antidotes can interrupt the momentum of the *kleshas*, thus we gather virtue.

Shantideva says we can gather virtue in three ways: *in the fields of qualities, of benefits, of sorrow.* The field of qualities refers to wisdom figures such as the teachers we've known or read about. Such men and women of wisdom are a field of excellence that awakens our devotion and veneration. The field of benefits refers to those who've been kind to us. And the field of sorrow includes all beings who are suffering.

One way to put this into action is the "three-bite practice." You can do this anytime you eat a meal. Before taking the first bite, just pause and think of those men and women of wisdom and mentally offer them your food. In this way, you connect with the virtue of devotion.

Before taking the second bite, pause and offer your food to all those who've been kind to you. This nurtures the virtues of gratitude and appreciation. The third bite is offered to those who are suffering: all the people and animals who are starving, or being tortured or neglected, without comfort or friends. Think, too, of all of us who suffer from aggression, craving, and indifference. This simple gesture awakens the virtue of compassion.

In this way—by relying on our teachers, our benefactors, and those in need—we gather the virtues of devotion, gratitude, and kindness.

5.82

Acting thus with faith and understanding,
You will always undertake good works.
And in whatever actions you perform,
You'll not be calculating, with your eye on others.

In this final verse on gathering virtue, Shantideva says that when we understand the chain reaction of karma, we will act wisely and not fall into the trap of comparing ourselves to others. Competitiveness can be a pitfall for bodhisattvas: hoping to do better than others, fearing that we'll do worse. To gain happiness, we train in awakening bodhichitta for its own sake, not to be more virtuous than others.

5.83

The six perfections, giving and the rest,
Progress in sequence, growing in importance.
The great should never be supplanted by the less,
And it is others' good that is the highest goal.

The six perfections are the six *paramitas*: generosity, discipline, and the rest. In verse 83, Shantideva says they are taught *in sequence,* with each one building on the one before: generosity is the foundation for discipline, and so forth. The *highest goal* of all the *paramitas* is *others' good*. This is the third discipline, benefiting others, which Shantideva presents in verses 83 through 107.

5.84

Therefore understand this well
And always labor for the benefit of beings.
The far-seeing masters of compassion
Permit, to this end, that which is proscribed.

In the mahayana teachings, to promote the welfare of others involves more than simply following a code of ethics or refraining from proscribed behaviors. There are times when that which is prohibited—lying or even killing—might be necessary to prevent harm. There is no set way to view this. The only guideline is to benefit beings by doing what's appropriate to the situation. Since we're left to figure this out for ourselves, we might begin to understand why Shantideva puts so much emphasis on taming the mind.

5.85

Eat only what is needful;
Share with those who have embraced the discipline.

To those, defenseless, fallen into evil states,
Give all except the three robes of religion.

These are some bodhisattva's guidelines: don't overindulge, share with everyone, and give generously even to those in *evil states*. Most of us find it is easy to feel kindly toward the defenseless, but not toward those who intentionally cause harm. Yet these people need our compassion. The Buddha taught that, because each of us experiences the consequences of our own acts, those who behave with cruelty and malice will reap the greatest misery and pain.

Shantideva tells us to give freely, even to those who hurt others; give all except your monks' robes, and in certain circumstances, I imagine even that would be permissible!

Another way to look at this verse is this: consider what it would take to go into the hells of this world and *give all* to those in seemingly inescapable pain. Until we've worked with our kleshas and judgmentalness, our bodhisattva aspirations will be sorely challenged in such places.

5.86

The body, apt to practice sacred teaching,
Should not be harmed in trivial pursuits.
If this advice is kept, the wishes of all beings
Will swiftly and completely be attained.

Here there is a shift in attitude toward the body. The body *should not be harmed in trivial pursuits*. We should take good care of it, so that we can continue to benefit beings for a long time.

5.87

They should not give up their bodies
Whose compassion is not pure and perfect.
But let them, in this world and those to come,
Subject their bodies to the service of the supreme goal.

Bodhisattvas should not prematurely feed themselves to starving tigers! They can, however, offer themselves continually for *the supreme goal,* the goal of full awakening.

5.88

Do not teach to those without respect,
To those who like the sick wear cloths around their
    heads,
To those who proudly carry weapons, staffs, or parasols,
And those who keep their hats upon their heads.

According to Indian custom in Shantideva's time, the various behaviors described here and in the following verses are disrespectful. The bodhisattva is encouraged to act in accord with the customs of the place and not do things considered inappropriate. In other words, a bodhisattva blends in and works within the cultural norm, rather than standing out like a sore thumb. In the best sense, a bodhisattva becomes invisible. Nobody knows you're a bodhisattva; you're just doing your best to wake up and benefit others.

5.89

Do not teach the vast and deep to those
Upon the lower paths, nor, as a monk,
To women unescorted. Teach with equal honor
Low and high according to their path.

5.90

Those suited to the teachings vast and deep,
Should not be introduced to lesser paths.
But basic practice you should not forsake,
Confused by talk of sutras and of mantras.

These days, a monk probably wouldn't have a problem teaching to *women unescorted*. But in Shantideva's time in India, it was considered shocking. So when in India, do as the Indians do. This is another bodhisattva guideline.

The important thing is to teach in such a way that your audience understands what you're saying. Don't teach too intellectually to those who just want to learn how to get through the day. But for those capable of hearing the profound truth of emptiness, don't hold back.

Do not bore people with the teachings. At the same time, never forsake basic teachings, such as causing no harm and benefiting others, preferring instead to impress people with your knowledge of sutras and mantras before they're ready.

5.91

Your spittle and your toothbrushes,
When thrown away, should be concealed.
And it is wrong to foul with urine
Public thoroughfares and water springs.

In response to this verse, Dzongsar Khyentse said, "In India to this very day, they still don't listen to Shantideva!" Here and in the following five verses, Shantideva gives advice for benefiting others by paying attention to all the details of your life.

5.92

When eating do not gobble noisily,
Nor stuff and cram your gaping mouth.
And do not sit with legs outstretched,
Nor rudely rub your hands together.

5.93

Do not sit upon a horse, on beds or seats,
With women of another house, alone.
All that you have seen, or have been told,
To be offensive—this you should avoid.

5.94

Not rudely pointing with your finger,
But rather with a reverent gesture showing,
With the whole right hand outstretched—
This is how to indicate the road.

5.95

Do not wave your arms with uncouth gestures.
With gentle sounds and finger snaps
Express yourself with modesty—
For acting otherwise is impolite excess.

5.96

Lie down to sleep with posture and direction
Of the Buddha when he passed into nirvana.
And first, with clear resolve,
Decide that you'll be swift to rise again.

In verse 96, Shantideva suggests we be mindful of how we go to sleep and how we rise. You might choose to lie on your right side, as the Buddha did when he died. The important point is to not mindlessly collapse into bed, and just as mindlessly arise.

5.97

The bodhisattva's acts
Are boundless, as the teachings say,
And all these practices that cleanse the mind
Embrace—until success has been attained.

5.98

Reciting thrice, by day, by night,
The Sutra in Three Sections,
Relying on the buddhas and the bodhisattvas,
Purify the rest of your transgressions.

The bodhisattva's acts aren't limited to rigid moral guidelines. We do whatever inspires people to help themselves, and whatever it takes to remove suffering. Because this is so open-ended, it's helpful to have books as guides. Here and in following verses, Shantideva gives some suggestions. *The Sutra in Three Sections* was translated by Stephen Batchelor, in his early days as a monk, as *The Sutra of the Three Heaps.* In some monasteries, nuns and monks recite this sutra three times a day. In this way, they acknowledge where they're stuck and where they've caused harm. Then they can start anew.

5.99

And therefore in whatever time or place,
For your own good and for the good of others,

Be diligent to implement
The teachings given for that situation.

If we memorize any of Shantideva's verses, we'll find they come to mind at appropriate times. This is what's meant by the *teachings given for that situation*. The dharma begins to come to life in our everyday experience when we take it out of the books and apply it on the spot.

5.100

There is indeed no virtue
That the buddhas' offspring should not learn.
To one with mastery therein,
There is no action destitute of merit.

Better to join in with humanity than to set ourselves apart. Aspiring bodhisattvas train by getting more involved, rather than more detached. In paintings of the six realms, there's a buddha standing in each realm, not just in a little bubble or looking down from above, but right in the middle of hell and the other realms.

Trungpa Rinpoche exemplified *no action destitute of merit*. He was interested in using everything as a path to enlightenment: calligraphy, filmmaking, poetry, flower arranging, tea ceremony, archery, horseback riding, theater, photography, and dance. Although he grew up as a titled person in a monastery, he knew how to make a drum and do gilding, *thangka* painting, and sculpture. And he wasn't afraid to take on the most difficult, out-of-control situations—in fact, he loved them.

5.101

Directly, then, or indirectly,
All you do must be for others' sake.

And solely for their welfare dedicate
Your actions for the gaining of enlightenment.

Working *indirectly* means that we benefit others by taming our own mind and kleshas. Working *directly* means we lend a helping hand in whatever way is needed: we give something away, sit by someone's bedside, teach the dharma. Then we dedicate the merit of whatever we do for the welfare of others, just as described in chapter 3.

5.102

Never, at the cost of life or limb,
Forsake your virtuous friend, your teacher,
Learned in the meaning of the Mahayana,
Supreme in practice of the bodhisattva path.

Although I have referred to *the Mahayana,* this is the first time Shantideva uses this term. *Maha* means "great," and *yana* means "vehicle." Mahayana Buddhism—which flourished in China, Korea, Japan, Mongolia, and Tibet—is the path of the bodhi-sattva. It emphasizes compassion and the wisdom of emptiness, the ultimate unfixed nature of everything. The mahayana in-spires us to expand our view. Instead of staying stuck in self-reference, we can open our minds to include ever greater numbers of beings.

On this path, the role of the teacher is very important. We need the example of someone who is fully awake or further along on the path. This is someone who does not get caught in fixed mind, someone who lives with a sense of equanimity and kindness, even under duress.

Just being around our spiritual friend can teach us more than any book. I was rarely alone with Trungpa Rinpoche, but I remember these times vividly, as well as the times I spent with great teachers such as the Sixteenth Karmapa and Dilgo Khyentse Rinpoche. I learned from everything they did: the way they spoke, ate their food, and related with people. Thus Shantideva says, *Never, at the cost of life or limb, forsake your virtuous friend, your teacher.*

5.103

For thus you must depend upon your guru,
As you will find described in Shri Sambhava's life,
And elsewhere in the teachings of the Buddha:
These be sure to study, reading in the sutras.

The biography referred to here tells us to regard our teachers as excellent and trustworthy physicians. When we're disabled by samsaric mind, the teachings are the best medicine. By digesting the instructions of our spiritual friends and putting them into practice, we will reconnect with our basic health and recover our strength and sanity.

5.104

The training you will find described
Within the sutras. Therefore, read and study them.
The Sutra of the Essence of the Sky—
This is the text that should be studied first.

5.105

The *Digest of All Disciplines*
Contains a detailed and extensive explanation
Of all that must be practiced come what may.
So this is something you should read repeatedly.

5.106

From time to time, for sake of brevity,
Consult the *Digest of the Sutras.*
And those two works peruse with diligence
That noble Nagarjuna has composed.

Unfortunately these texts are difficult to find or have not yet been translated. There are other books, however, that will inspire us and keep us from going astray. When times are tough, reading a dharma book or listening to a tape can help us to stay sane.

5.107

Whatever in these works is not proscribed
Be sure to undertake and implement.
And what you see there, perfectly fulfill,
And so safeguard the minds of worldly beings.

Since we may not have these texts, we could safely say that what-ever Shantideva does not prohibit in *The Way of the Bodhisattva,* we could *undertake and implement* and *so safeguard the minds of worldly beings,* including our own.

5.108

To keep a guard again and yet again
Upon the state and actions of our thoughts and deeds—
This and only this defines
The nature and the sense of mental watchfulness.

To conclude this chapter, Shantideva returns to taming the mind. In our daily activities, we can *again and yet again* practice mindfulness and alertness, recognizing when we're distracted and gently, even joyfully, coming back to being present. And when the kleshas begin to get their hooks in us, we can always do the noble practice of remaining like a log.

5.109

But all this must be acted out in truth,
For what is to be gained by mouthing syllables?
What invalid was ever helped
By merely reading in the doctor's treatises?

If we're just *mouthing syllables* from a book, nothing will ever change. Unless we're willing to apply Shantideva's instructions when and where they're needed, our minds will remain wild and we'll continue to be ruled by our kleshas.

Working with Anger

Patience, Part One

C HAPTER 6 OF *The Way of the Bodhisattva* gives further instructions for remaining steady when confronted by the kleshas. Here Shantideva presents the *paramita* of patience as the most effective way possible to work with anger. In verses 1 through 12, he presents his case against this powerful klesha.

6.1

Good works gathered in a thousand ages,
Such as deeds of generosity,
Or offerings to the blissful ones—
A single flash of anger shatters them.

Everyone already knows that anger is destructive. But to emphasize the immensity of this destruction, Shantideva makes a statement that generations of readers have found disturbing: one flash of anger can destroy years of ethical conduct and virtuous actions.

We know the familiar scenario of being in a harmonious relationship, when suddenly there's a nasty incident. One minute there's love and friendship; the next minute one of us is out of control. The physical or verbal abuse can wipe out months of goodness. And even if we apologize, it takes a long time to rebuild trust. So even *a single flash* of anger has long-term consequences.

According to some commentaries, this verse goes even further and addresses the anger that we *don't* regret and that we actually justify. We can stubbornly hold on to our anger for lifetimes, like the family feuds and ethnic rivalries that go on for centuries. I know two brothers who live next door to each other, but haven't spoken to each other in twenty-five years. This is what Shantideva talks about: anger we condone, hold on to, and remain unwilling to examine.

Once we recognize the unnecessary pain our anger causes, we are already on the way to undermining its power and its ability to shatter years of good will. That, of course, is precisely what Shantideva wants us to understand.

We all have parts of ourselves that seem unworkable and cause us grief. If we are habitually angry, then exploring this can become a major part of awakening bodhichitta. Shantideva assumes each of us has the ability to free ourselves from the tyranny of the kleshas. No matter what we've done, none of us are doomed.

But what are these *good works* that can be shattered in a flash? Good works that can be so quickly destroyed are superficial: superficial acts of generosity, superficial offerings to the buddhas. These are not the good works that transform us at the core. Fortunately, a fundamental change of heart can never be lost.

The merit gained from virtuous acts that are merely ritualistic is easily destroyed by angry outbursts. In Asia, for example, it's common for Buddhists to offer money to build temples. But if their generosity is simply an outer gesture to gain merit, it could actually increase self-importance rather than dissolve it. You could be a high-powered business person doing all kinds of shady deals, and think you're accumulating merit by performing conventional acts of virtue. But these superficial acts, while they might have some virtuous consequences, are destroyed by the power of rage.

If you're aggressive in your dealings, that's how you'll be regarded in the world. You might smile and give generously, but if you frequently explode in anger, people never feel comfortable in your presence and you'll never have peace of mind.

6.2

No evil is there similar to anger,
No austerity to be compared with patience.
Steep yourself, therefore, in patience—
In all ways, urgently, with zeal.

Verse 2 summarizes the theme of this chapter: the benefits of patience and the harm caused by anger. The underlying meaning of the word *evil* is to intentionally cause harm, to take pleasure in causing pain and, as Shantideva says, *no evil is there similar to anger.* Because striking out in anger can become a habitual response to stress and discomfort, Shantideva passionately encourages us to unwind this old habit rather than continue to strengthen it.

In his book *Healing Anger,* the Dalai Lama recommends using the word *hatred* instead of anger. There are times, he says, when anger is appropriate, but hatred is never justified. Anger can be motivated by compassion, but hatred is always accompanied by ill will. I find this distinction helpful.

Nevertheless, at times we may find ourselves consumed by hatred. To work with these times, Shantideva introduces us to the austerity of patience. I find it significant that he calls patience an *austerity.* It indicates that what we go through when we refrain from escalating the kleshas takes courage.

6.3

Those tormented by the pain of anger
Will never know tranquillity of mind—
Strangers they will be to every pleasure;
Sleep departs them, they can never rest.

When we're angry about something, most of us think about it feverishly; we can't sleep at night or find any peace of mind.

There are various ways you can deal with this situation. The first thing you can do is get in touch with how anger feels in your body. We don't usually pay attention to the physical anguish anger causes. Sensitizing yourself to that pain can motivate you to work more eagerly with aggression.

Another practice I recommend is done during meditation. If you've been angry, you can intentionally replay the whole story. Pay attention to your feelings and thoughts. Are they obsessive and repetitive? Do they fuel your grudges or judgments? Then, while gently breathing in and out, take the feeling of anger as the focus of your meditation. Give it your full attention, without moving away from it by repressing or acting it out. Try to experience the anger nonverbally by getting to know its qualities. What color is it? What temperature? How does it smell or taste? This practice puts us in touch with emotions very directly and lessens the sense of struggle.

Another instruction that I've found helpful is to stay with your soft spot. Below the anger is enormous tenderness, which most of us quickly cover over with the hardness of rage. Learning to touch that vulnerability isn't easy, but it can keep you from exploding and destroying everything in sight.

6.4

Noble chieftains full of hate
Will be attacked and slain

By even those who look to them
For honors and possessions.

6.5

From family and friends estranged,
And shunned by those attracted by their bounty,
Men of anger have no joy,
Forsaken by all happiness and peace.

This exemplifies the kind of rage that shatters our good works. *Noble chieftains full of hate* from *family and friends estranged—* these are the abusive parents or partners, the abusive bosses. They terrify everyone, even their own children and those who rely on them for food, promotions, and well-being. If you've ever been in such relationships, you know that any lack of gratitude for what these people provide outrages them even more. Because they're so explosive and unpredictable, even their gestures of friendliness or generosity are seen as untrustworthy. They aren't able to see how their anger destroys trust and respect.

Shantideva urges us to see that abusive people have no joy or peace of mind. They shatter their own happiness by justifying their anger; and the very people they expect to love and honor them have the strongest aversion.

The point, however, is not the noble chieftains. The point is to acknowledge our own anger and the way it harms us as much as it harms others.

6.6

All these ills are brought about by wrath,
Our sorrow-bearing enemy.
But those who seize and crush their anger down
Will find their joy in this and future lives.

The next time we want to justify our anger, if we think of it as *our sorrow-bearing enemy,* we might be motivated to refrain from fueling the fire. Of course, we don't literally *seize and crush* our anger; this language just makes it clear that we have to work with it assiduously.

The advice Shantideva gives here is advice for healing a universal dilemma: the dilemma of getting hooked and carried away by rage. We could do this work not only for our own sake but for all humanity. Instead of regarding ourselves as angry and messed up, we could identify with all those who are working to heal a universal illness. Siding with our courage instead of our neurosis is an important shift of allegiance.

6.7

Getting what I do not want,
And all that hinders my desire—
There my mind finds fuel for misery;
Anger springs from it, oppressing me.

6.8

Therefore I will utterly destroy
The sustenance of this my enemy,
My foe, whose sole intention is
To bring me injury and sorrow.

What triggers our anger? According to Shantideva, it's getting what we don't want and not getting what we desire. When we're heavily invested in our likes and dislikes, tiny reactions can escalate into violence and war. When we're afraid of getting stuck with something we don't want or deprived of what we need, our thoughts come in as reinforcements and escalate our anger and pain.

Full-blown, destructive anger starts with subtle *shenpa,* an uncomfortable feeling that things aren't going our way. It's helpful to recognize this uneasiness *before* it escalates. If, however, we've already gotten angry, we could still try to find the patience to not act or speak. It's never too late to put an embargo on the fuel of misery: at any point in the process, we can pause and practice patience.

Trungpa Rinpoche used to say that when something like anger arises, we should regard it as "not me." Just think of it as a little bug trying to land on you: if your mind remains open and free of bias, the bug has nowhere to light. Shantideva, in his own words, is saying the same thing. Anger is not "me," it's just dynamic energy. If we don't identify with it, that energy remains unfixated and free. If it freezes into "want" and "don't want," however, we can accurately predict the outcome. It will cause us, the basically good us, to suffer.

6.9

So come what may, I'll never harm
My cheerful happiness of mind.
Depression never brings me what I want;
My virtue will be warped and marred by it.

In his typically enthusiastic style, Shantideva rouses himself: *So come what may, I'll never harm my cheerful happiness of mind.* This joy is a feeling of workability: our life and mind are workable. Shantideva's intention is to help us realize this.

His cheerfulness comes in part from knowing that it never helps to indulge in depression and discontent. The instruction is to interrupt discouragement's momentum: interrupt the story line and return to the immediacy of your experience, no matter how unpleasant. A good description of patience is learning to relax with the edginess of our energy.

6.10

If there is a remedy when trouble strikes,
What reason is there for despondency?
And if there is no help for it,
What use is there in being sad?

Shantideva instructs us to stand back from the heat of our anger and not get entangled. If we're caught in a traffic jam, for example, what's the point of fuming? If there's a remedy like an off-ramp, there's no need to be upset. But if there are cars as far as the eye can see and no way out, then obsessing only makes us unhappier.

If you can do something about your situation, then do it. And if there's nothing to do, it's ridiculous to get all worked up. This is Shantideva's advice for stress reduction.

6.11

Pain, humiliation, insults, or rebukes—
We do not want them
Either for ourselves or those we love.
For those we do not like, it's quite the opposite!

Shantideva is teaching in an eighth-century Indian monastery, yet some things never change! He presents another situation that fuels our anger: not wanting insults or humiliation for ourselves or our loved ones, but being glad when bad things happen to those we dislike. Both extremes are kindling for the fire of remaining ornery.

6.12

The cause of happiness comes rarely,
And many are the seeds of suffering!

But if I have no pain, I'll never long for
    freedom;
Therefore, O my mind, be steadfast!

Verses 11 and 12 go together. We have the intelligence to understand that we cause suffering by rejecting pain for ourselves, while wanting it for others. If we remain in this self-absorbed state, then the *cause of happiness comes rarely, and many are the seeds of suffering!*

For angry people, the causes of suffering are everywhere. When they relate to others, they are easily provoked. The older they get, the touchier they become. More and more situations cause them discomfort, but fortunately this can shift. When the mind is less reactive, the causes of happiness increase. Then these very same situations no longer provoke us.

This is definitely the direction to go. If we think of ourselves ten years from now, don't we want fewer causes of suffering and more causes of happiness?

Shantideva then takes another tack: pain can also be helpful. Without pain, we would never *long for freedom.* This optimistic view can cheer us up. Without suffering, we would never look for a way out; we'd never be motivated to tame our minds or practice patience.

With verse 12, Shantideva concludes his discussion on the drawbacks of anger and the reasons to apply its antidote, patience.

Next, he explains three categories of patience. The first category is the patience that comes from reframing our attitude toward discomfort. The second category is the patience that comes from understanding the complexity of any situation. The third category is the patience that comes from developing tolerance.

6.13

The Karna folk, devoted to the Goddess,
Endure the meaningless austerities
Of being cut and burned.
Why am I so timid on the path of freedom?

Verse 13 begins the discussion on reframing our attitude toward discomfort. We all need this encouragement. Once we've refrained from escalating the kleshas, then what? As practitioners, we need some advice on how to remain steady with the edgy energy that often remains. We may not be acting out; we may be interrupting our thoughts, but then we're left to relate sanely with the withdrawal symptoms.

This method of developing patience is interesting to contemplate in a culture with such a low tolerance for mental or physical distress.

We are inundated with advertisements telling us we deserve to be comfortable and happy. But, believe me, with the austerity of patience, we will experience some pain. At the very least, the kleshas and their underlying restlessness will become more obvious and vivid. As I've said before, there's no way to get free of old addictions without going through the "detox period."

The Karna folk endured austerities of cutting and burning to attain spiritual insights. If they could endure such *meaningless austerities*—meaningless, in Shantideva's opinion, because they don't lead to irreversible liberation—*why am I so timid on the path of freedom?*

Maybe we are hesitant because we're not so sure about the payoff. The fruits of the spiritual path are ineffable and usually not immediate. Working patiently with the kleshas can be very uncomfortable. When our self-importance gets punctured, we might know intellectually that it's cause for rejoicing, but, at a gut level, it hurts and we don't like it. The only reason we put up with everyday hassles such as stressful jobs is the reassuring certainty of a salary or some other reward.

Shantideva cautions us, however, not to get discouraged by the discomfort of letting go of old habits. He has unshakable confidence that we can stop being slaves to the kleshas and experience the open, unbiased nature of our mind. He also knows that we have to discover this for ourselves, and that we'll never be able to do it if we give up every time we're challenged.

6.14

There's nothing that does not grow light
Through habit and familiarity.
Putting up with little cares
I'll train myself to bear with great adversity.

Having encouraged us to not be put off by the pain encountered on the path, Shantideva now gives more advice for working with this discomfort skillfully. The first instruction was to reframe the way we view this pain and regard it in a positive light.

Now he gives teachings on staying present with even the greatest misery. Because it's almost impossible to start training in times of *great adversity*, we're instructed to start with *little cares*. Being patient with slight irritations and annoyances prepares us to remain calm when challenges increase. Likewise, becoming familiar with the initial restlessness of impatience and milder forms of anger prepares us to relate wisely when kleshas intensify.

Dzongsar Khyentse calls our minor inconveniences "bourgeois suffering." We could practice patience when we arrive at our favorite restaurant and it's closed; or, when we reserve an aisle seat on the airplane and end up in the middle. In the next two verses, we're advised not to fret about the bourgeois suffering of insect bites, hunger pangs, or the weather. Fretting will only aggravate our troubles, until even little things seem like catastrophes. By practicing patience, we can learn to deescalate negativity while it's relatively easy to do.

6.15

And do I not already bear with common irritations—
Bites and stings of snakes and flies,
Experiences of hunger and of thirst,
And painful rashes on my skin?

6.16

Heat and cold, the wind and rain,
Sickness, prison, beatings—
I'll not fret about such things.
To do so only aggravates my trouble.

Homo sapiens are very good at making matters worse. We've practically perfected it. Shantideva is showing us how to change that by practicing patience rather than practicing fretting.

6.17

There are some whose bravery increases
At the sight of their own blood,
While some lose all their strength and faint
When it's another's blood they see!

6.18

This results from how the mind is set,
In steadfastness or cowardice.
And so I'll scorn all injury,
And hardships I will disregard!

Our first reactions to the world are based on many things: history, personality, and conditioning of all kinds. The sight of blood, to use Shantideva's example, will make one person faint and another feel strong.

The point here is to not mistake our relative reactions for absolute truth. If the sight of blood upsets us, we can't really blame the blood. It isn't what happens to us that makes us happy or unhappy; it is *how the mind is set*. What makes us suffer is the way we think about what's happening. This is another crucial message: our story lines aggravate our troubles.

6.19

When sorrows fall upon the wise,
Their minds remain serene and undisturbed.
For in their war against defiled emotion,
Many are the hardships, as in every battle.

Dzigar Kongtrul has an analogy for reframing our attitude toward hardships encountered on the path. He compares them to the pain of an injection, which we gladly accept in order to cure our illness. Likewise, we're not deterred by the short-term discomfort of refraining from the kleshas because we know this will heal the long-term suffering they cause. By encouraging ourselves this way, we gradually learn to relax and stay lucid, even in the most sorrowful times.

6.20

Thinking scorn of every pain,
And vanquishing such foes as hatred:
These are exploits of a conquering hero.
The rest is slaying what is dead already!

In ordinary battle, soldiers kill those who, like all of us, will die sooner or later. This is what Shantideva means by *slaying what is dead already*. By killing, however, they strengthen habits of aggression that will last far longer than any adversary.

The greatest heroes and heroines are not those who fight out of hatred, trapped in the bias of right and wrong, but those who patiently face hardships to gain victory over anger, prejudice, and war. The point of Shantideva's analogy is that no one is more worthy of respect than someone brave enough to refrain from escalating the kleshas.

Having made the point that awakening requires courage, Shantideva will now present a positive outlook on suffering.

6.21

Suffering also has its worth.
Through sorrow, pride is driven out
And pity felt for those who wander in samsara;
Evil is avoided, goodness seems delightful.

Shantideva cites three benefits of pain. First it is valuable because *through sorrow, pride is driven out*. No matter how arrogant and condescending we've been, great suffering can humble us. The pain of a serious illness or loss of a loved one can be transformative, softening us and making us less self-centered.

The second benefit of pain is empathy: the compassion *felt for those who wander in samsara*. Our personal suffering brings compassion for others in the same situation. A young woman was telling me that when her baby died, she felt a deep connection to all the other parents who had lost children. This was, as she put it, the unexpected blessing of her sorrow.

With sadness, we realize that we're all in the same predicament. We're all caught by the kleshas and continually blocking our basic goodness. Here Shantideva expresses compassion for everyone wandering in samsara, especially those with no interest in finding freedom.

The third value of suffering is that *evil is avoided* and *goodness seems delightful.* When we practice according to Shantideva's instructions, we can get smarter about cause and result. Based on this understanding, we'll have less inclination to cause harm, and more desire to gather virtue and benefit others. This is the "eager faith" I talked about before: we're eager to live our lives in ways that dismantle the habits that cause us so much grief. We are eager to increase our compassion, wisdom, and happiness.

These are the three values of suffering: it humbles us; it causes us to feel compassion for others in the same situation; and, because we begin to understand the workings of karma, it motivates us to not add to our burden of pain when we could lighten the load.

This ends the section on the first kind of patience: the patience that comes from reframing how we regard the vicissitudes of the spiritual path.

Verses 22 through 33 present the patience that comes from seeing the complex reality of any situation. These instructions can be used on the spot, whenever we realize we're hooked by the kleshas. They are reminders for remaining steady under pressure.

6.22

I am not angry with my bile and other humors—
Fertile source of pain and suffering!
So why should I resent my fellow creatures,
Victims, too, of like conditions?

Why is it that we don't get angry when suffering is caused by something inanimate, like an illness, but when suffering is caused by our fellow human beings, we're quick to feel resentment?

If a branch drops on our head, we assume it fell from a tree and rub our head, and that's that. But what if someone intentionally threw that branch? Could we cool down by remembering that this person is a victim of his habitual patterns, that we're all *victims, too, of like conditions*?

Until we start working with our mind, we are ruled by our emotions. They take us over until we're no longer in control. When we get angry with others, we could remember that, just like us, they do what they do for complex reasons, not the least of which is being controlled by their emotions. At times, we may feel completely justified in being hateful. Yet when someone harms us, we might ask ourselves this: Why aren't we just as enraged by falling branches?

If we reply that "the harm that person caused me is intentional," we might want to question our logic. For all of us, unpleasant feelings arise uninvited and quickly pull us in. If we don't see it happening, we won't refrain from acting out, and inevitably we'll cause harm.

It's so sadly predictable how everyone gets trapped. Reflecting on this cultivates understanding rather than resentment for all beings, including ourselves.

6.23

For though they are unlooked for, undesired,
These ills afflict us all the same.
And likewise, though unwanted and unsought,
Defilements nonetheless are quick to come.

6.24

Never thinking, "Now I will be angry,"
People are impulsively caught up in anger.
Irritation, likewise, comes—
Though never plans to be experienced!

A neutral event such as a fallen branch can result in various re-actions: an emotional explosion, relaxation, or even laughter. Our response depends on how we've worked with our emotions up to that point. We don't set out to be angry, and likewise anger doesn't set out to be experienced. But when causes and conditions come together, we impulsively get caught up and swept away. Patience, Shantideva infers, is the antidote: in particular, the patience that comes from having sympathy for the complexity of our current situation.

6.25

Every injury whatever,
The whole variety of evil deeds
Is brought about by circumstances.
None is independent, none autonomous.

Verse 25 presents the same idea. This moment is part of a con-tinuum; it doesn't exist in isolation from all that came before. Our reaction to it is based on how we worked with our emotions previ-ously, and our future depends on how we work with them right now. This is the crucial point.

6.26

Conditions, once assembled, have no thought
That now they will give rise to some result.
And that which is engendered does not think
That it has been produced by such conditions.

Our reactions are not as premeditated as we might think. They happen, Shantideva says again, because of past conditioning.

I once stayed with a friend whose dog has an uncontrollable fear of brooms. Just getting the broom out of the closet and starting to sweep sends the poor creature into a tailspin. Although he is no longer in danger of being harmed, he still reacts with terror. You can't convince a dog not to be afraid of brooms, but you can work with your own mind and phobias.

We all have our "brooms." We may never know what happened in the past to trigger our current response. But in this very moment, we can work with our mind and develop patience. We don't have to spend a lifetime building up a case about the badness of brooms or the wrongness of our emotions.

6.27

That which is referred to as the Primal Substance,
That which has been labeled as the Self
Do not come into being thinking
"That is how I will arise."

6.28

That which is not manifest is not yet there,
So what could want to come to be?
And permanently drawn toward its object,
It can never cease from being so.

6.29

Indeed! This Self, if permanent,
Is certainly impassible like space itself.
And should it meet with other factors,
How should they affect it, since it is unchanging?

6.30

If, when things occur, it stays unchanged and as before,
What influence has action had on it?

They say that this affects the Self,
But what connection could there be between
    them?

This section refutes the views of certain non-Buddhist schools of thought in Shantideva's time. One school believed in a "primal substance"; another, in the *atman,* or "Self," with a capital "S." In brief, these were beliefs in an absolute, unchanging principle, similar to notions of a "soul" or "God."

Because we long for certainty and something to hold on to, it's very reassuring to believe in some permanent, external essence that underlies everything. While we play out our relative dramas of hope and fear, there's no confusion in this underlying strata, which remains pure, unchanging, and undisturbed.

The Buddha, however, refuted such views. Nothing is unchanging or separate. The notion of an external, permanent essence is what Shantideva disproves here.

He is not, however, positing a belief in anything else. If we were to say "all is emptiness," Shantideva would refute that too. His intention is to pull the rug out from under any fixed view or solidified way of thinking. Instead, he points us toward the indescribable openness of mind: a mind free from any conceptualization whatsoever.

What is the day-to-day relevance of these verses? It's to give up creating more concepts. Don't get trapped by set ideas of self, or other, or anything else. Don't buy into the fixated thinking that results in anger.

Shantideva argues that any belief in a fixed or permanent entity doesn't make sense. If it hadn't yet manifested, then it could never come to be. If it already existed and was drawn in a certain direction, it could never cease from doing so. In other words, if things were fixed the way we think they are, then nothing could ever change!

6.31

All things, then, depend on something else;
On this depends the fact that none are
    independent.
Knowing this, we will not be annoyed at objects
That resemble magical appearances.

In the first two lines, Shantideva again says that all things are the result of complex causes and conditions: nothing exists independently. In the second two lines, he teaches on emptiness. Nothing is as it appears: we're like dream people getting annoyed at dream objects. Experiencing this, even momentarily, we see the absurdity of working ourselves into a frenzy.

This teaching on the insubstantial nature of everything is an important one to contemplate when going through the pain of detox.

6.32

"Resistance," you may say, "is out of place,
For what will be opposed by whom?"
The stream of suffering is cut through by
    patience;
There's nothing inappropriate in wanting
    that!

Using Shantideva's emptiness logic, we might say, "If everything is a magical appearance, what's the point of practicing patience?" But Shantideva doesn't buy this argument. Working with patience, he says, will end suffering. *There's nothing inappropriate in wanting that.* He drops the philosophy and gets right to the point: we can't use emptiness logic any more than we can use solidness logic to justify the continuation of suffering.

6.33

Thus, when enemies or friends
Are seen to act improperly,
Be calm and call to mind
That everything arises from conditions.

Here we experience Shantideva's kind heart. He asks us to *be calm*. No matter who behaves improperly, *enemies or friends*, don't get so heated up and opinionated. Be calm and practice patience, in this case, by reflecting on the fact that why they do what they do is not so obvious. It arises from a variety of causes and conditions.

This ends the section on the second kind of patience: the patience that comes from realizing the complex reality of all situations. Verses 34 through 51 explore the third kind of patience: the patience that comes from developing tolerance.

6.34

If things occurred to living beings
Following their wishes and intentions,
How could sorrow ever come to them—
For there is no one who desires to suffer?

The Buddha taught that all beings wish to be happy and free of suffering. If this is so, Shantideva asks, why do we do such crazy things? As he's pointed out before, our desire for comfort is not usually in sync with our methods for achieving it. In the following few verses he gives some poignant examples of our insanity.

6.35

Yet carelessly, all unaware,
They tear themselves on thorns and briars;

And ardent in pursuit of wives and goods,
They starve themselves of nourishment.

6.36

Some hang themselves or leap into the void,
Or eat bad food or swallow deadly poison,
Or by their evil conduct
Bring destruction on themselves.

6.37

For when affliction seizes them,
They kill themselves, the selves they love so much.
So how could they not be the cause
Of pain and suffering for others?

When consumed by passion, we stop eating and sleeping. We may break up marriages or betray our loved ones, oblivious to the pain we cause. We may even lie, steal, or kill ourselves. There are seemingly no limits to how far we'll go to achieve happiness, even when we know this happiness has never lasted in the past. If we're so willing to harm ourselves, it's not hard to understand how we could harm others.

6.38

And when, as victims of defilement,
Beings even cause their own destruction,
Even if compassion does not rise in us,
We can at least refrain from being angry.

We have to be honest with ourselves. At this point in our bodhisattva career, it may be asking too much to have compassion for some unlikable troublemaker. But we can at least refrain from speaking or acting out of anger. Even if we can't shed a tear over the ridiculousness of the human condition, by refraining from retaliation and the misery it causes, we will do what's best for everyone.

6.39

If those who are like wanton children
Are by nature prone to injure others,
What point is there in being angry—
Like resenting fire for its heat?

6.40

And if their faults are fleeting and contingent,
If living beings are by nature wholesome,
It's likewise senseless to resent them—
As well be angry at the sky for having clouds!

Verses 39 and 40 present two alternatives. If we believe that people are basically bad by nature, then why get angry with them? Why not simply accept that they're prone to causing harm, and let it go? Getting angry is *like resenting fire for its heat.*

If we see people as basically good and their faults as *fleeting and contingent,* then why get upset at their temporary lapses? That would be like getting *angry at the sky for having clouds.* Remembering this, we can cool down on the spot and avoid unnecessary pain.

My personal experience of working with Shantideva's instructions is that, even if some of them don't work for me, the willingness to simply pause—to create a gap and shift gears—always helps.

6.41

Although indeed it is the stick that hurts me,
I am angry at the one who wields it, striking me.
But he is driven and impelled by anger—
So it is his wrath I should resent.

This verse says more about developing patience through tolerance. How do we develop the willingness to not retaliate? Shantideva's approach is based on developing tenderness for the human
predicament and, if that's not possible, to at least realize that anger
increases our suffering. It's like eating poison seeds and wondering
why we get sicker.

To interrupt anger's momentum, he suggests these contemplations on the futility of our habitual responses. Ask yourself once
again: Why do I get angry at people and not inanimate things?
How much of my anger is caused by fixed views of good and bad,
right and wrong? And couldn't I have some tolerance for others
who, just like me, keep creating their own misery? The real culprits
are the kleshas themselves, and couldn't we all use some compassionate guidance in working with them?

6.42

I it was who in the past
Did harm to beings such as these.
And so, when others do me mischief,
It is only just that they should injure me.

Here is another way to reflect on being harmed. Consider the
law of karma: what goes around comes around. If you steal, you
can expect at some future time to be robbed. If you gossip, sooner
or later you'll be the one being slandered. When we ponder the
multiple factors coming together to cause an unfortunate event,

we should at least consider that one of them is our former deeds.

Westerners often have a hard time with this teaching because of guilt. When difficult things happen, they think it's because they're fundamentally bad or being punished.

My favorite clarification of this misunderstanding comes from Kelsang Gyatso's book *Meaningful to Behold*. If a child is told not to play with matches and does so anyway, it may result in her getting burned. Then the child has a chance to learn about cause and effect firsthand. As a result, she might conclude for herself that being careless with matches has painful results. She is wiser because of her mishap. But if the child feels she got burned as a punishment for not obeying Mommy and Daddy, then all she learns is guilt. Her intelligence is interfered with, and she doesn't profit from her mistake.

Understanding karma like this gives us tremendous freedom to create our own future. The way we relate to being hit on the head with a branch, right now, affects how we'll relate to being harmed at a later time.

6.43

Their weapons and my body—
Both are causes of my suffering!
They their weapons drew, while I held out my body.
Who then is more worthy of my anger?

The words or actions of others can wound us as much as any weapon. The meaning of this verse is that both *their* words and my reactivity are equally responsible for my pain.

A remark that provokes me may not affect you at all. We all have to work on our side of the equation. We can't stop others from saying mean words, but we can work on developing patience. We can work on relaxing with the restlessness of our energy by remaining like a log and not retaliating.

6.44

This human form is like a running sore;
Merely touched, it cannot stand the pain!
I'm the one who clings to it with blind attachment;
Whom should I resent when pain occurs?

Here Shantideva uses one of his familiar teaching devices: he repeats himself. My uptightness, he says, causes me as much pain as other people's deeds.

6.45

We who are like senseless children
Shrink from suffering, but love its causes.
We hurt ourselves; our pain is self-inflicted!
Why should *others* be the object of our anger?

Shantideva is speaking in a tender way. How sad it is that we, like children who don't know any better, continue doing the very things that cause us suffering. Moreover, we love these causes—the addictions, the gossip, the overwork, the feeding of our critical mind. We associate them with comfort, satisfaction, and well-being. Why don't we get angry with ourselves for hurting ourselves, rather than blaming others? Or, in our Western culture, where we're so prone to self-criticism, it might be better to ask, "Why don't we have some compassion for our situation?"

6.46

Who indeed should I be angry with?
This pain is all my own contriving—
Likewise all the janitors of hell
And all the groves of razor trees!

As has been said before, the hells in which we find ourselves are a projection of our mind. Our pain is for the most part self-inflicted. The good news is that once we see this, we might be motivated to free ourselves from our misery-producing ways.

6.47

Those who harm me come against me,
Summoned by my evil karma.
But they will be the ones who go to hell,
And so it is myself who bring *their* ruin.

Verses 47 through 51 are contemplations on the pain that purifies oneself, but hurts the person who inflicts it.

This is another idea that seems difficult for Westerners to accept: when someone harms us, they create the cause of their own suffering. They do this by strengthening habits that imprison them in a cycle of pain and confusion. It's not that we are responsible for what someone else does, and certainly not that we should feel guilty. But when they harm us, we unintentionally become the means of their undoing. Had they looked on us with loving-kindness, however, we'd be the cause of their gathering virtue.

What I find helpful in this teaching is that what's true for them is also true for me. The way I regard those who hurt me today will affect how I experience the world in the future. In any encounter, we have a choice: we can strengthen our resentment *or* our understanding and empathy. We can widen the gap between ourselves and others or lessen it.

6.48

Because of them, and through the exercise of patience,
My many sins are cleansed and purified.
But they will be the ones who, thanks to me,
Will have the long-drawn agonies of hell.

6.49

Therefore I am *their* tormentor!
Therefore it is they who bring me benefit!
Thus with what perversity, pernicious mind,
Will you be angry with your enemies?

The teaching here is the same. The troublemakers in our lives harm themselves, but benefit us by provoking us to practice patience. We can be grateful to whomever or whatever shows us we're still "provokable."

In any given situation, whoever justifies getting enraged loses and whoever uses that same situation to develop tolerance wins. Personally, I find this simple logic very helpful.

6.50

For if a patient quality of mind
Is mine, I shall avoid the pains of hell.
But though indeed I save myself,
What of my foes, what fate's in store for them?

At some point, we know we can work with our mind. We've listened to the dharma and pondered it. If someone is continually angry with us—a family member, for example—it occurs to us that we have tools to work with this intelligently and kindly. But what about our parents or siblings? Although *we* may have a long way to go, they may not have a clue that they're causing themselves unnecessary pain. What's in store for them if they keep strengthening the habit of anger? Remembering this can make us more compassionate toward them and motivate us to practice patience.

6.51

> If I repay them harm for harm,
> Indeed they'll not be saved thereby;
> And all my noble actions will be spoiled,
> Austerity of patience brought to nothing.

This very clearly states the same essential message. Retaliation doesn't help anyone: it doesn't help others and it definitely doesn't help me. This ends the section on the third kind of patience: patience that comes from developing the tolerance to not strike back.

Throughout all these teachings, Shantideva does his best to undermine our ordinary, commonsense attitude toward enemies and other irritants. He refutes our knee-jerk reaction that retaliation makes the most sense.

Specific Situations for Practicing Patience

Patience, Part Two

CONTINUING IN CHAPTER 6 of *The Way of the Bodhisattva*, Shantideva now lists various painful situations in which we can learn to relax and practice patience.

6.52

The mind is bodiless:
By no one can it be destroyed.
And yet it grasps the body tightly,
Falling victim to the body's pain.

6.53

Scorn and hostile words,
And comments that I do not like to hear—
My body is not harmed by them.
What reason do you have, O mind, for your resentment?

6.54

Contempt and scorn that others show me
Now and in my future lives—
Since none of it can bite and swallow me,
Why is it that I'm so averse to it?

The topic of verses 52 through 54 is practicing patience when
we're scorned, criticized, or treated condescendingly. When I was a
child we used to say "sticks and stones can break my bones, but
names can never hurt me." This is Shantideva's message: hostile
words are merely sounds coming out of someone's mouth. If they
were in a foreign language, we wouldn't even react. But because of
our past history and present state of mind, we interpret these
sounds in a way that causes us to fly into a rage. Could we even
consider not doing this?

6.55

Perhaps I turn from it because
It hinders me from having what I want.
But all my property I'll leave behind,
While sins will keep me steady company.

Perhaps, Shantideva muses, we resent hostile words because we
fear that if people dislike us, they may prevent us from acquiring
the possessions and wealth we desire. But this, he acknowledges,
doesn't make sense. When we die, we will leave all our property behind; only karmic consequences will keep us *steady company*.

It would be wise not to strengthen negative propensities, no
matter what their justification. Even if someone slanders us and
threatens our reputation, it would be better to lose everything than
to strengthen the causes of pain. In verses 56 through 61, he continues this reflection on "you can't take it with you."

6.56

Better far for me to die today,
Than live a long and evil life.
However great may be my length of days,
The pain of dying will be all the same.

6.57

One man dreams he lives a hundred years
Of happiness, but then he wakes.
Another dreams an instant's joy,
But then he, likewise, wakes.

6.58

And when they wake, the happiness of both
Is finished, never to return.
Likewise, when the hour of death comes round,
Our lives are over, whether brief or long.

6.59

Though we be rich in worldly goods,
Delighting in our wealth for many years,
Despoiled and stripped as though by thieves,
We must go naked and with empty hands.

Whether our dreamlike life is long or short, in the end we die.
Most of us hope for a long and happy dream and leave it at that.
But if our long, happy dream is built on other people's suffering,
the consequences won't be pleasant. A short dream in which we
shed destructive habits would be preferable.

6.60

Perhaps we'll claim that by our wealth we live,
And living, gather merit, dissipating evil.
But if we're ruthless for the sake of gain,
It's evil we will gather, dissipating merit!

6.61

What use then will our lives have been
When all is so degenerate and spoiled?
What use is there in living such a life
When evil is the only consequence?

These verses say more about *ruthlessness for the sake of gain*. We
might claim we need to gather wealth in order to do virtuous
deeds, like building temples or feeding the poor. With this Mafia-
style logic, we try to justify retaliating against those who would
keep us from getting rich. But Shantideva makes it clear that our
negative actions far outweigh any wholesome deeds we might perform in the hope of gathering a bit of merit.

6.62

If, when others slander us, we claim
Our anger is because they harm themselves,
How is it we do not resent
Their slander when it's aimed at someone else?

We could always use dharma logic to justify our anger: "I'm
angry because Mary is harming herself. When she slanders me,
look at the painful consequences she creates for herself!" Such an
argument might make us feel quite virtuous. But Shantideva re-

plies, "In that case, why don't I see you getting angry about Mary's bad karma when she slanders someone else?"

6.63

If we bear with such antipathy,
Remarking that it's due to other factors,
Why are we impatient when they slander us?
Emotion, after all, has been the cause of it.

We might claim that our not getting upset with Mary's antipathy toward someone else is *due to other factors*. For example, we think that the other person deserved to be told off. We say to ourselves, "He's so consumed by his emotions that Mary needed to point that out." To this, Shantideva is quick to reply: "Well then, since you also seem to be consumed by emotion, wouldn't Mary have every right to disapprove of *you?*" I sense he's having fun here with his logic and reasoning.

6.64

Even those who vilify and undermine
The sacred Doctrine, images, and stupas
Are not the proper objects of our anger;
The buddhas are themselves untouched
     thereby.

Perhaps we feel we could justify anger if someone harms the teachings or sacred images, but Shantideva disagrees. The buddhas themselves would not get upset; in fact, they would only feel compassion. So how can we presume to get self-righteous on their behalf?

6.65

And even if our teachers, relatives, and friends
Are now the object of aggression,
All derives from factors just explained.
This we should perceive, and curb our wrath.

Verse 65 discusses developing patience when those we love and admire are scorned. If our teacher is the object of aggression, it's ridiculous to get angry. This is exactly what our teacher wouldn't want us to do. If our loved one is being scorned, once again, we could reflect that, just like us, the aggressors are victims of their kleshas. If we become outraged, we become like mirror images of our foes. They, however, have no instructions for working with their emotions. Knowing that even *with* these instructions we still have difficulties, we might become more open-minded toward our adversaries and let this insight *curb our wrath.*

6.66

Beings suffer injury alike
From lifeless things as well as living beings;
So why be angry only with the latter?
Rather let us simply bear with harm.

This is now a familiar message. We don't hold grudges against fallen branches, and we'd be wise to have the same equanimity toward aggressive people.

6.67

Some do evil things because of ignorance,
Some respond with anger, being ignorant.
Which of them is faultless in his acts?
To whom shall error be attributed?

Someone might justify harming us, not realizing how much she's harming herself. We might retaliate out of the same ignorance. So who is right and who is wrong? Aren't we both in the same boat?

6.68

Rather, why did I do evil in the past,
That caused me harm at others' hands?
All that happens is the fruit of karma;
Why then should I now be angry?

To make this point clear, Shantideva reiterates his reflection on karmic consequences. This person and I have a karmic debt. I could respond in a way that erases that debt and benefits us both; or, I could keep the cycle of misery going. The choice is up to me.

6.69

This I see and therefore, come what may,
I'll hold fast to the virtuous path
And foster in the hearts of all
An attitude of mutual love.

Shantideva is clear that there's no valid justification for hatred. Rather than conning himself about his aggression, he'll devote himself to fostering *an attitude of mutual love.*

I once asked Thrangu Rinpoche how to work with my anger toward my mother. He told me I should experiment for awhile with resenting her and see how that felt. Then I should remember any kindness she showed me as a child and try appreciating her for a week or two. In the end, I could make my own decision about which attitude to cultivate for the rest of my life!

6.70

For when a building is ablaze
And flames leap out from house to house,
The wise course is to take and fling away
The straw and anything that spreads the fire.

6.71

In fear that merit might be all consumed,
We should at once cast far away
Our mind's attachments:
Tinder for the fiery flames of hate.

Here Shantideva gives clear instruction on how to cool off when anger is already aroused. He instructs us to remove the fuel that causes anger to escalate, the *tinder* of wanting things our way.

When we look closely at *our mind's attachments,* we can see they don't hold together without our story lines. When it comes to the *fiery flames of hate,* we could cool them down by acknowledging obsessive thoughts and letting them go. Our tool for doing this is the *shamatha* meditation that Shantideva introduced in chapter 5.

In meditation we recognize when our mind wanders and simply return to being present. To facilitate this process, we can add an additional step: we can label the thoughts "thinking." This technique gently and objectively dissolves the stream of habitual chatter and its underlying beliefs. Like removing the tinder from a burning building, it deflates the powerful surge of energy before we become enflamed.*

---

*For further instructions on meditation, see chapter 4 in my book *When Things Fall Apart.*

6.72

Is not a man relieved when, though condemned
    to death,
He's freed, his hand cut off in ransom for his life?
Enduring likewise merely human ills,
Am I not happy to avoid the pains of hell?

It's painful to refrain from anger; it takes courage. When the
hook of *shenpa* is strong, we long to talk indignantly among our
friends, to yell at our foes, and to fuel the anger with our thoughts.
Shantideva acknowledges the pain of not striking back by comparing it to the horror of having a hand cut off. But the pain of
refraining is well worth it: it's like losing only a hand instead of our
life. It allows us to calm down and *avoid the pains of hell.*

6.73

If pains of even this, my present life,
Are now beyond my strength to bear,
Why do I not overthrow my anger,
Cause of future sorrows in infernal torment?

The message here is the same: by putting up with the relatively
mild, short-term suffering of the detox period, we forgo far greater
agony. The key is taking responsibility for our actions. Our future
well-being depends on what we do right now.

6.74

For sake of gaining all that I desired,
A thousand times I underwent
The tortures of the realms of hell—
Achieving nothing for myself and others.

6.75

The present aches are nothing to compare with those,
And yet great benefits may come from them.
These troubles that dispel the pains of wanderers—
How could I not rejoice in them?

When I read this, I'm reminded of the earlier part of my life and
the suffering I went through around relationships. There was the
pain of getting into them, even more pain getting out of them—
and a tremendous amount of energy expended in between.

Likewise, our careers and the other things we pursue can feel
like *the tortures of the realms of hell,* and what do we have to show
for it, with the passage of time? We have even stronger habits of
striving, craving, hatred, and revenge. If we keep strengthening
these old patterns, our *present aches* are nothing compared to
those to come.

This is our chance to do something different. We've spent lifetimes trying to find happiness in ordinary, samsaric ways. Now,
let's try working straightforwardly with the mind itself. Let's also
recall that our ordinary human suffering has value. It can humble
us and teach us compassion. The pain we go through while changing old habits is not only worth tolerating, it's worth celebrating!

6.76

When others take delight
In giving praise to those endowed with talents,
Why, O mind, do you not find
A joy, likewise, in praising them?

Remember that all the teachings in this book are Shantideva's
instructions to himself. In verses 76 through 86, he gives himself a
pep talk about developing patience when his enemies are praised

and he isn't. It isn't easy when someone else gets the compliments—or job, or perks, or lover—we want. We can't pretend it
doesn't get to us. When the talents of others are being praised,
Shantideva asks, *Why, O mind, do you not find joy, likewise, in praising them?*

Now is not the time to go on automatic pilot. Instead you
could do something revolutionary. You could turn the tide and
rejoice in the good fortune of others; you could say to yourself:
"I'm glad for them, and if I were in their shoes, I'd want them to
be glad for me."

When the undertow of anger or resentment is pulling me under,
teaching myself the dharma like this is sometimes the only thing
that saves me from drowning.

6.77

The pleasure that you gain therefrom
Itself gives rise to stainless happiness.
It's urged on us by all the holy ones,
And is the perfect way of winning others.

This stanza refers to the "four joys" of practicing patience. First,
patience is stainless; second, it brings happiness; third, it is praised
by *the holy ones;* and fourth, it is the perfect way to help others.

So often when we achieve happiness, our gain is, intentionally
or unintentionally, someone else's loss. If we get the job, some
other person doesn't; if we win the Olympic gold, others are crying
because they lost. It's not that we're malicious or in any way at
fault. That's just the way it is. Even if we don't purposely step on
someone else's toes, our happiness is subtly "stained." The practice
of patience, on the other hand, is *stainless.* In every case, no one
loses and everyone gains.

The practice of patience brings happiness. This is the second
joy. It isn't always instant pleasure, of course; sometimes it's just

the great relief of lessening our burden of rage. Just being able to pause and relax instead of retaliating gradually brings unshakable well-being. We find that very few people provoke us and the world is a friendlier place.

The third joy is that patience is praised by the buddhas. In the most profound sense, this means it brings us closer to our buddha nature, or basic goodness.

The fourth joy is that patience enables us to communicate sanely. It allows us to be heard and is thus *the perfect way of winning others*. In other words, we can get our message across because no one feels threatened or accused.

6.78

"But they're the ones who'll have the happiness,"
    you say.
If this then is a joy you would resent,
Abandon paying wages and returning favors:
You will be the loser—both in this life and the next!

Sometimes we've had enough of hearing about the virtues of patience. On some level, we might buy it; but on a gut level, we prefer the conventional logic, the logic of "what about me?" Why shouldn't I feel envious when others get all the praise? Why shouldn't I feel left out, lonely, or miserable when they're the ones surrounded by friends? Samsaric reasoning says that someone else is going to get all the happiness, not me.

If this is the way we feel, Shantideva asks, why would we want happiness for anyone? Why even bother *paying wages and returning favors*? Just because people work for us or help us out, why do anything to make them happy?

His rebuttal may not be easy to grasp, but it's well worth considering: not practicing patience is like not paying wages or returning favors. In general, people won't like us very much; in terms of our kleshas, strengthening meanness and jealousy won't bring us any happiness. No matter how we look at it, we lose.

6.79

When praise is heaped upon your merits,
You're keen that others should rejoice in them.
But when the compliment is paid to others,
Your joy is oh so slow and grudging.

This is a very up-to-date little verse. We could read it anywhere in the world, to any cultural, economic, or racial group and everybody would get it. The last two lines describe a predictable human response: we resent it when others are praised instead of us. Shantideva's point is that nurturing this kind of response doesn't make anyone happy.

6.80

You who want the happiness of beings,
Have wished to be enlightened for their sake.
So why should others irk you when
They find some little pleasure for themselves?

6.81

If you truly wish that beings be enlightened,
Venerated by the triple world,
When petty marks of favor come their way,
Why, oh why, are you in torment?

How ironic to take the bodhisattva vow to work for the happiness of all sentient beings and get irked by the most trivial interactions. Sometimes all we can do is laugh at our all-too-predictable reactions. We'd rather travel around the world to help homeless orphans than deal with our own mother or spouse. Shantideva encourages us to fulfill our vow by working wholeheartedly with everyday provocations.

6.82

When dependents who rely on you,
To whom you are obliged to give support,
Find for themselves the means of livelihood,
Will you not be happy, will you once again be angry?

Here again Shantideva uses humor to point out our nonsensical foibles. At least one or two sentient beings are saving us some trouble on the bodhisattva path by finding happiness all by themselves, even if it's the happiness of getting compliments we don't feel they deserve. Just as we're relieved when dependent children get jobs and start taking care of themselves, we could be equally relieved when even one sentient being makes less work for this bodhisattva.

6.83

If even this you do not want for beings,
How could you want buddhahood for them?
And how can anyone have bodhichitta
And resent the good that others have?

He continues with the theme of practicing patience when others, particularly those we don't like, get praised or rewarded. How can we say we want people to get enlightened when we don't even want them to get compliments? And, again, Shantideva reminds us that justifying resentment—or feeling guilty about it, for that matter—stifles the bodhi heart.

There is no practice more important than relating honestly and sanely with the irritations that plague us in everyday life.

6.84

If someone else receives a gift,
Or if that gift stays in the benefactor's house,
In neither case will it be yours—
So, given or withheld, why is it your concern?

6.85

Tell me, why don't you resent yourself,
You who throw your merit, faith,
And all your qualities so far away?
Why do you not cultivate the cause of riches?

Shantideva says to himself and his fellow monks: if a gift is given, or not given, to someone else, in either case *we* are not receiving it. So let's not torture ourselves with envious or hateful thoughts. If we're so willing to throw away our peace of mind, we might as well resent ourselves.

He is not, of course, suggesting we denigrate ourselves. We could just acknowledge that the way our mind keeps cycling in the same old patterns is causing us problems. We have a choice here. When rewards are given to those we feel are unworthy, we can let it destroy our peace of mind or let it go.

6.86

All the evil you have done
You cheerfully neglect to purify.
And do you further wish to match yourself
With others who have earned their merit?

When we obliviously rant on about others' good fortune—How come they got the job? The pay increase? The winning lottery ticket?—we forget it may be due to their previous virtuous actions. Now they're experiencing the results and merit of those virtuous actions. Our resentment and gossip, on the other hand, won't bring us any positive results.

The next few verses address practicing patience when we find ourselves glad that our enemy has fallen on hard times.

6.87

If unhappiness befalls your enemy,
Why should this be a cause for your rejoicing?
The wishes of your mind alone,
Will not in fact contrive his injury.

6.88

And if your hostile wishes *were* to bring them harm,
Again, what cause of joy is that to you?
"Why, then I should be satisfied!"—are these your
    thoughts?
Is anything more ruinous than that?

6.89

Caught upon the hook, unbearable and sharp,
Cast by the fisherman, my own defilements,
I'll be flung into the cauldrons of the pit,
And surely parboiled by the janitors of hell!

It's definitely tempting to delight in the misfortune of our enemies. Shantideva likens us to a fish that spots a worm on a hook.

Whether or not we're conscious of the hook, we still want to bite into that juicy little worm. The consequences for us and the poor fish are the same: short-term gratification and a very unpleasant end. Getting caught on the sharp hook of hatred and jealously will never bring comfort and ease.

6.90

The rigmarole of praise and fame
Serves not to increase merit or one's span of life,
Bestowing neither health nor strength
And nothing for the body's ease.

6.91

If I am wise in what is good for me,
I'll ask what benefit these bring.
For if it's entertainment I desire,
I might as well resort to alcohol and cards!

Maybe our downfall isn't getting envious or insulted when others get what we feel we deserve; maybe our weakness is *the rigmarole of praise and fame.*

However, the things that we think will make a significant difference in our lives—fame, praise, status, a new house, the partner of our dreams—don't seem to remove unhappiness for very long. After the immediate gratification, we're usually back where we started.

This simple truth rarely penetrates. Even with clear-cut evidence to the contrary, we continue relying on possessions, relationships, reputation, or wealth to significantly alter our state of mind. Shantideva questions the wisdom of these habitual assumptions and states the obvious: no matter how successful we are at getting what we want, it won't increase our life span, long-term contentment, or merit. Expecting lasting happiness from a shift in outer circumstances will always disappoint us.

With his usual wit Shantideva says, in effect: If the reason for my addiction to praise and fame is a desire for gratification, I might as well give up my monastic vows and start drinking and gambling. It would give me the same fleeting satisfaction!

I always wonder if the monks in his audience were shocked or amused by Shantideva's humor.

6.92

We lose our lives, our wealth we squander,
All for reputation's sake.
What use are words, and whom will they delight
When we are dead and in our graves?

Some of us will go to any lengths to get ahead. Maybe even you have taken some crazy risks in hopes of being recognized and admired. But is the temporary elation worth it in the long run? And will you be able to look to it for help when you die?

6.93

Children can't help crying when
Their sand castles come crumbling down.
Our minds are so like them
When praise and reputation start to fail.

Life is transitory and passes quickly. People who've come close to death report seeing their whole lives flash before their eyes. We invest so much energy into getting people to admire us, but our reputations, like everything else, are as impermanent as sand castles, and attachment to them causes so much unnecessary pain.

There's a Charlie Brown cartoon that shows Lucy building an elaborate sand castle, saying proudly, "And a thousand years from now, people will see what I did here today and be totally amazed." It's this nonsensical attitude that Shantideva addresses here.

Better to regard yourself as a character in a play. You can take the part of a person who's famous or admired, without taking this identity too seriously. If praise and reputation are as fragile as sand castles, it's realistic to not be disturbed when they pass away with the changing tides. Then you can build a magnificent sand castle, covered with beautiful shells and stones. You can even get people to help you and enjoy it thoroughly, and when the waves come in, out it goes.

The creation of Tibetan sand mandalas exemplifies this process. These ceremonial mandalas require days of attentive work. At the end of the ritual, however, they are respectfully wiped away. The sand is placed in a bowl and returned to the sea, and nothing at all remains.

Once I was watching a TV documentary on Tibetan monks making a sand mandala. My friend was mesmerized by the beauty of the mandala, but knew nothing of how the ceremony ended. When the mandala was ultimately destroyed, I was unfazed, but she became almost hysterical with shock and disbelief. Understanding the impermanent nature of our lives is one key to equanimity.

6.94

Short-lived sound, devoid of intellect,
Can never in itself intend to praise us.
"But it's the joy that others take in me," you say—
Are these the shoddy causes of your pleasure?

6.95

What is it to me if others should delight
In someone else, or even in myself?
Their pleasure's theirs, and theirs alone.
What part of it could be for my enjoyment?

6.96

If I am happy at the joy of those who take delight,
Then everyone should be a source of joy to me.
Why, when glory goes elsewhere,
Am I not happy with this cause of happiness?

6.97

The satisfaction that is mine
From thinking "I am being praised,"
Is unacceptable to common sense,
And nothing but the silly ways of children.

In these four verses, Shantideva makes an important point. The many reasons we come up with to justify our need for praise are, in fact, just food for self-importance. Eventually we become enslaved by our childish craving for validation. Shantideva says that these hollow words are just *short-lived sound,* and it's silly to take them so seriously.

If we claim that our satisfaction comes not from being complimented but from bringing others the happiness of appreciating us, that reasoning is definitely "shoddy." First of all, pleasure is not transferable; secondly, if our bodhisattva motivation is to make others happy, why aren't we pleased when these same folks express appreciation for our enemy?

6.98

Praise and compliments disturb me,
Sapping my revulsion with samsara.
I start to covet others' qualities,
And thus all excellence degenerates.

In verse 98, Shantideva concludes this section with three reasons why it's futile to continually seek confirmation. First, we become dependent on *praise and compliments,* relying on the whims of other people's opinions to feel good about ourselves.

Second, too much admiration saps our *revulsion with samsara.* If we do manage to become esteemed and respected, we might start believing this feel-good state is equivalent to lasting happiness. We might kid ourselves into thinking we don't have any more foibles to work on, not even humility.

Third, our envy of others' good qualities increases. We may think we no longer need compliments, but watch out! When the praise we've gotten used to goes to someone else, envy can kick in. This is a warning sign alerting us to a blind spot.

6.99

Those who stay close by me, then,
To ruin my good name and cut me down to size
Are surely there protecting me
From falling into ruin in the realms of sorrow.

With verse 99, Shantideva starts a section on the value of troublemakers. Considering that he lived in a monastery where he was widely disrespected, this may have been one of his principle practices. He probably had ample opportunity to apply the advice he gives here.

Those who give us a hard time, who are difficult to be around or who constantly blow our cover, are the very ones who show us where we we're stuck. The great meditation master Atisha always traveled with his belligerent Bengali tea-boy because it kept him honest. Without his ill-tempered servant to test him, he might have been able to deceive himself about his degree of equanimity. Troublemakers up the ante: if we can practice patience with them, we can practice it with anyone.

6.100

For I am one who strives for freedom—
I must not be caught by wealth and honors.
How could I be angry with the ones
Who work to loose me from my fetters?

6.101

They, like Buddha's very blessing,
Bar my way, determined as I am
To plunge myself headlong in sorrow:
How could I be angry with them?

The next time you're irked, see if you can remember this logic: troublemakers show us things we don't want to see. They show us how we get trapped and continually create our own sorrow. Even the Buddhas could not bestow a greater blessing!

6.102

We should not be angry, saying,
"They are obstacles to virtue."
Is not patience the supreme austerity,
And is this not my chosen discipline?

Rather than considering troublemakers *obstacles to virtue,* we can see them as enhancements, the very means by which we learn to practice patience.

6.103

If I fail to practice patience,
Hindered by my own deficiency,
I am myself the obstacle to gaining
Merit, yet so close at hand.

When we lose our temper, it's a wake-up call: "Oh no! I just did it again!" Using levity instead of guilt, we can find the humor in the situation and go forward with a light heart because of what we've learned.

We should all expect relapses. No one ever said this unwinding of old patterns would be quick or easy. Better to simply acknowledge we're still provokable and not blame it on somebody else.

6.104

For nothing comes except through other
   factors,
And comes to be, those factors being present.
If one thing is the cause of something else,
How could it then be said to hinder it?

Developing patience depends upon having someone to provoke us. Because of his tea-boy, Atisha developed the ability to stay relaxed and awake even in the most provoking situations. So how can we say that our enemies and troublemakers are hindrances? Without them, we would never have the opportunity to practice nonaggression.

6.105

The beggars who arrive at proper times
Are not an obstacle to generosity.
We cannot say that those who give the vows
Are causing hindrances to ordination!

When we want to take monastic ordination, we need a precep-
tor to make it possible. When we want to practice generosity,
panhandlers provide the opportunity. When we want to practice
patience, there's no way to do so without troublemakers! Again,
Shantideva uses humor to make his point.

6.106

The beggars in this world are many,
Attackers are comparatively few.
For as I do no harm to others,
Those who do me injury are rare.

This is the bodhisattva's dilemma: we would like to practice patience, but by doing so, fewer and fewer people irritate us. *Those
who do me injury* are harder to find and opportunities for practice
are rare!

6.107

So like a treasure found at home,
Enriching me without fatigue,
All enemies are helpers in my bodhisattva work
And therefore they should be a joy to me.

The next time you're provoked by someone, pause and say to yourself: "*Like a treasure found at home, enriching me without fatigue*, you, my dear troublemaker, are the means by which a confused person like me will attain enlightenment." Even if it's not that convincing at first, this kind of thinking does a lot to deflate aggression.

6.108

The fruits of patience are for them and me,
For both of us have brought it into being.
And yet to them they must be offered first,
For of my patience they have been the cause.

What happens if you're confronted by someone who is always angry, and you don't retaliate? One, you don't fuel his anger. Two, you have the chance to practice patience and loving-kindness.

Therefore both of you bring this benefit into being: you, by being less reactive; and the angry person by giving you this opportunity. And so *the fruits of patience* are reaped by both of you. The merit, however, should be offered first to the one who provokes you. Because he was the cause of your patience, you gratefully wish him good fortune.

We might wonder if our practice of patience can actually save someone from his own karmic consequences. If not reinforcing his aggression helps him to pause and calm down, then the answer is definitely "yes, we can help someone escape from anger."

On the other hand, if he keeps getting worked up, the answer is "no, our patience doesn't help him at all." But even then we can say to ourselves: "May this connection between us, as unpleasant as it is, be the cause of our attaining enlightenment together." In this way, he will benefit in either case and so, of course, will we.

6.109

Yet if I say my foe should not be praised
Since he did not intend to stimulate my patience,
Why do I revere the sacred Doctrine,
Cause indeed of my attainment?

Many of us won't readily buy into Shantideva's reasoning. Why should we wish good fortune to our foes? Why be grateful to those who hurt us and certainly have no intention of stimulating our patience?

To this Shantideva replies, "Why then would you revere *the sacred Doctrine?* The dharma is just 'words,' with no more intention of stimulating your patience than your angry foes."

To determine what's worthy of your gratitude, look to the final result. What is the outcome of these dharmic words, or this encounter with an angry foe? If it's patience, we could be grateful to both of them. Instead of saying, "My boss didn't intend to make me patient, so he doesn't deserve my praise," we can say, "He didn't intend this, but I became more patient anyway. Therefore I'm grateful."

6.110

"This enemy conspired to harm me," I protest,
"And therefore should receive no honors."
But had he worked to help me, like a doctor,
How could I have brought forth patience?

Dzigar Kongtrul uses the expression "the illogical logic of self-importance." Shantideva's reasoning may sometimes be hard to accept, but does our usual logic of retaliation and spite make more sense?

We may protest cultivating patience toward those with malicious intentions. But Shantideva responds with this clever analogy: when a doctor helps us it may be painful, but we don't get angry because we know the pain will benefit us in the end. Couldn't we take this same attitude toward the pain caused by troublemakers? They, too, benefit us by giving us the opportunity to practice patience. If they had intentionally set out to help us, like a doctor, we wouldn't have this chance to heal our anger.

6.111

Because of those whose minds are full of anger,
I engender patience in myself.
They are thus the cause of patience,
Fit for veneration, like the Doctrine.

Shantideva concludes this section with a summary: because our enemies bring us benefit, they are as worthy of veneration as the dharma. If you've ever wondered about the mahayana teaching "Be grateful to everyone," these lines are an excellent commentary.

6.112

The worlds of beings are a buddhafield,
Thus the Mighty Lord has taught.
For many who have sought the happiness of others
Have gone beyond, attaining to perfection.

6.113

Thus the state of buddhahood depends
On beings and the buddhas equally.
By what tradition is it then
That buddhas, but not beings, are revered?

In these verses, Shantideva makes the remarkable statement that sentient beings like us are as worthy of veneration as fully awakened buddhas. When we hold sentient beings as the object of our practice—be it the practice of patience, compassion, generosity, or loving-kindness—they become the cause of our enlightenment, equal in value to the buddhas.

6.114

Their aims are not, of course, the same,
But it is by their fruits that we should know them.
And so we see the excellence of beings—
Beings and the buddhas are indeed the same!

It is tempting to dispute this teaching. Sentient beings are, after all, confused and self-absorbed; buddhas are completely sane. But Shantideva reiterates his previous point: *it is by their fruits that we should know them.* Since we constantly interact with each other and we rarely encounter a fully awakened buddha, then maybe sentient beings offer us even more opportunities for liberation!

6.115

Offerings made to one who loves
Reveal the eminence of living beings.
Merit that accrues from faith in Buddha
Reveals in turn the Buddha's eminence.

The *one who loves* refers to someone who has loving-kindness and compassion for everyone. To make offerings to such an evolved person reveals the *eminence of living beings.* Why is this so? It is because of the work they did with sentient beings—difficult, suffering beings like you and me—that this person's awakening occurred. Thus the eminence of living beings is as great as the eminence of the buddhas.

6.116

Since they are both the means of winning
    buddhahood,
We say that beings are the same as buddhas,
Even though they are not equal
In the boundless ocean of a buddha's merits.

6.117

Yet if a tiny part of that great merit
Were found to be contained in certain beings'
    hearts,
The three worlds made in offering to them
Would be a slight, a very little thing.

Certainly the enlightened ones have a great deal more merit and wakefulness available to them than you or I. But even the littlest bit of merit or wakefulness makes us worthy of unlimited offerings. The slightest recognition of bodhichitta, the slightest willingness to enter the bodhisattva path, makes us as worthy of offerings as the buddhas. I find these very encouraging words.

6.118

A share in bringing forth the supreme state of
    buddhahood
Is thus possessed by everyone.
This demonstrates the reason why
They are the proper object of my reverence.

Verse 118 is a concise summary of this section. The word *everyone* is important here: everyone shares in bringing forth the supreme state of buddhahood. And everyone, of course, includes us.

6.119

As buddhas are my constant friends,
Boundless in the benefits they bring to me,
How else may I repay their goodness,
But by making living beings happy?

6.120

By helping beings we repay the ones
Who gave themselves for us and plunged into the hells.
Should beings therefore do great harm to me,
I'll strive to bring them only benefit.

In verses 119 through 127, Shantideva gives tenderhearted advice on repaying the kindness of our teachers. These are the people who show us a bigger perspective and try to keep us on track. How do we repay their kindness? We do it, Shantideva says, by being patient with one another.

On an everyday level, other people do so much to save us from suffering. Even if we don't have a dharma teacher, we know what it is to be benefited by family, friends, or even strangers. There are people willing to go through personal inconvenience and pain to help us. And Shantideva is saying that now we can repay them, by treating each other with loving-kindness.

6.121

For if the ones who are my lords and teachers,
For beings' sake are careless even of their bodies,

Why should I, a fool, behave with such conceit?
Why should I not become the slave of others?

If our teachers and others have been willing to put themselves
out for us, why can't we do the same? Is it because of arrogance,
Shantideva ponders, that we can't bring ourselves to stoop
so low?

I've seen my son and his wife get up in the middle of the night
to care for my grandchildren, who were vomiting or shitting all
over themselves. They'd pick them up, clean them, and maybe lie
down with them next to the toilet. Even parents we may now resent probably did the very same things for us when we were young
and helpless.

As a bodhisattva-in-training, you could start today to put yourself out for others. Start with a close friend or loved one, then let
your willingness to tackle more demanding situations increase.
One day, you'll be able to extend yourself to anyone, as if they were
your own child. This is a gradual path of becoming more capable
of stretching further.

Shantideva says that those he reveres most never thought they
were too good to help *him*. Even if he thought of himself as foolish, his teachers never turned their backs on him. The best way he
can thank them is to follow their example.

6.122

Buddhas are made happy by the joy of beings;
They sorrow, they lament when beings suffer.
Bringing joy to beings, then, I please the buddhas
    also—
Offending them, the buddhas I offend.

The way to make one's spiritual teachers happy is not by making them meals or bringing them presents. It's by putting their

teachings into practice. Certainly, dharma teachers enjoy kindness and generosity as much as anyone. But it's definitely not going to compute if we're smiling and kind to them while being scornful and mean to others.

6.123

Just as when a man who's tortured in a fire,
Remains unmoved by little favors done to him,
There's no way to delight the great compassionate
    buddhas,
While we ourselves are causes of another's pain.

When a man's being burned at the stake, we can't really offer him a choice between pork chops and fried chicken, or bring him a pizza or video to alleviate his torment. These conventional gestures of generosity would be rather flimsy in the face of his agony. Likewise, when our teachers see us intentionally causing someone to suffer, it brings them so much pain that no matter how many *little favors* we offer them, it does nothing to ease their sorrow.

6.124

The damage I have done to wandering beings
Saddens all the buddhas in their great compassion.
Therefore, all these sins I will confess today
And pray that they will bear with me.

When we can really acknowledge the harm we've caused ourselves and others, this "positive sadness" heals us. We no longer get caught in justification or guilt and can go forward without a hangover. This kind of sadness is cleansing. With this spirit, we help ourselves and simultaneously repay the kindness of our teachers and friends.

6.125

And that I might rejoice the buddhas' hearts,
I will be master of myself, and be the servant of the
world—
And not respond though others trample, wound,
or kill me.
Now let the guardians of the world rejoice!

May Shantideva's enthusiasm for the practice of patience be contagious. No matter how challenged we are, may we take responsibility for our actions and develop our ability to care for others. May we train in nonaggression, even under fire.

6.126

The great compassionate lords consider as their own
All wanderers—of this there is no doubt.
Beings, then, are Buddha's very self.
Thus how can I not treat them with respect?

Here Shantideva explicitly says that all sentient beings *are Buddha's very self;* all beings have buddha nature.

Trungpa Rinpoche explained buddha nature in various ways. He taught that all beings have "enlightened genes"—murderers and buddhas alike. Beings suffering the agony of hell have exactly the same innate ability to wake up as those enjoying the bliss of enlightenment. All have equal potential.

He also presented this teaching as "basic goodness," saying that we could interact with one another in ways that connect us with this basic wisdom rather than obscuring it. Rather than triggering each other's aggression and discouragement, we could pause and allow some space for everyone to experience their soft spot.

I have a vivid memory of an irate man attacking Trungpa

Rinpoche about his teachings on basic goodness, saying that people were fundamentally flawed. Rinpoche calmly replied that the ultimate nature of everything tends toward goodness and there's no way to stop it, no matter what we believe.

6.127

Venerating them will please the buddhas' hearts,
And perfectly secure the welfare of myself.
This will drive away the sorrows of the world,
And therefore it will be my constant practice.

The best thing we can do for our teachers, ourselves, and the world is to think of benefiting rather than harming one another.

6.128

Imagine that the steward of a king
Does injury to multitudes of people.
Those among the injured who are wise
Will not respond with violence, even if they can.

6.129

For stewards, after all, are not alone.
They are supported by the kingly power.
Likewise I should not make light
Of lesser men who do me little injuries.

6.130

For they have guardians of hell for allies
And also the compassionate buddhas.
Therefore I'll respect all living beings,
As though they were the subjects of that wrathful king.

In verses 128 through 134, Shantideva perseveres in his attempt to make us see that it makes no sense to give in to the tug of aggression. His final teaching on the value of patience is to explain, once again, that our actions have karmic consequences. As our aggressive mind grows stronger, the world appears increasingly hellish.

He uses the analogy of not retaliating to harm done by *lesser men* supported by the power of a *wrathful king*. In other words, getting miffed at even little grievances strengthens the power of aggression; and the consequences will always be unpleasant.

Most of us feel it's OK to indulge in little irritations, lightweight gossiping, or a teensy-weensy bit of slander. But by doing so, Shantideva says, we're reinforcing negative mind. On the other hand, if we can catch the seduction of hostility and petty-mindedness at this subtle stage, it's much easier to nip it in the bud.

The *guardians of hell* and *the compassionate buddhas* are both our allies. If we're intelligent about the potential consequences of our actions, both pain and pleasure will motivate us to act wisely.

6.131

And yet, the pains of hell to be endured
Through making living beings suffer—
Could these ever be unleashed on us
By all the fury of an angry king?

6.132

And even if that king were pleased,
Enlightenment he could not give to us,
For this will only be achieved
By bringing happiness to living beings.

Is there anyone who can cause us as much pain as we cause ourselves by strengthening negative mind? A king might imprison or even kill us; but when our mind is seething with aggression, it will feel like eternal hell. On the positive side, even if he were pleased with us, what could a king really do? Give us a job, lots of money, a nice house? What are these transitory pleasures compared to finding ultimate freedom and unshakable happiness? Nothing can bring us as much suffering, or happiness, as our own mind.

6.133

Granted, then, that future buddhahood
Is forged through bringing happiness to beings;
How can I not see that glory, fame, and pleasure
Even in this life will likewise come?

6.134

For patience in samsara brings such things
As beauty, health, and good renown.
Its fruit is great longevity,
The vast contentment of a universal king.

Shantideva makes one last pitch. If unshakable, indestructible buddhahood isn't enough of a carrot, how's this? If we practice as he suggests, we will look good, feel good, and be famous!

When scowling and uptight, even conventionally beautiful people are disfigured. What's more, anger isn't good for our health or longevity and results in people not liking us. Even if nothing else penetrates, pondering these worldly benefits of patience might motivate us to take Shantideva's advice.

Should you find that this takes time and you relapse into aggression, never forget the importance of being patient and tolerant with yourself.

Enthusiasm

Heroic Perseverance

CHAPTER 7 BEGINS the third and final section of *The Way of the Bodhisattva*. The first three chapters present ways of connecting with bodhichitta. The next three chapters explain how to keep it from diminishing. In this third section, Shantideva tells us what causes bodhichitta to *grow and flourish ever more and more.*

The *paramita* of enthusiasm works like a miracle ingredient that brings eagerness to all we do. What the bodhisattva commits to isn't a trivial matter. Without enthusiasm, we might push too hard or give up altogether. As the Zen master Suzuki Roshi put it: "What we're doing here is so important we had better not take it too seriously!" The key is finding this balance between "not too tight" and "not too loose," not too zealous or too laid-back.

In this spirit, Trungpa Rinpoche encouraged us to lead our lives as an experiment, a suggestion that has been very important to me. When we approach life as an experiment, we're willing to try it this way and that way because, either way, we have nothing to lose.

This immense flexibility is something I learned from the example of Trungpa Rinpoche. His enthusiasm enabled him to accomplish an amazing amount in his life. When some things didn't work out, Rinpoche's attitude was "no big deal." If it's time for something to flourish, it will; if it's not time, it won't.

The trick is not getting caught in hope and fear. We can put our whole heart into whatever we do; but if we freeze our attitude into for or against, we're setting ourselves up for stress. Instead, we could just go forward with curiosity, wondering where this experiment will lead. This kind of open-ended inquisitiveness captures the spirit of enthusiasm, or heroic perseverance.

7.1

Thus with patience I will bravely persevere.
Through zeal it is that I shall reach enlightenment.
If no wind blows, then nothing stirs,
And neither is there merit without perseverance.

Wind is an apt metaphor for enthusiasm. Like wind in the sails of a ship, there's nothing heavy-handed about it. It doesn't take thousands of people to push a ship across the ocean; when the sails go up, the wind moves it forward naturally and easily.

At the same time, this verse conveys a feeling of urgency. As Suzuki Roshi said, the work we're doing is very important. The wind of delight and the urgency with which we apply it work together. There is no time to lose—but not to worry, we can do it.

7.2

Heroic perseverance means delight in virtue.
Its contrary may be defined as laziness:
An inclination for unwholesome ways,
Despondency, and self-contempt.

Two main topics are presented in verse 2. The first is the definition of enthusiasm, or heroic perseverance, as *delight in virtue*. The second is the opposite of enthusiasm: the klesha of laziness.

Once we have trust in the teachings, we'll naturally take delight in virtue. When I realized, for example, that Shantideva's instructions could cut through my unhappiness, I became enthusiastic about applying them. Delight in virtue, in this case, meant working wisely with my emotions and learning to gently tame my mind. It meant reaching out to offer kindness and support to as many beings as possible—and doing this eagerly, not out of a sense of duty.

I can tell you from experience that when there's a shift toward eagerness, life takes on a whole new meaning. Not the meaning that comes from careers or relationships, but the meaning that comes from using everything that happens as an opportunity to wake up. There will always be challenges, but they need not be seen as obstacles. It's all part of the path to enlightenment.

The opposite of enthusiasm is laziness. Here Shantideva presents three kinds: laziness, per se; not being willing to make an effort; and the despondency of self-contempt. In verse 2, he describes the first two together as *an inclination for unwholesome ways*.

Trungpa Rinpoche calls the first kind of laziness "comfort orientation." We use comfort to escape from our uneasiness. This doesn't mean we can't enjoy comfort in our lives; we just don't need to become addicted to it. This is what sentient beings predictably do, even little bugs and beetles. Did you ever wonder what those flies are doing, repeatedly struggling up a sunny window and falling down? Like most of us, they're looking for comfort.

There's a sutra in which beings from another galaxy visit the Buddha to discuss the dharma. They are shocked when the Buddha tells them he teaches the truth of suffering to get beings to enter the path. They find this an extremely crude technique and say that where they come from, enlightenment is directly introduced through pleasing smells. The Buddha replies that he'd be glad to use such an approach, but it would never work here because Earth beings immediately become attached to pleasure.

The second kind of laziness Trungpa Rinpoche calls "loss of heart." We feel we've tried and tried, but we never get it right. Things never seem to work out. We indulge in discouragement and lose our will to help ourselves or anyone else.

The third kind of laziness Trungpa Rinpoche calls "couldn't care less." This despondency of self-contempt takes the wind out of our sails. Doubting ourselves so profoundly is much more stubborn and bitter than merely losing heart.

7.3

Complacent pleasure in the joys of idleness,
A craving for repose and sleep,
No qualms about the sorrows of samsara:
These are the source and nurse of laziness.

In verse 3, Shantideva discusses the first kind of laziness: laziness, per se, or comfort orientation. This kind of laziness hopes to avoid the unpleasantness of life. If we could just get comfortable enough, if we could get that hot tub or go on that shopping spree, maybe we could outsmart samsara. Or, maybe the simple life would do it: a cabin in the woods, a life filled with beauty and peace. Of course, all that will quickly shatter when the doctor tells us our test results aren't good, but meanwhile, comfort looks like the solution to our discontent.

In the following verses Shantideva once again contemplates the certainty of his death. This is a traditional antidote to laziness: an antidote to investing so much hope in short-lived comforts and wasting our precious human birth.

7.4

Snared by the trapper of defiled emotion,
Enmeshed and taken in the toils of birth,
How could I not know that thus I've strayed
Into the mouth, the very jaws, of Death?

Verse 4 refers to the *nidana* chain, the chain of cause and effect that generates samsara. The wheel of samsara spins around and around, from birth to inevitable death. Like a poor animal *snared by the trapper of defiled emotion*, we're trapped in this cycle of suffering. Happily, we can interrupt the samsaric chain reaction by taming our mind and patiently refraining from escalating our kleshas. This, in fact, is what all Shantideva's teachings address: how to free ourselves from the vicious cycle of samsara.

7.5

Don't you see how one by one
Death comes to claim your fellow men?
And yet you slumber on so soundly,
Like a buffalo beside its butcher.

Lulled into comfort orientation, we prefer false security to facing the facts. Shielding ourselves from the disquieting realities of groundlessness, impermanence, and death, we *slumber on so soundly, like a buffalo beside its butcher.* But for how long will this strategy work?

7.6

All paths of flight are blocked,
The Lord of Death now has you in his sights.
How can you take pleasure in your food?
How can you delight to rest and sleep?

Imagine the feeble comfort of a feast just before we're lead to our death. By the same token, how can we be seduced by food and rest, if they're just further ways of cocooning in transitory pleasures? When *the Lord of Death has you in his sights,* the absurdity of this is obvious.

Of course, if we were able to experience the preciousness of each moment, we could genuinely enjoy our food and rest. Trungpa Rinpoche once said that enlightenment is like smelling tobacco or hearing a bugle for the very first time. We don't usually experience life this freshly. Instead of appreciating each unique and fleeting day, don't we generally use life's pleasures to numb or distract ourselves?

7.7

Death will be so quick to swoop on you;
Gather merit till that moment comes!
Wait till then to banish laziness?
Then there'll be no time, what will you do?

Once I heard a dharma practitioner boast: "*I* don't have to tame my mind or work with my kleshas because I received a special Tibetan transmission. At the moment of death, I'll just use those instructions to eject my consciousness into open space." But what a joke! If we can't even handle being told off or not getting what we want, how will we be able to handle death?

We still have time to prepare ourselves: this is precisely the reason for Shantideva's urgency. Our death could then be a liberating experience, a falling apart into openness.

7.8

"This I have not done. And this I'm only starting.
And this—I'm only halfway through. . . ."

Then is the sudden coming of the Lord of Death,
And oh, the thought "Alas, I'm finished!"

I saw a cartoon entitled "Reasons not to Meditate." First there's a drawing of an infant, with the caption "too young." Then there are students, parents with children, and people at work, with the caption "too busy." The next drawing shows an elderly person, with the words "too old." Finally there's a corpse, with the message "too late."

When we're about to die and we're having our last thoughts, will they be about the dream house we didn't build, the mortgage we didn't pay off, the novel we didn't finish? Feeling that we've failed to accomplish our worldly goals is not the frame of mind we want to be in when we die.

It's not uncommon to find ourselves thinking that we'll practice when we have more time. We'll start meditating when the conditions are better. Meanwhile, our kleshas only get stronger, and our mind is even less able to relax.

I was recently with a dying practitioner who admitted that her dharma practice now seemed meaningless. She didn't understand what relevance it had for her as the ground was slipping away. This could happen to any of us if we don't use our bodhichitta practices and meditation as a way of surrendering and letting go.

With each meditation session, you could train in opening to whatever arises, and relaxing with the immediacy of your experience. Just acknowledge your pleasant and unpleasant thoughts without bias and let them pass away. Then at the time of death, you will be ready to let go of your attachment to this life and surrender to the process of dissolving.

7.9

Your tear-stained cheeks, your red and swollen eyes,
Such will be the depths of your distress.
You'll gaze into the faces of your hopeless friends,
And see the coming servants of the Deadly Lord.

Shantideva presents death as the grim reaper. If we haven't relaxed with groundlessness during our life, death may well be terrifying. But if we've given birth to bodhichitta, death won't cause us to retreat into self-absorption, no matter now afraid we might be. Even fear will connect us with all the others who are equally terrified and alone. Right there, in what might be our darkest moment, we will be able to connect with the tenderness of basic goodness. Dying like this is said to be a joy.

7.10

The memory of former sins will torture you;
The screams and din of hell break on your ears.
With very terror you will foul yourself;
What will you do then, in such extremity of fear?

At a certain stage in the dying process there is an extremely loud and penetrating sound, as if *the screams and din of hell break on your ears.* This needn't be frightening, but if we've spent our life running from discomfort, it will be. And if we've been oblivious to the harm we've caused, we may be tortured by our memories at the time of death.

Because our whole life flashes before us in our last moments, nothing we've done remains hidden. If we've already looked honestly at our actions and been saddened by our misdeeds, there will be nothing left to haunt us when we die. This is the healing power of the practice of confession: it allows us to leave with a smile.

A cold-hearted, unrepentant Mafia man was once put into solitary confinement, a dark room that prisoners referred to as "the hole." After two hours alone with his mind in that darkness, visions of all the people he'd tortured or killed returned to haunt him. When they took him out eight hours later, he was raving and completely shattered. This is how we find ourselves in hell: it's a projection of our former harmful deeds that we've justified or repressed.

7.11

And if you are so scared while still alive,
Like fishes writhing on the open ground,
What need to speak of pain unbearable
In hells created by past evil deeds?

7.12

The hells in which the boiling molten bronze
Will burn your body, tender like a baby's flesh—
All is now prepared, your former deeds have done it!
How can you lie back, so free of care?

In the introduction to the Padmakara translation of *The Way of the Bodhisattva*, there's an excellent discussion of Shantideva's teaching technique. As I've mentioned before, he alternates between scaring us with the consequences of our evil actions and pointing out the wonder and benefit of practicing the dharma. The way to learn from this is to remember Shantideva's advice: there is no time to lose, so don't waste your life sowing seeds of misery.

Depending on the mental habits you've strengthened, you will find yourself in pleasant or unpleasant surroundings. Illusory though they may be, you will experience them as extremely real.

7.13

Much harm will come to those with small forbearance,
Who wish to have the fruit without endeavor.
Seized by death, they'll cry out like the gods:
"Alas I fall, by pain and sorrow crushed."

Wouldn't we all like to have *the fruit without endeavor*? If only we could attain enlightenment by lighting some candles or circumambulating a *stupa,* instead of committing to ongoing self-reflection and letting-go.

In the traditional teachings on the six realms of samsara, the god realm is depicted as a place of long-lasting pleasure, free from any pain. It's the kind of place the average person longs for. The catch, of course, is that everyone and everything is fleeting, even the long-lived pleasures of the gods.

The problem with the god-realm mentality is that we become complacent about pleasure and comfort. However, at some point, as with all samsaric existence, the good fortune of the god realm wears out. The teachings tell us that this degree of enjoyment is intensely painful to lose—as painful as the sufferings of hell.

7.14

Take advantage of this human boat;
Free yourself from sorrow's mighty stream!
This vessel will be later hard to find.
The time that you have now, you fool, is not
    for sleep!

Shantideva again teaches himself the dharma. This is not the time to be foolish, but to *take advantage of this human boat.* This precious human birth may be hard to find again. We have no way of knowing how long we will have these supportive outer conditions.

A human birth, however, is *always* precious for those who awaken bodhichitta. No matter how bad our circumstances are, no matter how sick or disabled we may be, it is still a precious birth if we use these difficulties to awaken our compassion and kindness. If we don't make use of these opportunities, of course, outer losses and mental anguish will inevitably throw us into a tailspin. Then we'll become too lost and despondent to think of others' pain and recall the good heart and open mind of bodhichitta.

7.15

You turn your back upon the sacred Doctrine,
The supreme joy and boundless source of bliss.
What pleasure can you have in mere amusement
Straying to the causes of your misery?

Having reflected on death, Shantideva here discusses the second kind of laziness: not being willing to make an effort, or loss of heart. The Dalai Lama describes this kind of laziness as "having no wish to do good." We feel too lazy to help ourselves or others. By turning our back on the dharma and aimlessly distracting ourselves with trivial pursuits, we are *straying to the causes of our misery*. In other words, we're doing the very things that make our loss of heart grow worse.

In verses 16 through 19, Shantideva will discuss the third kind of laziness: the despondency of self-contempt. This is an important topic for Western practitioners. Freeing ourselves from confusion and suffering depends on honest self-reflection. The practice of patience, for instance, depends on honestly acknowledging our impatience and aggression. It's essential, however, that this inquiry be based on respect and kindness for one's self.

Dzigar Kongtrul stresses the importance of having a good relationship with oneself; otherwise, the path of awakening can back-fire and fuel discouragement. Seeing our kleshas and the wildness of our mind, more clearly than ever before, can certainly heighten feelings of guilt and self-contempt. But buying into negative thinking only slows down our spiritual journey.

In verse 16, Shantideva gives us three antidotes for self-contempt. These are three ways to cheer up and develop a compassionate relationship with oneself: a relationship so respectful and loving, it can include clear-sighted recognition of our shortcomings.

7.16

Do not be downcast, but marshal all your strength;
Take heart and be the master of yourself!
Practice the equality of self and other;
Practice the exchange of self and other.

His first advice is to *marshal all your strength.* Instead of further denigrating yourself, teach yourself the dharma. To marshal your strength, remind yourself, in whatever way is personally meaningful, that it is not in your best interest to reinforce thoughts and feelings of unworthiness. Even if you've already taken the bait and feel the familiar pull of self-denigration, marshal your intelligence, courage, and humor in order to turn the tide.

Ask yourself: Do I want to strengthen what I'm feeling now? Do I want to cut myself off from my basic goodness? Remind yourself that your fundamental nature is unconditionally open and free. Kleshas are just relative, impermanent phenomena, whose transitory energy doesn't need to be solidified. In this way, we can teach ourselves the dharma and interrupt the chain reaction of discouragement.

We can cheer ourselves up by remembering that our mind is tamable. As Trungpa Rinpoche put it: "Whatever occurs in the confused mind is the path. Everything is workable. It is a fearless proclamation, the lion's roar!"

The second way to rouse your spirits is to take heart and *be the master of yourself.* This means taking responsibility for your moods. The instruction is to acknowledge that you're not a victim. Then find a way to interrupt discouragement's momentum, instead of mindlessly doing what you've always done before.

The third suggestion is to look beyond the narrow perspective of self-centeredness at *the equality of self and other.* This recognition of our sameness can be cultivated by doing the practice called "just like me." If you're burdened with self-contempt, remember:

just like me, many others are struggling with this same state of mind; just like me, all of them prefer comfort and ease, and to be free of misery and guilt.

This kind of reflection helps us look outward and open our heart to others. Instead of armoring ourselves, the softness of empathy can set in. With this as our ground, we can *practice the exchange of self and other.*

This practice is commonly known as *tonglen.* We begin by getting in touch with our own thoughts and emotions. Without doing this we have no idea what others also go through. This means contacting our feelings—of rage, self-contempt, resentment, envy, and so on—and realizing that these feelings are shared by everyone. They are not hindrances on the path. By leading us to a genuine understanding of others' distress, they are, in fact, necessary stepping-stones in the process of awakening genuine compassion.*

At any given moment, people all over the world are feeling exactly what you feel. If you're angry, you can remember the billions of people who feel exactly the same way. Then, for your sake and theirs, take in the feeling of rage, on the medium of the breath. Just breathe in the anger, with the aspiration that each and every angry person, including yourself, be relieved of it. Then breathe out spaciousness and relief to us all.

A more daring way to do this practice is to breathe in the pain with the intention of taking it into yourself. If you're angry, for instance, you might say to yourself, "Since I'm already suffering from this anger, may this pain ripen in me, so no one else has to feel it." This is a revolutionary way to ventilate self-absorption. On the in-breath, feel the pain and own it completely. On the out-breath, send out relief with the wish that everyone else could be free of their emotional distress.

---

*For more in-depth instruction on *tonglen,* see my book *When Things Fall Apart,* chapter 15.

If you don't feel ready for this more daring approach, it's not a problem. You don't have to jump into the deep end of the pool before you know how to swim. Just practice the form of *tonglen* that feels doable for you. It will still fulfill the same aspiration. Your ability to put yourself in other people's shoes will grow over time.

As we connect more profoundly with bodhichitta, the unchanging, nonconceptual openness of our being becomes more accessible. Because our basic nature is never altered by worldly confusion and pain, even glimpses of this skylike mind deepen our experience of *tonglen*. Knowing this, even intellectually, we breathe in, with the wish that all beings uncover their true nature; and we breathe out with the same aspiration.

7.17

"Oh, but how could *I* become enlightened?"
Don't excuse yourself with such despondency!
The buddhas, who declare the truth,
Have spoken and indeed proclaimed,

7.18

That if they bring forth strength of perseverance,
The very bees and flies and stinging gnats
Or grubs will find with ease
Enlightenment so hard to find!

Shantideva looks further into the unnecessary burden of self-contempt. Seeing our confusion, it's easy to wonder how we could ever become enlightened. When we feel really low, we doubt we have any potential at all. But Shantideva says, *Don't excuse yourself with such despondency!* Don't indulge in such negative thoughts, when you can train in letting them go. I can just see him giving us meditation instruction. As we start caving in, he says "Cheer up, if *stinging gnats or grubs* can persevere and reach enlightenment, so can we!"

7.19

Able to distinguish good from ill,
If I, by birth and lineage of human kind,
Devote myself to bodhisattva training,
Why should I not gain the state of buddhahood?

Shantideva is being very tender here. He's saying we can trust ourselves. Human beings, unlike gnats, bees, and our beloved pets, have a natural ability to know what's harmful or helpful. We can distinguish between actions that bring benefit and those that cause confusion and pain. We can see when we're hooked by the charge of *shenpa* and when we're not. Through trial and error, we know where these habitual urges lead; and we know the relief when, instead of acting them out, we just relax with our immediate experience.

Most importantly, we know that when we *do* lose it, we have the tools to recover. We can practice remaining like a log; we can do *tonglen;* we can teach ourselves the dharma; or we can relax with the ungraspable energy behind all the labels and words.

We discover we do have a choice: we can strengthen old habits and suffer, or interrupt them and break free. Frequently we miss this point, but the natural ability to know the difference never goes away.

7.20

"That I must give away my life and limbs
Alarms and frightens me"—if so you say,
Your terror is misplaced. Confused,
You fail to see what's hard and what is easy.

7.21

For myriads of ages, measureless, uncounted,
Your body has been cut, impaled,
Burned, flayed—for times past numbering!
Yet none of this has brought you buddhahood.

These verses begin a teaching on the power of gentleness to dissolve self-doubt. Someone who feels discouraged and hopeless might well say: I can't do this training. It's too painful and too frightening. It asks too much of me.

To this, Shantideva replies: Don't set your standards too high. This isn't an endurance test. If austerities like cutting or burning were all it took to attain enlightenment, you'd be there already. You've already suffered tremendously in this life, let alone in previous lives.

7.22

The hardships suffered on the path to buddhahood
Are different, for their span is limited,
And likened to the pain of an incision
Made to cure the harm of hidden ailments.

7.23

The doctors and those skilled in healing arts,
Use bitter remedies to cure our ills.
Likewise we, to uproot dreadful sorrow,
Should bear what are indeed but little pains.

7.24

And yet the Supreme Healer does not use,
Like them, these common remedies.

With antidotes of extreme tenderness
He soothes away intense and boundless suffering.

Of course, there are hardships on the bodhisattva path. But they are temporary, like taking small amounts of bitter medicine to ward off a life-threatening illness. The austerities commonly practiced in India were not recommended by the Buddha. His instructions encourage moderation and relaxation. We practice nonaggressively, catching ourselves when our mind wanders off and gently returning to this fleeting, ungraspable moment.

7.25

Our guide instructs us to begin
By giving food or other little charities,
That later, step by step, the habit once acquired,
We may be able to donate our very flesh.

The Buddha recommended a gradual path. We start where we are by giving food, small change, or whatever helps us to stretch a bit. We accustom ourselves to reaching out by doing practices such as "just like me," or visualizing giving away some of our cherished possessions.

Our ability to do more, in ever more challenging situations, naturally grows. We don't have to force it or expect more from ourselves than we can currently do. If our practice feels like an austerity, we need to look at what we're doing. If it's too harsh, we can lighten up and bring in more gentleness and humor.

A man I know had been trying to do the Tibetan prostration practice for ten years. The fact that he had managed to do only a few ate away at him, making him feel guilty and discouraged. Then his meditation instructor very wisely suggested that he do only three prostrations a day then stop. His first response was, "That's not enough." But his instructor insisted he give it a try. After one week, he asked to do fifty to one hundred prostrations each morning. Initially she said, "No, just do twenty-five." But within a month, he was eagerly doing hundreds of prostrations a day. This extremely moderate, relaxed approach broke through his resistance.

Bodhisattvas sometimes have to back off. This doesn't mean giving up. It means finding out what we can do with enthusiasm. This is something we have to experiment with. We discover for ourselves what's too tight and what's too loose; what brings us benefit and what causes further harm.

7.26

For when one has the view that sees
Equality between one's body and the food one gives,
Why then! What hardship can there be
In giving up, relinquishing, one's very flesh?

When we reach the point where we see no difference between our own flesh and hamburger meat, we will have no problem relinquishing our body to save another's life. Right now, however, we'd be wise to bring enthusiasm to whatever we *can* do and not worry too much about the future. Gentleness, again, is the key to progressing along the path.

This ends the section on the three kinds of laziness.

7.27

Sin has been abandoned, thus there is no pain.
Mind is skilled, and thus there is no sorrow.
For so it is that mind and body both
Are injured by false views and sinfulness.

Having contemplated the importance of a kind, step-by-step approach to awakening, Shantideva now points out two major causes of our suffering. One is creating negative karma, referred to here as *sin* and *sinfulness*. With even a little understanding of cause and effect, it dawns on us that the worst harm we can do to ourselves is to hurt others.

The second cause of our suffering is a closed, unskillful mind. This is a mind that fixates, conceptualizes, and compartmentalizes; a mind incapable of seeing things without bias. We have solid ideas about self and others, and equally fixed opinions about what's acceptable and unacceptable. This leads to what Shantideva calls *false views*. These misperceptions of reality result from tightly held notions of right and wrong. When we reify our experience, the true nature of all phenomena cannot be seen.

Conversely, when our mind is free of prejudice and self-righteousness we no longer act out of aggression and other neuroses and our suffering abates. To the extent that the mind returns to its natural flexibility and openness, we experience freedom.

With an understanding of karma and false views, even intellectually, we become more eager to loosen their destructive power.

7.28

Merit is the true cause of the body's ease,
While happiness of mind is brought about by training.
What can sadden those who have compassion,
Who linger in samsara for the sake of beings?

Shantideva then shifts his perspective and gives three causes for happiness. First, *the true cause of the body's ease* is merit, or the fortunate consequences of our wise and skillful actions, the positive results of letting go.

This raises an interesting question: Why, with all the time and energy we put into staying healthy, do we still have accidents and come down with painful or fatal diseases? The Buddhist teachings say that the merit of favorable circumstances, such as good health, is not ultimately the result of vitamins but of our previous positive actions. If this is true, then it follows that we'd be wise not to strengthen the negative habits that will only lead to suffering. This is something we can't dismiss as illogical; it's worth pondering and exploring. In any case, when we lead saner, more compassionate lives, there is one thing we can count on: when disaster strikes, we'll be able to fully incorporate it into our path of awakening.

Second, Shantideva says that mental well-being is the result not of outer pleasures but of taming our mind. The more we train in letting go of fixed ideas and opening ourselves to others, the happier we become. When discouragement or confusion does set in, instead of escalating it, we know to let the thoughts go, stay present, and relax.

The third cause of happiness is that nothing discourages those who choose to *linger in samsara for the sake of beings.* How can we get seriously despondent about samsara's challenges, once we've chosen to incorporate them into the path of awakening? When we're training to transform bad circumstances into the path of bodhi, we won't get bogged down in feelings of failure as soon as something goes wrong.

7.29

For through their power of bodhichitta,
Former sins are totally consumed,
And merit, ocean-vast, is gathered in;
Therefore we say they're higher than the
    shravakas.

The *shravakas* mentioned here take up the Buddhist path to escape samsara. One of the major differences between the bodhisattva and the *shravakas*, therefore, is their attitude toward chaos. A *shravaka* might regard *tonglen* practice, for example, as the antithesis of the Buddha's teachings: would the Buddha ever teach us to breathe in suffering, when his whole message was liberation from suffering? The *shravakas* have an aversion to samsara, which we can probably appreciate. Their goal is utter cessation and peace.

The bodhisattva, on the other hand, is constantly preparing to relate fearlessly with pain. The greater the suffering, the greater the need to go there, right into the hells of this world, if need be. Thus *merit, ocean-vast, is gathered in.* Of course, we have to be realistic; right now, we may barely be able to handle our credit card bills. Training with such everyday challenges, however, develops our courage to handle increasingly difficult situations in the future.

In the next verse, Shantideva cheers us on and helps us to see our options. Why be sad, once we've learned how to lean in to challenges, rather than avoid them? Why be dejected, when we've felt the possibility of inner strength?

7.30

For, mounted on the horse of bodhichitta,
That puts to flight all mournful weariness,
Who could ever be dejected,
Riding such a steed from joy to joy?

Wind was Shantideva's first metaphor for enthusiasm. Now he uses the image of a horse: the *horse of bodhichitta* that carries us *from joy to joy.* It's a beautiful image. Instead of trudging up a slippery slope in boots that hurt our feet, we're eagerly riding through this unique and precious training ground called "life."

7.31

The forces that secure the good of beings
Are aspiration, firmness, joy, and moderation.
Aspiration grows through fear of suffering
And contemplation of the benefits to be attained.

This verse begins a teaching on the four strengths that support our enthusiasm for benefiting others. These four strengths are aspiration, firmness, joy, and moderation. The first, aspiration, is discussed in verses 31 through 46.

Aspiration is a yearning to free ourselves from neurosis so that we can help alleviate the suffering of other people. This yearning is genuine and deep. It's not something we impose on ourselves just to look virtuous.

Aspiration is a deeply felt conviction that we express to ourselves in words: "May all sentient beings enjoy happiness and the root of happiness. May we all be free of suffering and the root of suffering." This isn't just empty rhetoric. Reaffirming our bodhisattva intention in this way becomes increasingly meaningful and supportive. Like the gasoline in our car, it makes it possible for us to go forward without hesitation.

But where does sincere aspiration come from? Shantideva says it comes from *fear of suffering*—fear of the consequences of continually giving in to habitual reactions. It comes as well from getting clear about the positive results of not getting swept away. You might ask if I know for sure that this path results in happiness. I'm glad to tell you that if you gently tame your mind and emotions, well-being, at the very least, is guaranteed.

7.32

Therefore leaving everything that is adverse to it,
I'll labor to increase my perseverance—
Through cheerful effort, keenness, self-control,
Through aspiration, firmness, joy, and moderation.

Once more, Shantideva expresses his enthusiasm for the bodhisattva's way of life. With so many tools to help him, he joyfully aspires to leave laziness behind and eagerly go forward. He voices his intention to call on the four strengths, as well as cheerfulness, keenness, and the self-control that comes from understanding karma and the benefits of liberation.

Hopefully we feel encouraged to join him. Let's do this together. Let's each do whatever we can to bring some light into this time of darkness.

7.33

Thus the boundless evils of myself and others—
I alone must bring them all to nothing,
Even though a single of these ills
May take unnumbered ages to exhaust!

7.34

And yet for this great enterprise I do not see
Within myself the slightest aptitude—
I whose destiny is boundless suffering,
Why does not my heart now burst asunder?

There are two sentiments expressed here. First Shantideva says that no matter how impossible this *great enterprise* may seem, he won't become discouraged. Then, like us, he has second thoughts: "Wait a minute. Who do I think I am, making such statements? I don't have what it takes for this job." Once again, however, we have the Shantideva twist: his ability for honest self-reflection, without letting it hold him back.

7.35

All virtues for my own and others' sake,
Though they be many, I must now accomplish,
Even if for each I must
Endeavor for unnumbered ages.

Shantideva sees his weak points but he doesn't become despondent. This is what makes the path possible. Because every last one of us has what it takes to wake up, Shantideva is willing to encourage all of us forever, if need be. It's not like polishing a lump of coal that can never become a diamond. Our true nature is like a precious jewel: although it may be temporarily buried in mud, it remains completely brilliant and unaffected. We simply have to uncover it.

In this spirit, Shantideva reaffirms his enthusiasm for the task. He will uncover his jewel-like nature in order to help others do the same. He then goes on to list his many imperfections, honestly acknowledging his laziness and self-importance. At the same time, he never doubts that he is as qualified as the Buddha himself to awaken the openness and warmth of his mind.

7.36

Acquaintance I have never gained
With even part of such great qualities.
So strange to waste in trivial pursuits
This life that chance has brought to me!

7.37

Offerings to the buddhas I have never made;
No feasts were ever held through my donations;
No works have I accomplished for the Teachings;
The wishes of the poor, alas, I left unsatisfied.

7.38

The frightened I have not encouraged,
And to the weary I have given no rest.
My mother's birth pangs and her womb's discomfort,
These alone are my accomplishments!

I so admire Shantideva's spirit. He honestly acknowledges that he's spent far too much time thinking only of himself. But rather than turn this into depression and self-loathing, he cracks a joke: "Looks like my only accomplishment in this life was *my mother's birth pangs and her womb's discomfort.*" A bit of humorous self-deprecation can be very useful on the bodhisattva's path!

7.39

Thus my poverty, my lack of fortune,
Come from failure to aspire to Dharma
In the past and likewise in the present!
Whoever would reject this aspiration?

Here Shantideva again describes the workings of karma: my present unfortunate circumstances are the consequences of closed-mindedness in the past. Right now, however, I can aspire to open my heart and reach out. How could I even consider not doing this, knowing the painful consequence of not applying these teachings in my daily life?

7.40

Aspiration is the root of every virtue,
Thus the Mighty One has said.
And aspiration's root in turn
Is constant meditation on the fruits of action.

He again states the benefit of voicing our sincere aspirations, words that become more heartfelt and genuine when we contemplate the inevitability of cause and effect.

7.41

The body's pains, anxieties of mind,
Our every fear and trepidation,
Separation from the objects of our wanting:
Such is the harvest of our sinful deeds.

7.42

If my acts are wholesome, mirroring my mind,
Then no matter where I turn my steps,
Respect and honor will be paid to me,
The fruit and recompense of merit.

7.43

But if, in search of happiness, my works are evil,
Then no matter where I turn my steps,
The knives of misery will cut me down—
The wage and retribution of a sinful life.

In short, virtuous actions have virtuous results; negative actions
lead only to pain. Shantideva repeats this so frequently because it's
not a teaching we catch on to all that quickly. If you're trapped in a
hellish situation, the only way to get relief is to calm your anguished
mind and reconsider self-absorbed solutions. When we cultivate
the bodhi heart, we experience a sympathetic world no matter
where we turn. This is Shantideva's recurring message.

Verse 44 describes birth in a pure land—the best-case scenario!

7.44

I will arise, through virtue, in the cool heart of a
    fragrant, spreading lotus,
Its petals opened in the Buddha's light,

With glory nourished by the sweet words of the
    Conqueror,
And live, the buddhas' heir, within the presence
    of Victorious Ones.

And in verse 45, we have the alternative.

7.45

Or else as wages for my sins, I'll be struck down,
    my skin flayed off by creatures
Of the Lord of Death, who on my body pour the liquid
    bronze that's melted in the dreadful blaze.
And pierced by burning swords and knives, my flesh
Dismembered in a hundred parts, will fall upon
    the white-hot iron ground.

Shantideva has presented his case. He's given us the facts, and
now we must choose our own destiny. Do you prefer *the cool heart
of a fragrant, spreading lotus* or being *pierced by burning swords
and knives?*

7.46

And so I will aspire and tend to virtue,
And steep myself in it with great devotion.
And with the method stated in the *Vajradhvaja,*
I will train in confident assurance.

In the *Vajradhvaja Sutra,* the Buddha says that just as the sun
illuminates the whole earth without bias, the bodhisattva is willing to work with anyone, no matter how ornery. In this spirit,
Shantideva aspires to go forward with his training.

This ends the teaching on the benefits of aspiration. The next two verses discuss firmness, the second of the four powers that support our enthusiasm.

7.47

Let me first consider my resources—
To start or not to start accordingly.
For it is better not to start at all,
Than to begin and then retrace my steps.

7.48

For, acting thus, the pattern will return
In later lives, and sin and pain will grow.
And other actions will be left undone
Or else will bear a meager fruit.

Firmness, or steadfastness, is based on commitment. Without commitment to what we're doing, it's easy to get seduced by self-doubt. Therefore Shantideva tells us to consider ahead of time whether we're up to a task. Youthful bodhisattvas are easily seduced by the idea of helping others and eager to begin. But when the job seriously challenges us, we draw back.

This is true in meditation practice as well. We set high goals, and then get bored or discouraged and give up. But *it is better not to start at all* than to change our mind halfway through. Whether we're inspired or in a slump, Shantideva's instruction is to stick with it. This is why we're encouraged to sit each day. Being steadfast, through emotional hurricanes as well as blue skies, is an important aspect of our training. It sets up a pattern of self-compassion that's not swayed by outer circumstance or moods.

Indecision and vacillation also set up a pattern. Not following through on the things we start strengthens this painful habit.

Eventually we think of ourselves as ineffectual when, ironically, we ourselves wrote the script.

Trungpa Rinpoche also taught that it's better not to start the spiritual journey, than to stop as soon as it gets challenging. He used the analogy of being on the operating table and deciding it's too painful to continue. Once we've been cut open and our guts are hanging out, getting up and leaving isn't a pretty picture.

7.49

Action, the afflictions, and ability:
Three things to which my pride should be applied.
"I will do this, I myself, alone!"
These words define my pride of action.

In verses 49 through 59, Shantideva discusses both negative and positive pride, inferring the latter is a component of genuine enthusiasm. In verse 49, *pride of action* is a synonym for confidence. How this confidence is applied to *action, the afflictions, and ability* may need some explanation. First, Shantideva knows which *actions* are helpful and which aren't. Second, he trusts that he can work skillfully and patiently with his *afflictions*. And finally, he has confidence that the *ability* to connect with basic goodness is his birthright.

This positive pride is energizing: like the spark of life, it inspires and encourages us. Ordinary pride—the sense of being superior and looking down on others—only makes us feel weaker.

7.50

Enfeebled by their minds' afflictions,
Worldly folk are helpless to secure their happiness.
Compared to those who wander, I am able—
This indeed shall be my chosen task.

Even though Shantideva has claimed not to have any aptitude for this path, he now rouses his positive pride. Looking around him, he realizes he has a much better chance than most. Some people don't consider it a problem to slander or hate or even murder their enemies. They've never even remotely considered working with their mind and emotions. Compared to these unfortunate folk, he is confident he can follow the way of the bodhisattva.

7.51

When others give themselves to base activities,
How can I connive as their companion?
But I shall not refrain through pride or arrogance;
My best way is to give up such conceit.

We all know how easy it is to get caught in neurotic relationships or addictions when we hang out with certain people. If we have a history with drugs or alcohol, it's lethal to go back and fraternize with the old crowd. But how do we draw the line between ourselves and unhealthy situations without looking down on others as bad or inferior? It's important to contemplate this point.

The longer we stick with the bodhisattva path, the more it breaks our heart to see others trapped in confusion. Instead of feeling condescending or arrogant, we see how much they're like us. We just happen to be lucky; they, for whatever reasons, haven't yet been able to abandon their addictions or get out of their destructive relationships.

It's not arrogant, therefore, to keep our distance; we're simply wise enough to know we can't handle some situations yet. We aspire to be able to go anywhere in the future, but we accept the fact that we don't have the strength right now.

7.52

When they find a dying serpent,
Even crows behave like soaring eagles.
Therefore if I'm weak and feeble-hearted,
Even little faults will strike and injure me.

Poverty mentality is a setup for feeling under attack. The smallest things cause us to doubt ourselves; the slightest comment can make us feel inadequate and weak.

Shantideva uses the analogy of a dying serpent. When the serpent is alive and well, it's like a confident person; it can't be easily wounded. But when it loses its strength, it's like someone with low self-esteem. Suddenly the smallest bird has the devastating power of a soaring eagle. The tiniest slight feels like a major slander campaign.

7.53

How will those who basely flee the conflict,
Ever free themselves from their debility?
But those who stand their ground with proud resolve
Are hard to vanquish even by the mighty.

Those who basely flee the conflict are in the majority. At the least sign of discomfort, we run away as fast as our little feet or little mind can carry us. Shantideva asks how we will ever free ourselves if we always cave in to feelings of inadequacy.

Limitations can be acknowledged without exaggerating or succumbing to them. When we're confident that our mind is workable, our failings don't seem like such a big deal. They're as temporary as clouds, and in no way diminish the skylike nature of our mind. With this kind of confidence in our limitless potential, the mightiest challenges won't cause us to lose heart.

7.54

Therefore with a steadfast heart
I'll get the better of my weaknesses.
But if my failings get the upper hand,
My wish to overcome the world is laughable indeed.

If we have big ideas about saving others, but are easily triggered ourselves, then something is wrong with this picture. If we want *to overcome the world,* the first step is to have steadfast trust that we can work wisely with our kleshas. Then we can put that confidence into action.

7.55

"I *will* be the victor over all;
Nothing shall prevail and bring me down!"
The lion-offspring of the Conqueror
Should constantly abide in this proud confidence.

Proud confidence isn't anything tangible or solid. It grows as we lighten up and shed our self-righteousness. We needn't make such a big deal about our emotions or thoughts. Because they're essentially empty, we don't have to struggle against them; we can let them dissolve. From this point of view, what could ever *prevail and bring me down?* The experience of nonconceptual emptiness brings the proud confidence that we have absolutely nothing to lose but our chains!

7.56

Those whom arrogance and pride destroy
Are thus defiled; they lack proud confidence.
They fall into the power of an evil pride,
But those with true pride will escape the enemy.

Verse 56 clearly distinguishes arrogant pride from the pride of confidence and succinctly states which is preferable.

7.57

When arrogance inflates the mind,
It draws it down to states of misery,
Or else it ruins human birth, should this be gained.
Thus one is born a slave, dependent for one's
    food—

7.58

Or feebleminded, ugly, without strength,
The butt and laughingstock of everyone.
Hapless creatures puffed up with conceit!
If these you call the proud, then tell me who are
    wretched?

The main thing about being proud and arrogant is that people don't like us. These aren't attractive qualities, and they do not make for a happy life. They certainly won't get us the job. Because no one will hire us, we might end up bereft, *a slave, dependent for one's food*.

Proud confidence, on the other hand, is uplifting. It comes from the understanding that all of us are buddhas in disguise.

7.59

Those who uphold pride to vanquish pride, the enemy,
Are truly proud, the victors in the war.
Those who overwhelm the progress of that evil pride,
Perfect the fruit of buddhahood and satisfy the longings
    of the world.

This verse plays further with the word pride. Shantideva concludes this section by saying that we can use pride to undermine pride. Joyful confidence has more power than the klesha of pride. Dismantling negative pride, he affirms, brings the greatest possible benefit to oneself and to the world.

7.60

When you are beleaguered by defilements,
Fight them in a thousand ways.
Do not surrender to the host of the afflictions;
Be like a lion in a crowd of foxes.

7.61

However great may be their peril,
People will by reflex guard their eyes.
And likewise I, regardless of all hardship,
Must not fall beneath defilement's power.

7.62

Even though I may be burned to death,
And though I may be killed, my head cut off,
At no time will I bow and scrape
Before that foe of mine, defiled emotion.

7.62A

Thus in every time and place
I will not wander from the wholesome path.

Shantideva fearlessly proclaims what's possible for all of us. To identify with our neurosis instead of our basic goodness would be very sad: like being born a queen, but thinking of yourself as a beggar.

In my own training, I've been taught to look for the gaps: the gap at the end of each out-breath; the space between thoughts; the naturally occurring, nonconceptual pause after a sudden shock, unexpected noise, or moment of awe. Trungpa Rinpoche advised intentionally creating these gaps by pausing to look at the sky or stopping to listen intently. He called this "poking holes in the clouds."

These fleeting moments of no-big-deal me, no internal conversations, no frozen opinions, are very simple yet powerful. The utter freshness of just being present introduces us to unshakable confidence: a lionlike pride that refuses to buy into any negative or limiting story lines.

Would that we could catch this Shantideva spirit. Then no outer challenge or emotional distress could lure us into ignorance and confusion. Just as *people will by reflex guard their eyes* in time of peril, we would instinctively interrupt the momentum of getting hooked. *In every time and place,* we would keep an open heart. Even if tortured or threatened with death, we'd never surrender to the lure of the kleshas or cut ourselves off from our birthright.

7.63

Like those who take great pleasure in their games,
The bodhisattvas in their every deed
Will feel the greatest joy, exhilaration,
Pleasure that will never fade or pass.

7.64

People labor hard to gain contentment
Though success is very far from sure;
But how can they be happy if they do not labor,
Those whose joy is in the work itself?

The third of the four powers, the power of joy, is described in verses 63 through 66. Along with aspiration and steadfastness, joy is an essential ingredient of enthusiasm.

Dzongsar Khyentse remarked that when we do something we don't enjoy, we drag our feet. But doing something we love—Let's go swimming! Let's eat popcorn and watch videos!—makes us feel happy and light. Could we bring the same enthusiasm to freeing ourselves from pain? Could we approach awakening from self-absorption *like those who take great pleasure in their games*? With this kind of enthusiasm for challenge, life becomes a constant source of happiness. "The greater the challenge, the better" is the bodhisattva's motto.

Trungpa Rinpoche's mother-in-law initially hated him. She had been raised in apartheid South Africa and, as far as she was concerned, her daughter had married a black man. Rinpoche was absolutely delighted with the challenge of winning her over. When she was most antagonistic, he had his wife invite her to a holiday dinner. She refused to come unless he invited her personally. So he went to her house and when she opened the door, he got down on his knees and pleaded with her to join them. He courted her like this for years, and eventually she grew to love him without reservation.

The love of challenge is the bodhisattva's secret weapon. While most of us try to avoid the slightest anxiety, hint of groundlessness, or twinge of insecurity, bodhisattvas develop a healthy appetite for difficulty.

7.65

And since I never have enough of pleasure,
Honey on the razor's edge,
How could I have enough of merit,
Fruits of which are happiness and peace?

This image—licking *honey on a razor's edge*—has become a famous analogy for addictive behavior. Because the honey tastes so delicious, we don't want to stop; meanwhile our poor tongue is being cut to shreds. Where do we want to put our enthusiasm, into short-term gratification or the long-range happiness of a bodhisattva's life? This is the question.

7.66

The elephant, tormented by the noonday sun,
Will dive into the waters of a lake,
And likewise I must plunge into this work
That I might bring it to completion.

This is the spirit! Like an overheated elephant diving into the waters of a lake, we can take delight in living a life that frees us from confusion. Knowing it will heal us, how could we not want to plunge into the task of cooling the heat of our kleshas?

7.67

If impaired by weakness or fatigue,
I'll lay the work aside, the better to resume.
And I will leave tasks completed,
Anticipating thus the work to come.

The subject here is the importance of moderation and rest. Before making any commitments, we can consider our capabilities and learn to pace ourselves. We sentient beings habitually drive ourselves or flop, both of which lead to burnout. The key to remaining eager and inspired on the bodhisattva path is knowing when to take a break. On this wise and compassionate note, Shantideva ends his presentation of the four powers: aspiration, firmness, joy, and moderation.

7.68

As seasoned fighters face the swords
Of enemies upon the battle line,
Lightly dodge the weapons of defilement,
And overcome the foe with nimble skill!

The final verses of this chapter present various attributes of enthusiasm. First, the quality of nimbleness, or lightness, is introduced. It's easy to become deadly serious about freeing ourselves from suffering. People need help now, and we have to get ourselves in shape fast! But in the so-called war against the kleshas, heavy-handedness is just another ego trip. Instead of struggling, Shantideva suggests bringing some lightness into the equation. Like children at play, like a hot elephant diving into a lake, like a joyful horse, or a breeze of delight—bring enthusiasm to the task.

In the beginning, of course, this may not seem possible; it's the *seasoned fighters* who can do this. But that's no reason to get discouraged. It may be hard work now; but refraining from kleshas and being open to whatever arises is like learning to drive a car: it gets easier with practice.

On the bodhisattva path, even after a direct experience of emptiness, it takes a long time to become skilled in helping others. Meanwhile, if you keep your sense of humor and playfully catch yourself whenever you get uptight, your lightness and confidence can't help but grow.

7.69

If, in the fray, the soldier drops his sword,
In fright, he swiftly takes it up again.
So likewise, if the arm of mindfulness is lost,
In fear of hell be quick to get it back.

The next quality of enthusiasm is urgency. The combination of lightness and urgency is unbeatable. On one hand, it's critical to your well-being to dismantle the kleshas; on the other hand, if you're too driven, you simply create another form of self-absorption. The trick is to see when you get hooked, then gently but urgently come back to the present moment.

Just as a soldier can't be nonchalant about dropping his sword in battle, we can't be complacent about losing our mindfulness. When our mind is distracted, the kleshas move in like a band of robbers. But if we bring our mind back with harshness or panic, we'll never generate the self-compassion we need to progress along the path.

7.70

> Just as seeping venom fills the body,
> Carried on the current of the blood,
> An evil thought that finds its chance,
> Will spread and permeate the mind.

This is very true. We can't underestimate the *seeping venom* of even tiny grudges or subtle resentments. Unacknowledged, they will spread and permeate our minds. In this and the following verses, Shantideva emphasizes the importance of mindfulness as a component of enthusiasm.

7.71

> Be like a frightened man, a brimming oil jar
>   in his hand,
> And menaced by a swordsman saying:
> "Spill one drop and you shall die!"
> This is how the disciplined should hold themselves.

At the time of the Buddha, there was a king who discredited the power of mindfulness practice. To show the skeptical king his error, the Buddha had several men walk into the palace, carrying jars brimming with oil. Behind each of them walked a swordsman ready to strike if they spilled a drop. Although the room was filled with dancing maidens, musicians, and other distractions, none of them spilled a bit of that brimming oil. Not even a three-ring circus is distracting when there's a sword at your back! Thus, the tremendous power of a stabilized mind was convincingly demonstrated to the king.

7.72

> As such a man would leap in fright
> To find a snake coiled in his lap,
> If sleep and sluggishness beset me,
> I will instantly dispel them.

This is yet another image for enthusiasm that puts the emphasis on urgency. When a snake lands in your lap, you don't just sit there admiring its stripes; you leap up without hesitation. I've always been encouraged to practice like this: as if a snake had just landed in my lap or my hair were on fire!

7.73

> Every time, then, that I fail,
> I will reprove and vilify myself,
> Thinking long that by whatever means
> Such faults in future shall no more occur.

Here Shantideva refers back to the practice of confession. Although the word *vilify* sounds aggressive, his point is that honest self-reflection is crucial. On the spiritual path, we need to make friends with ourselves. Otherwise, Shantideva's recommendations will backfire into utterly useless guilt and self-contempt.

The only way to heal ourselves is to build on the foundation of loving-kindness. Then it's not a problem to recognize neurosis as neurosis and connect with our genuine heartbreak. This tender, broken-hearted longing to stop harming ourselves naturally leads to *thinking long* that in the future *such faults shall no more occur*.

I think the best way to understand this approach is through the hilarious stories of the Tibetan yogi Geshe Ben. Whenever this eccentric fellow saw in himself any kindness or wisdom, he referred to himself as "Venerable Geshe." When he saw himself getting hooked by *shenpa*, he addressed himself as "you fool."

Once when he was visiting some patrons, Geshe Ben saw an open bag of barley flour hanging on the wall. He needed some flour, and when he was left alone he unconsciously started dipping in. Suddenly, realizing what he was doing, he screamed at the top of his lungs, "Thief, thief, I've caught a thief!" When his hosts rushed in, there he was with his hand in the bag.

Another time, the patrons invited all the monks for a meal. Geshe Ben was seated last. As the servers were doling out his favorite yogurt, he began to panic: "What if there's none left for me?" "How can that fat monk take such a huge helping?" As feelings of resentment grew, he began to connive how he could move ahead of the other monks before it was too late. Then he realized, with remorse, what he was doing and patiently waited his turn. When they finally got to him, he put his hand over his bowl and yelled, "No yogurt for this greedy fellow. This yogurt addict has already had enough."

Personally, these humorous tales have often helped me acknowledge my small-mindedness, without getting too heavy-handed or judgmental.

7.74

At all times and in any situation,
Mindfulness will be my constant habit.
This will be the cause whereby I aim
To meet with teachers and fulfill the proper
    tasks.

7.75

By all means, then, before I start this work,
That I might have the strength sufficient to the
    task,
I will reflect upon these words on mindfulness
And lightly rise to what is to be done.

Shantideva concludes with praises for mindfulness. When we're
fully awake and present, we can better fulfill our tasks and hear
what our teachers have to say. Usually, we miss a lot: our mind
wanders and large segments of our experience are lost. It would
be wise, therefore, to contemplate Shantideva's teachings on mindfulness and lightly, not sternly, put them into practice.

7.76

The lichen hanging in the trees wafts to
    and fro,
Stirred by every breath of wind;
Likewise, all I do will be achieved,
Enlivened by the movements of a joyful
    heart.

This beautiful verse is an image of fruition enthusiasm and gives
us a feeling of what is possible for all of us. Despite the heartbreak

of seeing the world's suffering, we're joyful that we can do our part to alleviate rather than add to that misery. This happiness gives us access to a tremendous bank of energy that was previously bound up in self-absorption. Now everything that took effort happens spontaneously and naturally. Imagine the upliftedness of a life where everything *will be achieved, enlivened by the movements of a joyful heart.*

Heartbreak with Samsara

Meditation, Part One

I N THE OPENING VERSE of chapter 8 of *The Way of the Bodhisattva,* Shantideva makes reference to the linear development of the *paramitas,* with each one building on the one before: based on our cultivation of enthusiasm, or diligence, we can now practice the *paramita* of meditation. Our spiritual development, however, doesn't always go in such a straight line. Sometimes our mind is stable and alert; at other times, it's all over the place. Sometimes we reach out to one another, and sometimes we retreat into our cocoon. Nevertheless, if our intention remains strong, we do become progressively more present and less distracted, progressively more compassionate and less self-centered.

8.1

After cultivating diligence,
Set your mind to concentrate.
For those whose minds are slack and wandering
Are caught between the fangs of the afflictions.

In verses 1 through 24, Shantideva discusses the reasons to tame the mind and avoid distractions. The message is similar to the teachings in chapter 5. There the analogy for wild mind was a crazed elephant. Here, being ruled by a wandering mind is compared to being *caught between the fangs of the afflictions*. The point of both examples is that an untamed mind causes us to suffer.

8.2

In solitude, the mind and body
Are not troubled by distraction.
Therefore, leave this worldly life
And totally abandon mental wandering.

With this verse, Shantideva begins a discussion on the need for solitude. In contemplating this section, it is helpful to remember three topics: *dunzi*, or wasting our lives with useless distractions; *shenpa*, the experience of being hooked; and heartbreak or nausea with samsara.

When Shantideva tells us to *leave this worldly life*, he's addressing how hooked we become by the things of this world, and how we need to find time to be free of distractions. After a while, nausea with getting hooked becomes like an ache in the heart that never goes away.

Shantideva is not making an ultimate statement about how to live one's life. He's just saying that in order for the mind to become steady, we'll need to remove ourselves from *dunzi*, at least for short periods of time. Outer solitude is a support for inner solitude. This is his point.

We can't kid ourselves: if we never take a break from our busy lives, it's going to be extremely difficult to tame our minds. This is why it's recommended to take time every day to meditate. Even short periods of sitting silently with ourselves allow the mind to settle down. Longer periods are even better.

8.3

Because of loved ones and desire for gain,
Disgust with worldly life does not arise.
These, then, are the first things to renounce.
Such are the reflections of a prudent man.

Verse 3 addresses a common addiction: seeking happiness in outer things, as though a partner, food, or some possession could provide the joy lacking in our lives. Our tendency to be overtaken by these drives is what concerns Shantideva here. It isn't the *loved ones* and *gain*, per se, that need to be renounced; it's the unrealistic hopes we place in these things.

Wishful thinking can easily become more compelling than the longing of the bodhi heart.

8.4

Penetrative insight joined with calm abiding
Utterly eradicates afflicted states.
Knowing this, first search for calm abiding,
Found by those who joyfully renounce the world.

Calm abiding again refers to the mental stability of *shamatha* meditation. The *penetrative insight* of a calm and steady mind is the basis for working with the kleshas. To cultivate this stability and wakefulness, we'll need to find time for solitude.

8.5

Beings, brief, ephemeral,
Who fiercely cling to what is also passing,
Will catch no glimpse of happiness
For many thousands of their future lives.

8.6

And thus their minds will have no joy
And therefore will not rest in equanimity.
But even if they taste it, they are not content—
And as before, the pain of longing stays.

When we *beings, brief, ephemeral* cling to things that are equally
impermanent, it's a setup for dissatisfaction. This isn't a particularly religious statement; we can see that everything is constantly
changing, including ourselves.

Since impermanence defies our attempts to hold on to anything, outer pleasures can never bring lasting joy. Even when we
manage to get short-term gratification, it doesn't heal our longing
for happiness; it only enhances our *shenpa*. As Dzigar Kongtrul
once said, "Trying to find lasting happiness from relationships or
possessions is like drinking saltwater to quench your thirst."

8.7

If I long and crave for other beings,
A veil is cast upon the perfect truth.
Wholesome disillusion melts away,
And finally there comes the sting of pain.

8.8

My thoughts are all for them . . .
And by degrees my life is frittered by.
My family and friends all fade and pass, for whom
The Doctrine is destroyed that leads to indestructibility.

Driving the point home again and again is one of Shantideva's
teaching methods. These verses say once again that when we *long*

and crave for other beings, *a veil is cast upon the perfect truth.* In other words, this craving blinds us to the unbiased nature of mind and thus our *wholesome disillusion* with samsara melts away.

Nausea with doing the same thing over and over is called *wholesome disillusion* because it motivates us to break our habits. By contrast, ordinary disillusionment is ego-based disgust—I don't like this, I don't want that—that keeps our habits well entrenched. Shantideva says that when seeking security in outer things clouds our perception of the fleeting, uncertain nature of reality, our longing to wake up may well evaporate. Then sooner or later it's too late to wake up, because *there comes the sting of pain.* In other words, we die.

Even hundreds of years later, we can easil/ understand when Shantideva says *my thoughts are all for them.* We're always thinking about others: loved ones, family, and the people we like and dislike. We fritter away whole lifetimes preoccupied with these objects of our craving and disdain. Meanwhile *family and friends all fade and pass,* leaving us, sadly, with a well entrenched craving "habit." Sadder still, we may have lost our passion for liberation in the process.

8.9

For if I act like those who are like children,
Sure it is that I shall fall to lower states.
So why keep company with infants
And go with them in ways so far from virtue?

8.10

One moment friends,
The next, they're bitter enemies.
Even pleasant things arouse their discontent:
Worldly people—hard it is to please them!

8.11

A beneficial word and they resent it,
While all they do is turn me from the good.
And if to what they say I close my ears,
Their anger burns, the cause of lower states.

The Buddha often likened sentient beings like us to children
or childish beings. We're childish in the way we constantly run
after the objects of our desire. Shantideva isn't implying he's
gone beyond this childishness. He's saying this is the way we all
are, and if we keep going like this, there's no way to weaken our
craving.

The time we spend getting hooked into our personal dramas
only creates more confusion. One day we childish beings are
friends, the next day we're bitter enemies. Even the nice things
we do for one another can create trouble. Have you ever tried to
comfort someone or give them a word of encouragement, and get
hostility in return? If you close your ears, people get angrier still. At
a party, for example, if there's some really good gossip circulating
but you don't go along with it, people find it very irritating. That's
just the way it is, and it never seems to change.

Reading these verses, you might decide that Shantideva's a real
curmudgeon. But if you take time to contemplate your experiences in the last twelve months, you'll probably find he's just stat-
ing the obvious.

8.12

Jealous of superiors, they vie with equals,
Proud to those below, they strut when praised.
Say something untoward, they seethe with rage:
What good was ever had from childish folk?

8.13

Keep company with them and what will follow?
Self-aggrandizement and scorn for others,
Talk about the "good things" of samsara—
Every kind of vice is sure to come.

These verses describe how we so often get it wrong. We are jealous of those who are wealthier, more popular, better looking, or have better jobs. We are competitive with our equals. To those "beneath" us, we're scornful and proud.

It would be so simple to turn these biases into the practice of dharma. With our *superiors,* we could practice sympathetic joy; thus, by awakening our bodhi heart, their station would bring us benefit. Instead of being competitive *with equals,* we could practice kindness and respect. With *those below,* we could practice compassion. We only get it wrong out of habit, and by doing so we miss valuable opportunities.

What often happens when we get emotionally entangled with *childish folk* is that we egg each other on. Building ourselves up, putting others down, regaling in the *"good things" of samsara—* our wonderful vacation, an excellent bottle of wine—we get further enmeshed in transitory pleasures. At this stage of the path it is very easy to get hooked into each other's dramas, and it is very dangerous.

The support we need to dissolve these old patterns, Shantideva says again, will come from finding time for solitude.

8.14

Only ruin can result
From links like these, between yourself and others.
For they will bring no benefit to you,
And you in turn can bring them nothing good.

8.15

Therefore flee the company of childish
    people.
Greet them, when you meet, with smiles
That keep on terms of pleasant courtesy,
While not inviting close familiarity.

8.16

Like bees that get their honey from the
    flowers,
Take only what is consonant with Dharma.
Treat them like first-time acquaintances,
Without encouraging a close relationship.

The way we get hooked by relationships always pulls us down.
No one benefits and no good comes of it. Like a bee that gets stuck
extracting honey from flowers, when we overindulge in gossiping,
boasting, and slander, it's lethal. We could stay on good terms with
each other without getting hooked. Like wise bees, we can get what
sustains our good heart without getting hopelessly trapped.

These teachings can be very challenging, and somewhat insulting or disturbing. But truthfully, do we use our current relationships to awaken bodhichitta? Most of us have no desire to be
malicious or cause harm. We see our practice as a way of involving
ourselves with sentient beings, not avoiding them. But as long as
we are so easily triggered and seduced, we need solitude to deepen
our stability and awareness.

It's like becoming a brain surgeon: if this were truly our aspiration, we'd go to medical school for intensive training, and not try
it out at home. Shantideva isn't saying not to have friends or keep
company with others. He is giving us advice for becoming less
reactive and more wise.

The stability of mind is like a candle flame that at this point is very vulnerable. Solitude is like a glass chimney that keeps it from blowing out in the wind. When the flame is stable, we can take the cover off. The wind is no longer a threat; now, in fact, it will make the flame burn like a bonfire.

The older I get, the more drawn I am to longer periods of retreat, yet I know that spending months in solitude isn't realistic for many people. You could, however, meditate each day and do daylong or weekend retreats whenever possible. If you can take more time, I certainly encourage you to do so. The main point is to make solitude a part of your life.

In order to work with difficult outer circumstances, we need to gather our inner strength. If even ten or twenty minutes of meditation a day helps us to do this, let's go for it!

Making good use of our limited time—the limited time from birth until death, as well as our limited time each day—is the key to developing inner steadiness and calm.

One of the most inspiring stories I've heard in this regard concerns Dzigar Kongtrul's grandmother. Her life was extremely demanding. But even though she worked hard from early morning until late at night, she became a highly realized person by practicing in the gaps. Whenever she wasn't talking to somebody, she would relax her mind and be present. Whether she was milking cows, washing dishes, or walking from here to there, she used any opportunity to settle and expand her mind. With every pause, she found outer solitude and thus discovered an inner solitude that was unshakable and profound.

8.17

"Oh, I am rich, surrounded by attention,
I have so much, and life is wonderful!"
Nourish such complacency and later,
After death, your fears will start!

8.18

Indeed, O foolish and afflicted mind,
You want, you crave for everything,
This "everything" will grow and turn
To suffering increased a thousandfold.

Verses 17 to 21 address the way we get distracted by good fortune. The great meditation master Dilgo Khyentse Rinpoche taught that sometimes good circumstances are more difficult to work with than bad ones, because they're so much fun. He called them "positive obstacles."

When someone is angry with us, it might remind us to meditate on patience. When we get sick, our suffering can put us in touch with the pain of others. When things go well, however, our mind easily accepts this. Like oil absorbing into our skin, attachment to favorable circumstances blends smoothly and invisibly into our thoughts and feelings. Without realizing what's happening, we can become infatuated with our achievements, fame, and wealth. It's difficult to extricate ourselves from positive obstacles. If we could have everything we wish for—wealth, a comfortable house, nice clothing—he advises us to view this good fortune as illusory, like a beautiful dream, and not let it seduce us into complacency.

As Shantideva says, *O foolish and afflicted mind, you want, you crave for everything,* but everything is never enough. As those in advertising well know, the more we get, the more we feel we need.

8.19

Since this is so, the wise man does not crave,
For from such craving fear and anguish come.
And fix this firmly in your understanding:
All that may be wished for will by nature fade
   to nothing.

8.20

For people may have gained a wealth of riches,
Enjoying reputation, sweet renown.
But who can say where they have gone to now,
With all the baggage of their gold and fame?

All those people throughout history who've gained riches, fame, and good reputations, where are they now? They're gone forever. And in the end, what use was *all the baggage of their gold and fame?* It didn't help them at death and it won't help us.

Worldly delights could, of course, support our awakening. When we are comfortable and at ease, we can devote more time to meditation and benefiting others. Usually, however, they lure us into further busyness and *shenpa*. As Trungpa Rinpoche put it, "Aren't we ridiculous?"

8.21

Why should I be pleased when people praise me?
Others there will be who scorn and criticize.
And why despondent when I'm blamed,
Since there'll be others who think well of me?

Shantideva refers here to the "eight worldly concerns": praise and blame, pleasure and pain, fame and obscurity, gain and loss. He asks why be happy *when people praise me,* or unhappy when they condemn me, since there'll always be those with other opinions. Nevertheless, these worldly concerns are the very things we constantly strive to get or get away from. The *shenpa* tug of want and don't want keeps us spinning in samsara.

Just the thought of someone saying something nice about us makes us feel good. If someone treats us in a neutral way, maybe has a deadpan response to our story, just remembering this makes us a little depressed. It's insane to be enslaved by such hopes and fears, but we can all count on it happening.

This is not just personal neurosis; it's another example of our universal dilemma.

8.22

So many are the wants and tendencies of beings,
Even Buddha could not please them all—
Of such an evil man as me no need to speak!
Better to give up such worldly thoughts.

8.23

People scorn the poor who have no wealth,
They also criticize the rich who have it.
What pleasure can derive from keeping
    company
With people such as these, so difficult to
    please?

8.24

Unless they have their way in everything,
These children are bereft of happiness.
And so, shun friendship with the childish,
Thus the Tathagata has declared.

Here Shantideva wraps up the section on getting hooked by people and good fortune. There is no wisdom in trying to satisfy worldly cravings—our own or anyone else's. The fact that *even Buddha could not please them all* is sobering. Shantideva advises us once again to not get sucked into the drama.

8.25

In woodlands, haunt of stag and bird,
Among the trees where no dissension jars,
It's there I would keep pleasant company!
When might I be off to make my dwelling there?

8.26

When shall I depart to make my home
In cave or empty shrine or under spreading tree,
With, in my breast, a free, unfettered heart,
Which never turns to cast a backward glance?

8.27

When might I abide in such a place,
A place unclaimed, by nature ownerless,
That's wide and unconfined, a place where I might stay
At liberty without attachment?

8.28

When might I be free of fear,
Without the need to hide from anyone,
With just a begging bowl and few belongings,
Dressed in garments coveted by none?

When Shantideva praises solitude, he is not suggesting we run
away and hide from all unpleasantness. Even if this were possible,
he wouldn't recommend it. One could spend years alone in a cave
without really letting go of anything. The question is how best to
attain the inner solitude that will bring lasting happiness.

There's a story about Patrul Rinpoche visiting a yogi who had been meditating in retreat for many years. His main practice was the perfection of patience. Rinpoche arrived unexpectedly and immediately started needling the yogi, ridiculing his practice, and calling him a charlatan. Finally the man got furious and screamed at Patrul Rinpoche to go away and leave him alone. As Rinpoche took his leave, he said to the yogi, "I was just testing your perfection of patience."

8.29

And going to the charnel ground,
When shall I compare
My body with the dry bones there,
So soon to fall to nothing, all alike?

8.30

This form of mine, this very flesh,
Is soon to give out such a stench
That even jackals won't come close—
For that indeed is all its destiny.

Yet again, Shantideva contemplates the impermanence of his life. In charnel grounds filled with exposed corpses, he compares his body with *the dry bones there* and understands that after death, *this form of mine, this very flesh,* will give off such a stink that even the jackals won't come near. In this pensive mood, Shantideva then teaches himself the dharma.

8.31

This body, now so whole and integral,
This flesh and bone that life has knit together,

Will drift apart, disintegrate.
And how much more will friend depart from friend?

8.32

Alone we're born, alone we come into the world,
And when we die, alone we pass away.
For no one shares our fate, and none our suffering.
So what are they to me, such "friends" and all their
hindrances?

Our very life depends on *this body* being relatively healthy and together. But our body will disintegrate, and that's it. It will leave us, just as a friend departs from a friend. In a kind of "ashes to ashes" verse, he says that we're born alone, and when we die, no matter how much we love people or they love us, we will go through that transition without company. There is nothing our dear ones can do to help us. Clinging to them will only hinder our ability to let go and move on with ease.

8.33

Like those who journey on the road,
Who halt and make a pause along the way,
Beings on the pathways of the world,
All halt, and pause, and take their birth.

8.34

Until the time comes round
When four men carry me away,
Amid the tears and sighs of worldly folk—
Till then, I will away and go into the forest.

This life is like a rest stop on a journey. We could think of our body as a hotel room: we rent it, we rest for a while, and we move on. Shantideva aspires to not waste his brief life running after meaningless distractions. Until the time comes for his corpse to be carried away, he'll put his days to good use and go into retreat.

8.35

There, with no befriending or begrudging,
I will stay alone in solitude,
Considered from the outset as already dead,
Thus, when I die, a source of pain to none.

8.36

And likewise, staying all alone,
The sound of mourning will not hinder me.
And no one will be there distracting me
From thinking of the Buddha and the practice.

This is instruction for dying. If, due to our training during life, we can connect with the openness of our mind, the experience of death will be joyful and expansive. But what if our mind is all over the place and easily distracted by emotional entanglement? Then the death process will be confusing and frightening. Shantideva's aspiration is to die alone, in hope of avoiding these unnecessary complications.

8.37

Therefore in these lovely gleaming woods,
With joy that's marred by few afflictions,
I shall pacify all mental wandering,
And there remain in blissful solitude.

8.38

Relinquishing all other aspirations,
Focusing myself on one intent alone,
I'll strive to still my mind,
And, calming it, to bring it to subjection.

This aspiration ends the section on seeking outer and inner solitude. Calming the mind refers to *shamatha* meditation; bringing it
to subjection means taming the wildness of the mind. Despite the
harshness of the language, we already know that doing this depends on gentleness, patience, and enthusiasm.

In the next section, Shantideva teaches at length about abandoning distractions that disturb the mind, particularly sexual
desire.

What is especially noteworthy about this section is Shantideva's
breathtaking logic. He relentlessly undermines the reasoning of
craving. No matter what we lust for—a lover, a car, a hot fudge
sundae—it's always much ado about nothing.

8.39

In this and every other world,
Desire's the fertile parent of all conflict.
Here in this world, bonds and wounds and
    death,
And in the next, a hell is all prepared.

8.40

You send your go-betweens, both boy and maid,
With many invitations for the prize,
Avoiding, in the quest, no sin,
No deed that brings an ill renown,

8.41

Nor acts of frightful risk,
Nor loss and ruin of both goods and wealth—
And all for pleasure and the perfect bliss,
That utmost penetrating kiss.

Some of what's being discussed is the way people in Shanti-deva's time went about finding partners—hence the *go-betweens* and *invitations*. It is interesting to note that, unlike many of the Nalanda monks, Shantideva was well acquainted with the customs of lay people. As a prince, he most likely had had intimate relations and was not a sexual prude.

What he's addressing here is not sexual passion itself, but how obsessed we become and the crazy things we do to satisfy our desires. As he says in verse 39, out-of-control passion can result in jail, injuries, or even death. Sadly, the O. J. Simpson syndrome is not all that uncommon.

In the following verses, Shantideva asks us to look intelligently at the nature of our lover's body, as he challenges the logic of our unreasonable preoccupation with sex.

8.42

Of what in truth is nothing but a heap of bones,
Devoid of self, without its own existence!
Is this the only object of desire and lust?
Sooner pass beyond all suffering and grief!

8.43

Oh what pains you went through just to draw
    the veil,
And lift the face that modestly looked down.

That face which, looked upon or not,
Was always carefully concealed.

8.44

That face for which you languished so . . .
Well, here it is, now nakedly exposed.
The crows have done their work for you to see.
What's this? You run away so soon?

8.45

That body that you guarded jealously
And shielded from the eyes of other men,
What, miser that you are, you don't protect it,
Now that it's the food of graveyard birds?

8.46

Look, this mass of human flesh,
Soon to be the fare of carrion beasts,
You deck with flowers, sandalwood, and jewels,
And yet it is the provender of others!

There are two traditional antidotes for lust. The first is to re-place lust with aversion. Shantideva uses this approach when he looks at the body after death and asks us to contemplate the un-reasonable craving for this *mass of human flesh*. Desire, he says, fades quickly when your lover becomes a rotting corpse.

The other antidote relies on seeing the body's insubstantial, dreamlike nature. As he remarks in verse 42, those we lust after are *nothing but a heap of bones*, with no permanent or solid existence.

From this point of view, it's helpful to question the solid pic-ture we hold of our sexual partner. Maybe we see them as sexy and irresistibly attractive; but catch them when they're unwashed and smelly, and passion may rapidly change to aversion. What if we desire them fully dressed, but are shocked when they take off their clothes? Maybe they're fatter or thinner than expected, or we don't like their choice of tattoos. If passion can evaporate so quickly, what is it we're really obsessed with?

A friend of mine quickly ended a relationship after coming down with mumps. When her partner saw her so disfigured, he temporarily lost all interest in her. By the time she recovered her beauty, she had lost all interest in him!

8.47

Look again, these heaps of bones—
Inert and dead. Why, what are you so scared of?
Why did you not fear them when they walked around
And moved with ease, like deadly revenants?

Here again is Shantideva's wit. Why, he asks, are we so afraid of a dead body, when this same body when it's up and moving about doesn't freak us out at all?

8.48

You loved them once, when clothed and draped they
    were.
Well, now they're naked, why do you not want them?
Ah, you say, your lust is no more there,
But why did you embrace them, all bedecked and
    covered?

He's referring again to seeing our lover's body as a corpse. What is it we're so hooked on? If we think it's their body, then why does everything change when that body is dead?

8.49

From food, a single source, come equally
Their bodies' filth, the honey-nectar of their mouths.
So why are you delighted by saliva,
And yet revolted by their excrement?

It may be obvious why our lover's saliva is more appealing than
their shit. But think of it: a fly would find that shit very desirable.
Is anything really intrinsically desirable or revolting?

8.50

Taking no delight in pillows,
Soft though they may be to touch and stroke,
You claim the human form emits no evil stench;
You don't know what is clean, befooled by lust!

8.51

Lustful ones, befuddled by desire,
Because you cannot copulate with them,
You angrily find fault with pillows,
Even though they're smooth and soft to touch!

When Shantideva speaks of being *befooled by lust* and *befuddled
by desire,* he addresses the heart of the problem. It's not the sexual
object that's at fault, it's our unreasonable degree of *shenpa.*

8.52

And if you have no love for filth,
How can you coddle on your lap
A cage of bones tied fast with sinews
Plastered over with the mud of flesh?

8.53

The reason is you're full of filth yourself,
And wallow in it constantly.
It is indeed just dirt that you desire,
And therefore long for other sacks of filth!

Maybe this is where the expression "you're full of shit" comes from! One has to have a sense of humor about Shantideva's arguments. Here he's saying that we contain plenty of unclean stuff ourselves, so why hanker after other's impurities!

8.54

"But it's the skin and flesh I love
To touch and look upon."
Then why do you not wish for flesh alone,
Inanimate and in its natural state?

Verse 54 begins a classic analysis done to expose the nature of emptiness. The traditional example is a chariot: Where do we find the chariot's true nature? Is it in the left wheel, the right wheel, or the seat? We can ask these same questions using the example of the body.

Shantideva is questioning where the object of our lust resides. Is it in the flesh or the perfume? If so, then why don't we lust for raw meat or pleasant smells? If it's the sandalwood smell that turns us on, we'd be foolish to confuse that smell with the body.

In the same way the Buddha analyzed the chariot, Shantideva analyzes the body to find out where "it" is. Where is this "self" or other? He then goes on to describe how we not only imbue these dreamlike lovers with desirability, we then covet them, long to copulate with them, and so on.

8.55

The mind of the beloved you so much desire
Eludes your touch; this mind you cannot see.
Nothing that the sense perceives is mind,
So why indulge in pointless copulation?

If I say it's my lover's mind I'm attracted to, well then, where exactly is that?

8.56

To fail to understand the unclean nature
Of another's flesh is not perhaps so strange.
But not to see the filthy nature
Of oneself is very strange indeed!

8.57

Why does the mind, intent on filthiness,
Neglect the fresh young lotus blossom,
Opened in the sunlight of a cloudless sky,
To take joy rather in a sack of dirt?

If it's beauty we want, why don't we lust after a lotus blossom?

8.58

And since you're disinclined to touch
A place or object grimed with excrement,
Why wish to touch the body
Whence such excrement has come?

8.59

And if you have no craving for impurity,
Why will you now embrace and kiss
What comes from such an unclean place,
Engendered likewise from an unclean seed?

The *unclean place* referred to here is the womb, and the *unclean seed* is semen. In our culture, many people don't have aversion to these things, but in India in Shantideva's time, apparently everyone did. This, in fact, proves Shantideva's point. Aversion and attraction are frequently based on cultural bias and are not in any way absolute realities.

8.60

The fetid worms that live in filth—
You have no love for them, not even little ones.
And yet you're lusting for a human form,
From filth arisen and replete with it!

8.61

Toward your own impurity
Disgust you do not feel; but what is more,
Attracted to the ordure of an unclean sack,
You long to touch the body of another!

In our low-self-esteem culture it's not helpful to encourage disgust for our own body. Nevertheless, Shantideva continues to do his best to deflate the irresistible urge of lust. It is lust, not sexual passion, per se, that he hopes to undermine with his logic and reasoning.

8.62

Pleasant substances like camphor,
Rice, and fresh green herbs—
Put them in your mouth and spit them out:
The ground itself is rendered foul with it!

8.63

If still you doubt such filthiness,
Though it is very plain for all to see,
Go off into the charnel grounds, observe
The fetid bodies there abandoned.

8.64

If when their skins are peeled away,
They make you feel great horror and
    revulsion,
How, having seen this, later on,
Can you desire and crave for such an
    object?

The basic point is this: once we've seen a dead body, how can we
become so obsessed with a live one?

8.65

The scent that now perfumes the skin
Is sandalwood and nothing else.
Yet how is it that one thing's fragrance
Causes you to long for something else?

8.66

Surely it is best to cease to long
For what by nature gives off evil smells.
Yet worldly people's lusts are all confused—
To what end do they daub the flesh with
    perfumes?

8.67

For if this scent in fact is sandalwood,
How will we now describe the body's odors?
And how is it that one thing's fragrance
Causes you to long for something else?

8.68

With lanky hair, with long nails overgrown,
With dirty teeth, and reeking with the stink
    of slime,
This body, naked, as it is, untended,
Is indeed a nightmare to behold!

8.69

Why go to such excess to clean and polish
What is but a weapon that will injure us?
The cares that people squander on themselves in
    ignorance
Convulse the universe with madness.

Looking good isn't the problem. Getting caught in hope and
fear about our appearance is what fills *the universe with madness.*

8.70

Did you see the heaps of human bones
And feel revulsion in the charnel ground?
Then why such pleasure in your cities of the dead,
Frequented by such skeletons that live and move?

Shantideva repeats his question: If dead bodies in the charnel ground freak us out, why aren't we repelled by whole cities filled with bodies walking around?

8.71

What's more, possession of another's filth
Is not to be acquired free of charge.
All is at a price: exhaustion in this life,
And in the next, the sufferings of hell!

8.72

To pay the bride-price young men are unable.
So while they're young, what joy is there for them?
Their lives are spent to gain sufficient wealth,
By then they're old—too old to satisfy their lust!

In eighth-century India, it was not uncommon for lower-caste men in certain tribes to borrow money to get married. They then became indentured to the lender. To gather enough wealth to attract a bride, whole generations of a family could become indebted. The son inherits the debt of the father, and so on; and in this way they became slaves. By the time the poor man gets his bride, he might be too old to satisfy his lust.

In these and the following verses, Shantideva's main concern is how we get completely hooked and distracted by our cravings.

Since his audience consisted of celibate monks, he has spent a long time trying to deflate their sexual fantasies. In monasteries, working sanely with sexual energy is often a hot topic.

8.73

Some are miserable as well as lustful.
For worn out by their day-long work,
They go home broken with fatigue,
To sleep the slumbers of a corpse!

8.74

Some, obliged to travel far abroad,
Must suffer separation from their wives,
From children whom they love and long to see.
They do not meet with them for years on end.

8.75

Some, ambitious for advancement,
Not knowing how to get it, sell themselves.
Happiness eludes their grasp, and pointlessly
They live, in bondage to their masters.

8.76

Some completely sell themselves,
No longer free, in slavery to others.
And, destitute, their wives give birth
With only trees for shelter, in the wilderness.

We have an idea, a dream, of what would bring us comfort and pleasure, somehow missing the point that what we go through to achieve that dream is painful and absurd. The goal of happiness eludes us despite all our worries and toil.

Next Shantideva discusses the futility of obsession with wealth and possessions. The craving that these things generate in us gets us in a lot of trouble.

8.77

Fools ensnared by craving for a livelihood
Decide that they will make their fortune
In the wars, though fearful for their lives.
And seeking gain, it's slavery they get.

People often join the army for money and other benefits. But once you sign up, there's no way out. If you're sent to war, off you go.

8.78

Some, as fruits of their ambition,
Have their bodies slashed, impaled on pointed stakes.
Some are wounded, run through by the lance,
While some are put to death by fire.

Dealing drugs may seem like an easy way to get rich. But it soon turns out to be a very dangerous lifestyle and not so easy after all.

8.79

The trouble guarding what we have, the pain of
     losing all!
See the endless hardships brought on us by wealth!
Those distracted by their love of riches
Never have a moment's rest from sorrows of existence.

We experience this pointlessness constantly. The anguish we go through to get our *wealth*—our livelihood, good circumstances, and possessions—doesn't make us happy in the end. We buy a beautiful silk shirt and accidentally splatter it with salad dressing. We save up money and buy our dream car; but when it's parked on the street, we worry ourselves sick that someone might scratch it. Of course, having no money is also extremely painful. But unfortunately, it's rare for any of us to be content with just enough to meet our basic needs.

8.80

They indeed, possessed of many wants,
Will suffer many troubles, all for very little:
Mouthfuls of the hay the oxen get
As recompense for having pulled the cart!

8.81

The cattle's fodder!—not so very rare—
And for the sake of such a petty thing,
Tormented by their karma they destroy
This precious human life so hard to find.

We'll go through great discomfort to get a raise or an extra week of vacation. To get on the boss's good side, we'll work overtime without pay or whatever else it takes. Isn't this similar to the ox that pulls the cart, sweating and miserable, only to be rewarded by a mouthful of hay? This is Shantideva's analogy for the pain we cause ourselves for even the smallest of pleasures. Meanwhile, we're wasting the precious opportunity of this fleeting human life.

8.82

All that we desire is sure to perish,
And afterwards we fall to hellish torment.
The constant, minor troubles we endure
Are all for what amounts to very little!

This refers to the pain of samsaric existence. As one Buddhist verse says: friends, wealth, homes, and other transitory comforts are like a banquet before the executioner leads us to our death.

We may get everything we want, but the pleasure is fleeting. What's more, if we harm anyone in the process, the end result will be pain. Even if we harm no one, we still strengthen our craving habit, which is never in our best interest.

8.83

But with a millionth part of such vexation
Enlightenment itself could be attained!
The pains the lustful take exceed by far the trials
    encountered on the path,
And at the end the fruit is very far from
    buddhahood!

This is so painfully true. With a fraction of the time and effort we spend on our worldly existence, what tremendous progress we could make on the bodhisattva path. I remember hearing one teacher say: "If I gave you all a pack of cards and a case of beer, you could stay up—enthusiastic, alert, and energetic—for days on end. But ask you to sit for a couple of hours in the evening, and you all fall sound asleep!"

8.84

Reflect upon the horrors of the states of sorrow!
Weapons, poisons, fires, and yawning chasms,
Hostile foes—these worldly pains are slight
Compared with what we get as fruit of our desire!

8.85

And so, revolted by our lust and wanting,
Let us now rejoice in solitude,
In places where all strife and conflict cease,
The peace and stillness of the greenwood.

These verses refer again to the genuine heartbreak and revulsion
we may come to feel for our repeating samsaric patterns.

8.86

In pleasant dwellings formed of massive stone,
And cooled by sandal trees beneath the moon,
In woodlands wafted by the gentle breeze,
Our minds intent on bringing good to others,

8.87

In caves, beneath the trees, in houses left abandoned
May we linger long as we might wish.
Relinquishing the pain of guarding our possessions,
Let us live in freedom, unconfined by cares.

8.88

To have such liberty unmarred by craving,
And loosed from every bond and tie—

A life of such contentment and such bliss,
The gods like Indra would be pressed to find!

8.89

Reflecting in such ways as these,
Upon the excellence of solitude,
Pacify completely all discursiveness
And cultivate the mind of bodhichitta.

With this beautiful and peaceful rallying cry, Shantideva reminds us again of the benefits of solitude and concludes the first section of this chapter on the *paramita* of meditation.

Dissolving the Barriers

Meditation, Part Two

W ITH VERSE 90 of chapter 8, we enter one of the
most famous sections of *The Way of the Bodhi-*
sattva. Here Shantideva talks about the equality of self and other,
and gives us specific practices for standing in another person's
shoes. These instructions are antidotes for the narrow, confused
perspective of "me" and "mine."

8.90

Strive at first to meditate
Upon the sameness of yourself and others.
In joy and sorrow all are equal.
Thus be guardian of all, as of yourself.

We begin by contemplating the sameness of ourselves and others. Philosophically, we might discuss the insubstantiality and false
security of a separate "self." But, when it comes to actually dissolving the illusory barrier between this self and others, we work on a
practical level and keep it real.

The myth of separateness is very convincing. Even though it causes us enormous pain, it's definitely not easy to shake. This myth is addressed very directly by the practices and teachings on the equality of self and other. They expose the agendas and strategies of self-importance, and change the way we see one another.

Simply put, if you've ever lived on the streets, you can never look at a panhandler the same way again. You've been there; you know what it's like to be down and out and to ask for money. This experience automatically brings down the barrier. Likewise, if you've ever been hospitalized with a serious illness, you know how people can pass in and out of your room without seeing you or treating you as a person. In the movie *Wit*, the dying heroine is seen vomiting into a basin while a staff person asks, "How are we feeling today?" Having experienced this kind of depersonalization yourself, it's difficult to relate superficially to someone else who is very ill.

Imagining ourselves in another person's situation shakes up our indifference. We begin to realize that *in joy and sorrow,* we are equals. Our suffering and happiness are the same: misery is misery and joy is joy; therefore, whether we feel sorrow *or* relief, we understand how others feel.

Understanding the equality of our joys and sorrows widens our perspective. Somehow staying caught in the web of self-centered thinking is not as easy as before.

8.91

The hand and other limbs are many and distinct,
But all are one—one body to be kept and guarded.
Likewise, different beings in their joys and sorrows,
Are, like me, all one in wanting happiness.

The analogy of the body represents one whole with many unique parts. The ear is not the toe, the tooth is not the eye, yet these individual parts also aren't separate. If our toe hurts, our whole body feels it; if our leg is cut, our hand reaches out to help. We don't experience our leg as "other" and say, "How interesting, look at the blood pouring out."

Shantideva uses the analogy of the wholeness of the body in several contexts. Here it refers to the interdependence of human beings: all of us unique but not separate, and, just like me, all of us wanting to feel good and not bad.

8.92

My pain does not in fact afflict
Or cause discomfort to another's body.
Through clinging to my "I," this suffering is mine.
And, being mine, is very hard to bear.

The cause of our suffering is our concept of ourselves as a separate, continuous self. Whatever we cling to as "me" or "mine"—our body, spouse, emotions, possessions, or friends—causes us to suffer. The *intensity* of our pain, according to the Buddha and Shantideva, is dependent on the intensity of our clinging to an impermanent, ungraspable "I."

If this is true, how can we go beyond this central reference point of self? We do it simply and directly by recognizing that other people are just like me. This practice reveals that we all have the same fear of suffering and the same desire for happiness. This realization frees up the kindness of our heart.

8.93

And other beings' pain
I do not feel, and yet
Because I take them for my own
Their suffering is likewise hard to bear.

Maybe we feel that our own suffering is already more than we can bear. Maybe this is why we don't want to relate to someone else's pain. When we understand that their suffering is no different than ours, however, something shifts. The fearful heart of ego begins to melt.

8.94

And therefore I'll dispel the pain of others,
For it is simply pain, just like my own.
And others I will aid and benefit,
For they are living beings, just like me.

8.95

Since I and other beings both,
In wanting happiness, are equal and alike,
What difference is there to distinguish us,
That I should strive to have my bliss alone?

These verses summarize the reasons for practicing the equality of self and other.

8.96

Since I and other beings both,
In fleeing suffering, are equal and alike,
What difference is there to distinguish us,
That I should save myself and not the other?

Do you ever wonder why people do such crazy things? They do them for the same reasons you do: to avoid pain and make their lives more comfortable. No sentient being wants anxiety, stress, or physical pain. In this, we're all alike: we want security, predictability, and happiness in our lives—and to get it, we can do some very mean things.

8.97

Since pains of others do no harm to me,
What reason do I have to shield myself?
But why to guard against "my" future pain
    which
Does no harm to this, my present "me"?

Shantideva once again enters into a debate with himself. In the first lines of verse 97, he presents *shenpa* logic: "Since someone else's pain doesn't hurt me, why should I care about it?" And then wisdom responds.

8.98

To think that "I will have to suffer it"
In fact is but a false conception—
In the present moment, "I" will perish;
At a later time, another will be born.

Logically we might say: "If a knife cuts me, it hurts. This is obviously why I protect myself. But if the knife cuts you, I don't feel a thing. So why should I be concerned?" Shantideva refutes this argument by saying that the "I" we're constantly trying to protect from harm, today, tomorrow, or next week, is not the same "I" of this moment. It is constantly changing and perishing. Every second, another "I" is born. It's worth pondering this idea.

8.99

It's for the sufferer himself, you'll say,
To shield himself from injuries that come!
The pain felt in my foot is not my hand's,
So why, in fact, does one protect the other?

From a conventional point of view, the practices of equality appear foolish. Whoever suffers should take care of him- or herself. This rationale makes sense from our ordinary perspective: I'll take care of me, you take care of you.

Shantideva's reply comes in the last two lines of this verse. Again he uses the analogy of the body: obviously the hand will protect the foot from harm. If we accept this as reasonable, why would we dismiss the idea that separate beings could also relate as parts of a whole?

When someone is hurting, we see them as "other." So how do we come to know we're not isolated beings? One way is to reflect that by not helping them, we are harming ourselves. Working with this notion again and again, what starts as a practice becomes real understanding. Whatever happens to any one of us affects the whole.

If you think about it seriously, this type of interdependent thinking makes perfect sense. When we don't take care of one another, I suffer, you suffer, the whole world suffers.

8.100

"This may be irrational," you'll say.
"It happens simply through the force of ego-clinging."
But that which is illogical for both of us
Should be refuted and dispensed with utterly!

Shantideva continues debating with himself. *Shenpa* logic says, "Let's not get too philosophical. *Ego-clinging* is the only reason I want to protect *my* hand and not your hand." To which wisdom responds, "That is exactly the point!"

Let's stop justifying ourselves with such illogical excuses. We live in a painful, self-centered prison called "me." This misperception causes pain for everyone. How do we undercut the self-absorption that separates us? How do we become more broad-minded and openhearted? We do the practice of "just like me."

8.101

Labeled continuities and aggregates,
Like strings of beads and armies, are like mirages.
Likewise, there is no one hurt by suffering,
For who is there to be oppressed by it?

8.102

And if there is no subject suffering,
Mine and other's pain—how are they different?
Simply, then, since pain is pain, I will dispel it.
What grounds have you for all your strong
    distinctions?

In verse 101, we have the third rationale for not practicing the equality of self and other. This is the rationale of emptiness: if everything is illusory like a mirage, why worry about nonexistent suffering?

"Good thinking," Shantideva might respond, "but if you weren't stuck in a solid sense of 'me,' you'd understand the sameness of our pain. There's no difference between my pain and yours." In this way, he uses the emptiness argument to support, rather than refute, the need for compassion, concluding, *since pain is pain, I will dispel it.*

8.103

Thus the suffering of everyone
Should be dispelled, and here there's no debate.
To free myself from pain means freeing all;
Contrariwise, I suffer with the pain of beings.

At the level of absolute truth, there is no reason to suffer. But at the relative level, we're all in considerable pain. The cause of our discontent, Shantideva insists, is our mistaken feeling of separateness. This isn't based on anything tangible. It's based on beliefs and concepts. The duality of subject and object, self and other, is an illusion imputed by the mind.

This absolute understanding is arrived at through the practice of letting go. Meanwhile, we can work at the level of everyday pain and treat other people's suffering as our own.

8.104

"The sorrow felt in pity aggravates," you say,
"The pain already felt, so why engender it?"
But can the sting of pity be compared
With all that other beings have to suffer?

I frequently hear this response to the practice of putting oneself in another's shoes. It's a conventional argument against experiencing the pain of others. The opponent of pity—a better word might be empathy or compassion—says, "I can't bear my own sorrow, let alone someone else's." But Shantideva replies that the *sting* of empathy is nothing compared to the suffering—the hunger, thirst, violence, neglect, and fundamental ignorance—of sentient beings.

The pain of compassion can make us decidedly more loving and tender-hearted toward others. Certainly it hurts not to shut out their pain, but it heals the even greater pain of self-absorption.

8.105

And if through such a single pain
A multitude of sorrows can be remedied,
Such pain as this a loving being
Strives to foster in himself and others.

Someone asked a Tibetan lama if he was afraid that by breathing in others' suffering during *tonglen* meditation practice, he would catch it. To this he replied that nothing would make him happier than to take on their pain so they could be free of it. When someone can say this, a profound shift has taken place. His greatest happiness comes from realizing the equality of himself and others. Whatever pain he experiences in the process is not a deterrent.

8.106

Even thus, Supushpachandra
Knowing how the king would cause him harm
Did nothing to escape from tribulation,
That the pains of many should be overthrown.

This verse refers to the story of a man who was threatened with death if he taught the dharma. In order to benefit hundreds of people, he gladly risked his life. Supushpachandra is a bodhisattva role model. His example may be a hard act to follow, but it could inspire us to stretch a bit further each day.

8.107

Those whose minds are practiced in this way,
Whose happiness it is to soothe the pain of others,
Will venture in the hell of unremitting agony,
As swans sweep down upon a lotus lake.

8.108

The oceanlike immensity of joy
Arising when all beings will be freed,
Will this not be enough? Will this not satisfy?
The wish for my own freedom, what is that to me?

Could we become fearless enough to venture into places of *unremitting agony*? Could we do this as enthusiastically *as swans sweep down upon a lotus lake*? Nothing gave Mother Teresa more pleasure than relieving suffering. Happiness for her was helping people to die knowing they weren't alone.

You and I are like fledglings just learning to fly. We can foster the heart of bodhi in smaller ways: giving a beggar money with the enthusiasm of those swans would be a major step forward.

I've benefited greatly from Shantideva's advice to start with little cares and minor challenges and let daring unfold naturally. This isn't playing it safe; it's the wisdom of starting with what's doable and expanding our courage a little bit at a time. If you've ever wondered how to get there from here, this teaching provides an answer.

In earlier chapters, Shantideva's instructions were primarily for working with our personal confusion. Building on that foundation, he now emphasizes a more advanced stage of our journey. It's always wise, however, to use the teachings that apply to where you are right now as your guide to daily living. This is the way to avoid discouragement and burnout.

8.109

The work of bringing benefit to beings
Will not, then, make me proud and self-admiring.
The happiness of others is itself my satisfaction;
I do not expect another recompense.

8.110

Just as I defend myself
From all unpleasant happenings, however small,
Likewise I shall act for others' sake
To guard and shield them with compassion.

Perhaps the easiest way to appreciate what Shantideva says is to think of our relationship with animals. It's not that complicated. We'd happily save an animal from a cruel situation, not to be seen as virtuous, but just to *guard and shield* them from pain. We might easily be more protective of their welfare than our own.

8.111

Although the drop of sperm and blood
Is alien and in itself devoid of entity,
Yet, because of strong habituation,
I recognize and claim it as my "I."

8.112

Why, then, not identify
Another's body, calling *it* my "I"?
And vice versa, why should it be hard,
To think of this my body as another's?

The relentless sense of "me" and "mine" is an acquired habit: the strongest habit we have. Realizing the absurdity of this, is it too comical to think of "I" as someone else and not me? If this "I" is insulting someone, is it too big a stretch to imagine how the other person feels? If we were to literally exchange places for even an instant, we would feel the full force of our own cruel words and without a doubt, instantly stop hurting them.

8.113

Seeing then the faults that come from cherishing
    myself,
The oceanic qualities that come from loving
    others,
I shall lay aside all love of self
And gain the habit of adopting others.

When Shantideva uses the expressions *cherishing myself* or *love of self*, he's referring to the cocoon, the prison of separateness. This is the opposite of a compassionate relationship with oneself. The way out of the pain of self-absorption is to think of others.

8.114

Hands and other limbs
Are thought of as the members of a body.
Shall we not consider others likewise—
Limbs and members of a living whole?

8.115

Just as in this form, devoid of "I,"
The thought of self arose through long
    habituation,
Why, upon the aggregate of living beings,
Should not the thought of "I," through habit,
    be imputed?

What would a family or a city be like if, instead of "me first," we all cared about one another and were open to regarding others as "just like me"?

8.116

Thus when I work for others' sake,
No reason can there be for boasting or
    amazement.
For it is just as when I feed myself—
I don't expect to be rewarded.

We don't need applause for feeding a starving puppy; it's as natural as feeding ourselves. We don't expect to be congratulated or win a Noble Peace Prize for our efforts.

8.117

Just as I defend myself, therefore,
From all unpleasant happenings however small,
Likewise I shall act for others' sake
To guard and to protect them with compassion.

This is reminiscent of Jesus's teaching to "do unto others as you would have them do unto you." It would be heartwarming, indeed, to be on the receiving end of such actions.

8.118

This is why the Lord Avalokita
Out of great compassion blessed his name,
That those caught in the midst of multitudes
Might be released and freed from every fear.

The bodhisattva Avalokiteshvara said that in times of danger, if we call out his name three times, we'll be released from fear. His story serves as an analogy for the vast potential of our own selfless compassion.

8.119

And so we should be undeterred by hardships,
For by influence of use and habit,
People even come to grieve for one
Whose very name strikes terror in their hearts!

Shantideva presents the unusual idea of grieving for those *whose very name strikes terror* in our hearts. If we start practicing now for the people we like, we can move on to those we find neutral or mildly irritating. Over time our compassion can expand, until we reach the point where grieving for those we dislike and fear doesn't seem so far-fetched.

The Dalai Lama was teaching in front of a large audience when he received word that Mao Tse-tung had died. He paused and then started to weep. For most Tibetan people, nobody was more feared than Mao Tse-tung, yet the Dalai Lama's first reaction was to weep—perhaps, in part, because of the suffering Mao Tse-tung would go through as a result of his cruelty to the Chinese and Tibetan people.

8.120

Those desiring speedily to be
A refuge for themselves and other beings
Should interchange the terms of "I" and "other,"
And thus embrace a sacred mystery.

Sometimes the sun is obscured by clouds. It may not even seem to be shining. This, of course, isn't the case; the sun is simply hidden. In the same way, the unobscured nature of mind is always with us, but it is blocked by self-absorption. It's hidden by opinions, biases, and concepts, and obscured by kleshas. When we reflect on this verse, it's helpful to keep this in mind.

The clouds of self-centeredness mysteriously part when we put ourselves in another person's place and imagine what he or she feels. In *tonglen* practice, we breathe *in* what we usually push away and send *out* what we usually cling to. This dissolves the ego's strategies and reveals the clarity of our mind. It may be a mystery how this simple practice frees us, but it's definitely a mystery worth embracing.

8.121

Because of our attachment to our bodies,
We're terrified by even little things.
This body, then, this source of so much fear—
Who would not revile it as the worst of enemies?

Sometimes Shantideva refers to the body as a precious vehicle for attaining enlightenment, and sometimes he points out its drawbacks. Here he says that our bodily obsessions create tremendous fear.

8.122

Wishing to relieve our bodies' ills,
Our hungry mouths, the dryness of our throats,
We lie in wait along the road
And steal the lives of fishes, birds, and deer.

8.123

And for the body's service and advantage,
Some there are who even kill their parents,
Or steal what has been offered to the Triple Gem,
Because of which, they'll burn in deepest hell.

8.124

Where then is the prudent man
Who wants to pamper and protect his body?
Who will not ignore and treat with scorn
What is for him a dangerous enemy?

People can be so afraid of coming to harm, they're willing to kill and steal to protect themselves. These self-protective tendencies can be dangerous—as dangerous as treating ourselves with scorn. Either way, I hope Shantideva's message about the harm caused by self-centeredness is clear.

The mahayana teachings say the reason we don't harm others is that we care about them. We don't kill because we cherish the lives of others; we don't steal because we respect their possessions. We don't just refrain from negative actions, we also practice loving-kindness.

8.125

"If I give this, what will be left for me?"
Thinking of oneself—the way of evil ghosts.
"If I keep this, what will be left to give?"
Concern for others is the way of heaven.

Our actions lead to happiness or grief, but our usual understanding of how this works is misguided. We think, for instance, that saving our money will make us wealthy and giving too generously will make us poor. In this and the following verses, Shantideva turns this everyday logic upside down. He begins in verse 125 by pointing out that richness is a state of mind. Giving freely is *the way of heaven;* holding back increases neediness and fear.

Verses 126 through 128 describe three pairs of contrasting destinies reflecting different relationships between self and other.

8.126

If to serve myself I harm another,
I'll suffer later in the realms of hell.
If for others' sake I harm myself,
Every excellence will be my heritage.

8.127

Wanting what is best for me—
Stupidity and lower realms result!
Let this be changed, applied to others—
Honors and the realms of bliss will come!

8.128

Enslaving others, forcing them to serve me,
I will come to know the state of servitude.
But if I labor for the good of others,
Mastery and leadership will come to me.

When Shantideva says *for others' sake I harm myself,* it simply means he's willing to undergo hardships to help someone out. The result of this is happiness. Wanting only *what is best for me* and using others for our own profit result in our own suffering. This sentiment is summarized below in a verse often quoted by the Dalai Lama.

8.129

All the joy the world contains
Has come through wishing happiness for others.
All the misery the world contains
Has come through wanting pleasure for oneself.

I think Shantideva would have appreciated the film *Groundhog Day*, because it illustrates verse 129 so perfectly. An angry man lives one day over and over again, until he gets it right. He tries every possible selfish strategy for happiness, which only increases his frustration and discontent.

Finally, he begins spending his day helping people. Why? Not to be seen as the good guy, but because it's the only thing that brings him pleasure. Every day he catches the same little boy falling out of a tree, and every day the little boy runs off without saying thank you! Every morning he tries to save the life of a homeless man he's come to love, and every day he doesn't succeed. But as this day is relived again and again, he becomes more flexible and warm-hearted. And people understandably come to love him.

As Shantideva says, the more we benefit others, the more happiness comes our way.

8.130

Is there need for lengthy explanation?
Childish beings look out for themselves,
While Buddhas labor for the good of others:
See the difference that divides them!

Childish beings like ourselves are ignorant about the causes of happiness. Optimistically, both Shantideva and *Groundhog Day* suggest that we can wise up and get it right.

8.131

If I do not give away
My happiness for others' pain,
Enlightenment will never be attained,
And even in samsara, joy will fly from me.

8.132

Leaving future lives outside the reckoning,
Even this life's needs are not fulfilled—
When servants do not do their work,
And masters do not pay the wages earned.

Forget about enlightenment; even worldly joy will elude us if we
don't care for one another. In this life, if *servants*, or employees,
don't do their work and *masters*, or employers, have no concern for
them, then the values of society begin to break down.

Verse 132 is the story behind all revolutions. I think of South
Africa when I read it. For years, cruel masters didn't pay the wages
earned. Apartheid, or separateness, was legalized and deeply ingrained. Yet many people worked with the same principles Shantideva is proclaiming and eventually something shifted for the
better.

As a result of years of oppression, however, the former "servants" now attack the former "masters." This is a familiar story: the
roles of the oppressor and the oppressed switch back and forth.
Lasting happiness, Shantideva says, depends on a true shift in the
human heart, one that begins with wanting what's best for others
because we see their joys and sorrows as our own.

8.133

Casting far away abundant joys
That may be gained in this or future lives,
Because of bringing harm to other beings,
I ignorantly bring myself intolerable pain.

Shantideva reiterates this pivotal teaching: by harming others
we're setting ourselves up for future pain.

8.134

All the harm with which this world is rife,
All fear and suffering that there is,
Clinging to the "I" has caused it!
What am I to do with this great demon?

8.135

If this "I" is not relinquished wholly,
Sorrow likewise cannot be avoided.
For if he does not keep away from fire,
A man cannot escape from being burned.

When we play with fire, we *cannot escape from being burned.*
This describes life in the cocoon: the more self-absorbed we are,
the more we suffer. But we can't just snap our fingers and say, "This
'I' is just a label; I'm not going to think that way anymore." Our ego
trips are deeply ingrained. They are, in fact, the very means that
keep the six realms well oiled and running.

So, how do we get out of this? As Shantideva has said again and
again, seeing the sameness of ourselves and others is the key.

8.136

To free myself from harm
And others from their sufferings,
Let me give myself away,
And cherish others as I love myself.

Loving ourselves provides the foundation for cherishing others.
If we feed our low self-esteem, we won't have anything to build on.
Reflecting on this will keep us from getting off track.

8.137

"For I am now beneath the rule of others,"
Of this you must be certain, O my mind.
And now no longer shall you have a thought
That does not wish the benefit of beings.

8.138

My sight and other senses, now the property of others—
To use them for myself would be illicit.
How much more so is it disallowed to use
My faculties against their rightful owners?

To be *beneath the rule of others* means to be at their service. Shantideva's greatest joy is helping others. If his *sight and other senses* could benefit someone, this would make him happy. To use them for harm is not an option. He knows that self-absorption blinds us to the preciousness and fragility of other beings.

8.139

Thus others will be now my chief concern.
And everything I see my body has
Will all be seized and given
For the use and service of all other beings.

Like a houseguest who enjoys a friend's possessions without forgetting they belong to someone else, you could just as easily appreciate your body but have no problem letting it be used to benefit *all other beings*.

From verse 140 until the end of the chapter, Shantideva teaches a practice that is only found in *The Way of the Bodhisattva:* his unique version of "exchanging self for other."

8.140

Take others—lower, higher, equal—as yourself;
Identify yourself as "other."
Then, without another thought,
Experience envy, pride, and rivalry.

Shantideva begins with an overview of the practice. He asks us to exchange places with others—*lower, higher, equal*—and *without another thought*, experience their kleshas. He encourages us to intensify these emotions and experience their energy directly, using them as our vehicle for awakening insight and compassion.

In verse 141, we begin by identifying with someone we might consider "lower," such as a homeless person. As a mind-training practice, he asks us to imagine ourselves in this person's place.

This serves two purposes. First, you intentionally experience an emotion we all normally avoid: the *envy* that someone with nothing could easily feel. Imagine a well-off person passing by and condescendingly handing you down a few coins. See this fortunate person, clean and well-clothed, maybe chatting with friends and going into a restaurant or movie . . . and don't hold back. Get in touch with your envy. Exaggerate it with your thoughts and allow it to escalate, just as Shantideva does. Feel its intensity, seductiveness, obsessiveness, and pain. That's the first purpose of this practice.

The second purpose is to experience being on the receiving end of such intense emotion. This is a radical thing to do. Normally we see things exclusively from our own perspectives. Reflecting on the other person's experience is a far more expansive and compassionate stance and a straightforward, practical way to awaken bodhichitta.

In the next few verses, Shantideva sets up dialogues between people—*lower, higher, equal*—and has some fun playing all the parts. It may seem, in these verses, that he's interacting with others, but he's just describing himself from various vantage points.

8.141

He's the center of attention; I am nothing,
And unlike him, I'm poor without possessions.
Everyone looks up to him, despising me;
All goes well for him, for me there's only bitterness!

Here he's the homeless person watching the well-off Shantideva walk by. And as the homeless person, he intentionally indulges in his envy and aversion.

8.142

All I have is sweat and drudgery,
While he's there, sitting at his ease.
He's great, respected in the world,
While I'm the underdog, a well-known nobody.

8.143

What! A nobody without distinction?
Not true! I do have some good qualities.
He's not the best, he's lower down than some;
While, when compared with some, I do excel!

Building ourselves up is part of the envy syndrome. When we're not feeling victimized, our haughtiness steps in.

8.144

My discipline, my understanding have declined,
But I am helpless, ruled by my defilements.
As much as he is able, he should cure me,
And I should be submissive even to his punishments.

8.145

The fact is he does nothing of the sort!
By what right, then, does he despise me?
What use, then, are his qualities to me,
Those qualities of which he's so possessed?

8.146

Indifferent to the plight of living beings,
Who tread the brink of evil destinies,
He makes an outward show of virtues,
Even sets himself among the perfect!

When a beggar looks at someone like me, someone who's taken the bodhisattva vow and should not be so unfeeling, he must wonder why I have no empathy. Why don't I do something to help his predicament?

It must be like that when you live on the streets: middle-class people, with all their ideas about helping others, scoot by without even noticing you're there. Imagining yourself in this position changes the way you see those less fortunate: "just like me," this person would appreciate some understanding and kindness.

This ends the section on getting in touch with the pain of poverty mind, as well as the pain our dislike and envy causes other people.

Some commentaries refer to these and the following verses as dialogues between ego and wisdom. But, for the most part, I won't teach it that way. For me, the value of working with this practice is not philosophical; the value comes from making the effort to put myself in someone else's place.

Then I can, first, connect vividly with the klesha energy shared by all sentient beings. And secondly, I can experience the unpleas-

antness of being on the receiving end of negativity, and therefore
stop myself before I denigrate another human being.

8.147

That I might excel, outstripping him,
Him, regarded as my peer and equal!
In contests I will certainly secure
My fame and fortune, public renown.

8.148

By every means I'll advertise
My gifts to all the world,
Ensuring that *his* qualities
Remain unknown, ignored by everyone.

8.149

My faults I will conceal, dissimulate.
For I, not he, will be the object of devotion;
I, not he, will gain possessions and renown;
I will be the center of attention.

8.150

I will take such satisfaction
In his shame and degradation.
I will render him despicable,
The butt and laughingstock of everyone.

In these verses Shantideva exchanges places with a rival. Looking over at his former self, this is what he has to say: Now *I will be
the center of attention,* not he. I will render Shantideva *the butt and*

laughingstock of everyone. The point is to feel the discomfort of the competitive frame of mind, as well as what it's like to have that bitterness directed at you.

8.151

People say this pitiful nonentity
Is trying to compete with me!
But how can he resemble me, they ask,
In learning, beauty, wealth, or pedigree?

8.152

Just to hear them talk about my qualities,
My reputation on the lips of all,
The thrill of it sends shivers down my spine,
The pleasure that I bask and revel in!

8.153

Granted, even if he does have something,
I'm the one he's working for!
He can keep enough just to survive,
But with my strength I'll steal away the rest.

8.154

I will wear his happiness away;
I will always hurt and injure him.
He's the one who in samsara
Did me mischiefs by the hundreds!

In verses 151 through 154, Shantideva changes places with someone who looks down on him, someone who finds him unworthy of attention. He allows himself to experience full-blown arrogance as well as being on the receiving end of that degree of scorn and condescension.

In this practice, you get to play all the roles and use your own words to make the situation personal and real. Let's say I'm a homeless person, and there's Pema walking by with all her good fortune. What if she treated me as a human being, instead of just giving me money? What if she asked how I was doing or where I was going to sleep that night? In a relationship between two equal human beings, both the unfortunate person's resentment and Pema's indifference have a chance to melt away.

With the last two lines in verse 154—*He's the one who in samsara / Did me mischiefs by the hundreds!*—Shantideva begins a dialogue with the fearful, uptight mind of self-absorption.

8.155

O my mind, what countless ages
Have you spent in working for yourself?
And what great weariness it was,
While your reward was only misery!

Here, he also plays two roles: his innate wisdom talks sense to his confused, neurotic self. We all have this guiding wisdom mind and, like Shantideva, we can call on it at any time.

8.156

The truth, therefore, is this:
That you must wholly give yourself and take the
    other's place.
The Buddha did not lie in what he said—
You'll see the benefits that come from it.

He talks kindly to his poor, confused mind: What will best serve you is serving others. If you follow the Buddha's instructions, it will go much better for everyone.

8.157

If, indeed, you had in former times
Embraced this work and undertaken it,
You could not still be lacking
In the perfect bliss of buddhahood.

What's more, oh neurotic mind, if you had started on this path even a month ago, you'd be that much closer to Buddhahood!

8.158

Just as you identify
A drop of other's blood and sperm,
And cling to it as though it were yourself,
Now take sentient beings—others—as your self.

8.159

Now be covetous for others' sake,
Of everything you see that you possess.
Steal it, take it all away,
And use it for the benefit of others.

So much of what we do builds up selfishness and destroys our happiness. Exchanging ourselves with others brings contentment into our lives. It's as simple as that.

Herbert Guenther defines ego as a "fictitious self." Here this fictitious self is being advised by wisdom mind to free itself and benefit others, by whatever means possible. If your neurotic tendency is to steal, turn stealing into benefit for others. In order to be free of covetousness, imaging stealing whatever your fictitious self is most attached to, and then giving that to those in need. This is a unique instruction for escaping the trap of self-centered grasping.

8.160

I indeed am happy, others sad;
I am high and mighty, others low;
I am helped while others are abandoned:
Why am I not jealous of myself?

8.161

Happiness, fulfillment: these I leave aside.
The pain of others: this I will embrace.
Inquiring of myself repeatedly,
I will become aware of all my faults.

8.162

When others are at fault, I'll take
And turn the blame upon myself.
And all my sins, however slight,
Confess, and make them known to many.

With these verses, we begin a section on directing all blame toward the cause of our misery: our neurotic self-absorption. Rather than blaming others for our unhappiness or blaming ourselves in a harsh, mean-spirited way, we take a clear, compassionate look at how self-centeredness ruins our chances of lasting happiness. Our relentless self-importance causes us to suffer far more than any other culprit.

8.163

The fame of others I will magnify
That it might thus outshine my own.
Among them I will be as one who serves,
My lowly labor for their benefit.

8.164

This ego is by nature rife with defects,
Its accidental talents I should hide, not praise.
Whatever qualities it has I will conceal,
That they remain unknown to everyone.

These verses could easily be misunderstood as guidelines for masochism. We need to be very clear that Shantideva is not advising us to denigrate ourselves. He is encouraging us to acknowledge the misery caused by our ego trips, and to use our innate wisdom to turn that around. Instead of generating self-loathing, this practice promotes confidence in our basic goodness. When driving all the blame into ego, it's important to keep this in mind.

8.165

All the harm, in short, my ego does
To its advantage and to others' cost,
May all of it descend upon itself,
To its own hurt—to others' benefit.

Shantideva wants his ego to experience all the harm it's selfishly caused others. This would certainly be a surefire method for curing our self-centered aggressive tendencies.

8.166

Do not let it strut about the place,
So arrogant, so overbearing.
But like a newly wedded bride,
Let it be demure and blushing, timorous
    and shy!

8.167

That's how it should be and stay!
And if it lapses, bring it forcibly to heel
With antidotes, and if these fail,
Well then, apply the lash!

Here Shantideva continues to refer to the self-centeredness of
ego and recommends the Geshe Ben approach. If gentle techniques aren't working for you, then be more forceful. Life is too
short to stay addicted to ego.

8.168

And so, O mind, if still you will refuse,
Though you have been so lengthily advised,
Since every evil has its roots in you,
You are indeed now ripe for punishment!

8.169

The time when you could do me harm
Is in the past, and now is here no more.
Now I see you! Where will you escape?
I'll bring you down, and all your haughty
    insolence.

"Your time is up!" the wisdom of buddha nature says to ego. "I'm not going to let old patterns keep bringing me down." If Shantideva's language—*ripe for punishment, apply the lash*— doesn't do it for you, then put this sentiment into your own words. But don't sweeten the message too much. Indulging in self-absorption is dangerous to our health.

At some point, we need to stop identifying with our weaknesses and shift our allegiance to our basic goodness. It's highly beneficial to understand that our limitations are not absolute and monolithic, but relative and removable. The wisdom of buddha nature is available to us at any time.

8.170

Every thought of working for myself
Is utterly rejected, cast aside.
"Now that you've been sold to others,
Stop your whining, be of service!"

Remember that! But when you say to yourself, *Stop your whining, be of service!* say it with a smile. Remember, too, that this is something you say to your sorrow-bearing ego, not to others.

8.171

For if, through being inattentive,
I do not deliver you to others,
You will hand me over, it is certain,
To the dreadful guardians of hell.

Because of our mindlessness and many kleshas, we often find ourselves in very familiar hot water. For best results, therefore, stay awake! The bodhisattva delights in resisting the seduction of self-absorption and in benefiting others.

8.172

For this is how so many times
You have betrayed me, and how long I've
    suffered!
Now my memory is full of rancor;
I will crush your selfish schemes!

Here we have an example of wrathful compassion. When this very abrupt, anger-against-anger approach is used skillfully as a tool of loving-kindness, it can be very helpful.

8.173

And so it is that if I want contentment,
I should never seek to please myself.
And likewise, if I wish to save myself,
I'll always be the guardian of others.

The line *I should never seek to please myself* refers to acting selfishly. Shantideva says that by benefiting others we will achieve personal contentment. The Dalai Lama calls this "wise selfishness." Foolish selfishness is not concerned with others' welfare and thus perpetuates our discontent.

8.174

To the extent this human form
Is cosseted and saved from hurt,
Just so, just so, to that degree,
It grows so sensitive and peevish.

8.175

For those who fall to such a state,
The earth itself and all it holds
Are powerless to satisfy.
For who can give them all they crave?

8.176

Their hopeless craving brings them misery,
And evil policies invade their minds.
While those with free, untrammeled hearts,
Will never know an end of excellence.

Shantideva makes the point that desires are endless. To think
that comfort and security could come from satisfying them is as
comical as trying to put out a fire by adding more wood.

8.177

Therefore, for the increase of my body's wants,
I'll give no space, no opportunity.
And of possessions, those things are the best
That do not captivate by their attractiveness.

Again, there is nothing wrong with possessions. The problem
lies in our addiction to them.

8.178

Dust and ashes are the body's final state,
This body which, inert, is moved by other forces.
This insupportable and unclean form—
Why do I regard it as my "I," my "self"?

The body *moved by other forces* refers to the body that is carried away after death. This body will fade away. It is not a permanent entity now, and it won't be when we die.

8.179

Alive or dead, what difference does it make?
What good to me is this machinery?
What difference will divide it from a clod of earth?
Oh, why not rid myself of this conceit of "self"?

Our body can, of course, be very useful, but not if we're obsessed with it. Hopefully this now familiar message is sinking in.

8.180

Through lavishing attention on this body,
Such sorrow have I brought myself so senselessly.
What use is all my wanting, all my hating—
For what indeed is like a log of wood?

By the time we die, we can get really good at all our wanting and hating. But to what end? Let's not wait until we're dying before we ask this question.

8.181

Whether I protect and pamper it,
Or whether it is torn by beaks of carrion birds,
This body feels no pleasure, no aversion—
Why then do I cherish it so much?

8.182

Resentment when it is reviled,
Or pleasure when it is esteemed,
Neither of these two the body feels—
So why do I exhaust myself?

8.183

Because of the appreciation, you will say,
That others, all my friends, will have of it.
They all appreciate the bodies that they have,
So why do I not like them as my own?

When people say, "You're looking so good, so radiant!" or, "You seem to have more wrinkles since last I saw you," we're drawn into joy or depression. Our fictitious self gets very worked up over a bit of praise or blame. *So why do I exhaust myself?* Shantideva asks in verse 182. Why do this to ourselves, our fleeting, momentary selves?

In verse 183, we have another familiar dialogue. We claim that we *protect and pamper* our body to bring delight to others. But if that's the case, why not protect and pamper their bodies? This would surely delight others as well.

8.184

Therefore, free from all attachment,
I will give this body for the benefit of beings;
Thus, though many blemishes afflict it,
I shall take it as my necessary tool.

8.185

And so, enough of all my childish ways.
I'll follow in the footsteps of the wise,

Recalling their advice on vigilance,
I'll shun all sleep and mental dullness.

Here Shantideva vows to take this body as his working basis, his *necessary tool*. When we do likewise and enthusiastically *follow in the footsteps of the wise*, it will serve us well and carry us to unsurpassable enlightenment.

8.186

Like the buddhas' heirs, in their compassion,
I will take the burden, all that should be borne.
For if I do not labor night and day,
When will all my sorrows have an end?

Trungpa Rinpoche often used the word *burden* in a positive sense. The great burden he felt to benefit sentient beings was one he carried joyfully. *To labor night and day* doesn't mean striving and struggling. It means persevering with the eagerness of an elephant diving into cool water, or with the delight of a swan descending on a lotus lake. Ultimately it means getting our priorities straight, so that everything is done with the intention of awakening the heart of bodhi.

8.187

Thus to banish all obscuring veils
I'll bend my mind from the mistaken path;
And constantly upon this perfect object
I shall rest my mind in even meditation.

Dedication

I N CHAPTER 10 of *The Way of the Bodhisattva*, Shanti-deva dedicates any merit he has accumulated from composing this text for the benefit of himself and all other beings. By reading these verses of dedication we can use his expert help to voice our own deepest wishes.

This is a simple yet profound way to engage in enlightened activity. At the end of any activity—a meal, a meeting, or a dharma teaching—we can make the aspiration that any benefit we've received be shared by others. We might think of one particular person who could use some help, or the men, women, and children living in war-torn countries, or all beings everywhere without exception.

I once asked Trungpa Rinpoche about sharing the merit at the end of a meal. Since I often ate mindlessly, it seemed a bit hypocritical to think I'd accumulated anything but further self-absorption. He replied that since I had the good fortune to have nourishing food, which I enjoyed in a safe and comfortable environment, I actually had plenty of good fortune to share.

He also reminded me of the three noble principles: good in the beginning, good in the middle, and good in the end. If we start an activity with the clear intention that it be of benefit, and if we continue with as open a mind as we can manage, then we will always have something to share at the end. Even if we become completely distracted from what we're doing, the clear aspiration we begin with transforms any action into bodhisattva activity.

Dedicating merit shifts our attitude. Instead of just focusing on ourselves, we start thinking beyond "me" and "mine." Remembering the distress and hardships of others, and that enlightenment is possible for everyone, opens us to a bigger perspective.

Dedicating merit also softens us. The suffering of all the people and animals we share this planet with becomes more real. They need help as much or more than we do. Even the ones we don't like and the ones we feel "got what they deserved" become the focus of dedication. These seemingly small gestures of love and concern can help heal the suffering of the world. The most significant step any one of us can make toward global peace is to soften what's rigid in our heart.

10.1

By all the virtue I have now amassed
By composition of this book, which speaks
Of entry to the bodhisattva way,
May every being tread the path to buddhahood.

Shantideva begins with this brief dedication. As a result of his commendable activity, he aspires for every being to have the chance to live the life of a bodhisattva: *May every being tread the path to buddhahood,* including those we currently feel don't deserve it.

The wish for all beings to awaken has two parts. One is the sincere longing that it happen sooner rather than later. The second is the growing confidence that this is not only possible but inevitable. The only question is whether we choose to slow down or speed up the process.

10.2

May beings everywhere who suffer
Torment in their minds and bodies
Have, by virtue of my merit,
Joy and happiness in boundless measure.

10.3

As long as they may linger in samsara,
May their present joy know no decline,
And may they taste of unsurpassed beatitude
In constant and unbroken continuity.

Shantideva makes aspirations for all beings in the six realms: By the virtue of his merit may people and animals who are suffering have physical comfort and mental joy *in boundless measure.* May they enjoy good health and other worldly benefits as well as the ultimate joy of realizing their true nature. When we share the merit, we can think of *all* people everywhere and wish them *unsurpassed beatitude,* not just for an afternoon, but forever. In other words, we think as big as possible.

10.4

Throughout the spheres and reaches of the
    world,
In hellish states wherever they may be,
May beings fettered there, tormented,
Taste the bliss and peace of Sukhavati.

First, Shantideva directs his compassion toward those suffering in hell. He wishes well even to those we consider despicable. The minds of beings who have done horrific things, very likely enjoying them thoroughly, project the hellish environments described here. This is the kind of scenario in which Hitler, Pol Pot, or serial killers might find themselves imprisoned.

One reason we're taught about the hell realms is to awaken our compassion. Another reason is to shake up our hard-hearted, conventional thinking. Generally, we're glad when abusers get what's coming to them. However, these aspirations mark a profound change in the way we see things. We realize that if the abusers of the world could awaken bodhichitta, cruelty would be impossible. The hell realms would be emptied, and our inhumanity to one another would cease.

Many of us may not feel ready to make this wish right now. We may be in a place where resentment or bitterness prevents us from making such aspirations for those we dislike or fear. I find it humbling that Shantideva holds no such grudges. I make the aspiration that eventually we may all be able to say these words: May those in hellish states *taste the bliss and peace* of perceiving the world with a clear and open mind. May they perceive the world as the pure land of Sukhavati.

10.5

May those caught in the freezing ice be warmed.
And from the massing clouds of bodhisattvas' prayers
May torrents rain in boundless streams
To cool those burning in infernal fires.

10.6

May forests where the leaves are blades and swords
Become sweet groves and pleasant woodland glades.

And may the trees of miracles appear,
Supplanting those upon the hill of shalmali.

10.7

And may the very pits of hell be sweet
With fragrant pools all perfumed with the scent
    of lotuses,
Be lovely with the cries of swan and goose
And water fowl so pleasing to the ear.

10.8

May fiery coals turn into heaps of jewels,
The burning ground become a crystal floor,
The crushing hills celestial abodes,
Adorned with offerings, the dwelling place of buddhas.

10.9

May the hail of lava, fiery stones, and weapons
Henceforth become a rain of blossom.
May those whose hell it is to fight and wound
Be turned to lovers offering their flowers.

10.10

And those engulfed in fiery Vaitarani,
Their flesh destroyed, their bones bleached white
    as kunda flowers,
May they, through all my merit's strength, have
    godlike forms,
And sport with goddesses in Mandakini's peaceful
    streams.

These verses refer to traditional descriptions of hell, where, similar to Dante's *Inferno*, the intensity of the suffering makes it seem endless. Whether it's the agony of cold hatred or hot hatred, Shantideva aspires that this agony be relieved.

How can hell beings come to have a shift in their hatred, a change in their aggression, a movement away from cruelty? How can a glimmer of tenderness awaken in their hearts? This rarely happens in the midst of incessant torment.

The key is the phrase *from the massing clouds of bodhisattvas' prayers.*

One reason these tortured beings can have a change of heart, as unlikely as it seems, is that bodhisattvas, even people like ourselves, make aspirations on their behalf. This is the power of directing our compassion toward those trapped in mindsets that are almost impossible to escape.

Affected by our aspirations, someone trapped in a closed-hearted, closed-minded reality might suddenly feel a glimmer of kindness, a glimmer of possibility for living some other way. This person might experience this as a refreshing change in her environment. Instead of being engulfed in rivers of fire, she might find herself in the *peaceful streams* of the Pure Land.

10.11

"What fear is it," they'll ask, "that grips the henchmen
    of the Deadly Lord, the frightful vultures and
    the carrion crows?
What noble strength is it that brings us joy and
    drives away our dreadful night?"
And looking skyward they will see the shining
    form of Vajrapani.
Then may their sins be quenched in joy, and may
    they go to him.

10.12

And when they see the seething lava-flood of hell
Extinguished in a rain of blossoms, drenched in
　　scented water,
At once fulfilled in bliss, they'll ask, "How can this be?"
And thus the denizens of hell will see the One Who
　　Holds the Lotus.

10.13

"Friends, throw away your fears and quickly
　　gather here.
For who is it who comes to banish dread, this youth
　　with bound up, gleaming hair,
This loving bodhisattva saving and protecting
　　every being,
Whose power relieves all pain, increasing joy?

10.14

"Do you see the splendor of his house that echoes
　　praises of a thousand goddesses,
The hundred gods who lay their diadems before his
　　lotus feet,
The rain of flowers falling on his head, his eyes moist
　　with compassion?"
Thus may those in hell cry out on seeing
　　Manjughosha.

10.15

And likewise when, through these my roots of virtue,
They see the joyful clouds let fall their cooling scented
　　rain,

> Their obscurations cleansed by bodhisattvas like
>   Samantabhadra,
> May all those languishing in hell come now to
>   perfect happiness.

Bodhisattvas enter into places of unspeakable darkness to help and inspire those living there. As a result, these tortured beings might well experience a newfound openness. It's not that our buddha nature disappears when we're in hell; it's just very hard to access. When bodhisattvas appear in our lives, they awaken our wisdom and compassion. Whether in hell or some lesser form of torment, something resonates with our inborn strength and goodness when we're with them.

10.16

> And may the stooping animals be freed
> From fear of being preyed upon, each other's food.
> And may the famished spirits have such joy
> As those who dwell within the northern continent.

10.17

> And may they be replete and satisfied
> By streams of milk that pour
> From noble Lord Avalokita's hand,
> And bathing in it, may they be refreshed and cooled.

The first lines of verse 16 address the fear and suffering of animals. The next lines, along with verse 17, refer to the hungry ghost realm, where beings are tormented by a hunger and thirst that can never be satisfied.

According to ancient Indian mythology, *the northern continent* is called Uttarakuru, a place of great harmony and peace. We live in the southern continent, called Jambudvipa, which is less harmonious and peaceful but still not a bad place to be born. Having addressed the suffering of the lower realms, Shantideva now shows compassion for human beings, such as you and me. He enumerates our woes and makes the wish that they all might end: may all of us be free of suffering and the causes of suffering.

10.18

And may the blind receive their sight,
And may the deaf begin to hear,
And women near their time bring forth
Like Mayadevi, free from any pain.

10.19

And may the naked now be clothed,
And all the hungry eat their fill.
And may those parched with thirst receive
Pure waters and delicious drink.

10.20

May the poor and destitute find wealth,
The haggard and the careworn, joy.
May confidence relieve those in despair
And bring them steadfastness and every excellence.

10.21

May every being ailing with disease
Be freed at once from every malady.
May all the sickness that afflicts the living
Be instantly and permanently healed.

10.22

May those who go in dread have no more fear.
May captives be unchained and now set free.
And may the weak receive their strength.
May living beings help each other in kindness.

10.23

May travelers upon the road
Find happiness no matter where they go,
And may they gain, without the need of toil,
The goals on which they set their hearts.

10.24

May those who put to sea in boat or ship
Attain the ports that they desire,
And may they safely come to shore
And sweet reunion with their kith and kin.

10.25

May those who lose their way and stray
In misery, find fellow travelers,
And safe from threat of thieves and savage beasts,
Be tireless, and their journey light.

10.26

May children and the old, the weak, protectorless,
Bewildered in the wild and pathless wastes,
And those whose minds are dulled, and all who are
    insane,
Have pure celestial beings as their guardians.

Shantideva aspires that all the people he can possibly think of be comfortable and at their ease. By thinking this way, genuinely and from the heart, the one making the aspiration is as blessed as those for whom it's being made. You may ask why this is so. By feeling empathy and loving-kindness for others, we are softened and changed. In this way both giver and receiver are deeply benefited.

Studies have shown that aspirations and prayers *do* have a positive effect on people. Even if you're a skeptic, just make your wish with the hope that those you have in mind receive this blessing. Then you, too, will definitely benefit from doing this practice of dedication.

10.27

May all attain the human state,
And be possessed of wisdom, faith, and love.
With perfect livelihood and sustenance,
May they have mindfulness throughout
    their lives.

10.28

May everyone have unrestricted wealth,
Just like the treasury of space,
Enjoying it according to their wish,
Without a trace of harm or enmity.

The aspiration *may everyone have unrestricted wealth* could be a dangerous one. Shantideva therefore adds an important stipulation: without it creating enmity toward anyone or triggering selfishness, greed, or meanness, may all beings have their needs fulfilled.

10.29

May beings destitute of splendor,
Become magnificent and bright.
And those worn down by toil and drudgery
Acquire great beauty and perfection.

10.30

May all the women in this world
Attain the strength of masculinity.
And may the lowly come to excellence,
The proud and haughty lose their
    arrogance.

May those who are exhausted by their work be restored to health and beauty. May the downcast be uplifted and the arrogant find humility, and may *women attain the strength of masculinity*.

To understand this last line, we have to know the context in which Shantideva was teaching. To be born a woman in eighth-century India was not an asset. Even if you were wealthy, you were valued little more than a work animal—and often treated worse. If you had spiritual aspirations to practice the dharma, your gender was a great hindrance. Even today, nuns in parts of Southeast Asia are treated very badly; because of cultural prejudice, nobody feeds them or takes care of their needs.

This is the kind of inequity that Shantideva is addressing. His aspiration is for women to be relieved of this injustice and the pain it causes, and for them to be born into a situation free of prejudice.

The message here is highly compassionate. If we suffer from any prejudice—such as gender, race, or religion—may we escape that injustice, with all its inevitable difficulties and obstacles.

10.31

And thus by all the merit I have gained,
May every being, leaving none aside,
Abandon all their evil ways
Embracing goodness now and ever more.

10.32

From bodhichitta may they never separate,
And constantly engage in bodhisattva deeds.
And may they be accepted as disciples by the buddhas,
And turn aside from what is demons' work.

In these two verses, there is a shift. In previous and later verses, Shantideva wishes that our outer circumstances be comfortable and supportive. Here, he wishes us spiritual inspiration as well. The bodhisattva's challenge is to work through every last prejudice and bias. Then the power of our aspiration can influence all living beings in the most positive way possible.

10.33

And may these beings, each and every one,
Enjoy an unsurpassed longevity.
Living always in contentment,
May the very name of death be strange to them.

10.34

On every side, in all the ten directions,
May groves of wish-fulfilling trees abound,
Resounding with the sweetness of the Teachings,
Spoken by the buddhas and their bodhisattva children.

10.35

And may the earth be wholesome everywhere,
Free from boulders, cliffs, and chasms,
Flat and even like a level palm
And smooth like lapis lazuli.

10.36

And for many circles of disciples,
May multitudes of bodhisattvas
Rise in every land,
Adorning them with every excellence.

10.37

From bird song and the sighing of the trees,
From shafts of light and from the sky itself,
May living beings, each and every one,
Perceive the constant sound of Dharma.

10.38

May they come into the presence of the buddhas,
And meet with bodhisattvas, offspring of the same.
With clouds of offerings unbounded,
May the teachers of the world be worshiped.

10.39

May kindly spirits bring the rains on time,
For harvests to be rich and plentiful.
May princes rule according to the Truth,
And may the world be blessed with all prosperity.

May there be good governments. May we have an enlightened society, whose rulers have everyone's best interest in mind.

10.40

May medicines be strong and full of virtue;
May healing spells be chanted with success.
May spirits of the air that feed on flesh
Be kind, their minds imbued with pity.

10.41

And let no being ever suffer pain;
Let them neither ail nor languish, never doing evil.
May they have no fear, nor suffer insults,
And may their minds be ever free from sorrow.

The following few verses are specifically dedicated to monks and nuns, Shantideva's sangha brothers and sisters.

10.42

In monasteries, temples, and the like,
May reading and reciting widely flourish.
May harmony prevail among the Sangha,
And may its purpose be all fulfilled.

10.43

May ordained monks intent upon the practice
Find perfect places for retreat in solitude,
Abandon every vagrant thought,
And meditate with trained and serviceable minds.

10.44

May nuns have all their wants supplied;
May quarreling, vindictiveness be strange to them.
Let all who have embraced monastic life
Uphold a pure and unimpaired observance.

10.45

May they feel regret when discipline is broken,
And always may they strive to cleanse away their faults.
May they thus obtain a fortunate rebirth,
Wherein to undertake unfailing discipline.

Shantideva aspires for wisdom to flourish in the monasteries; for the monastics to live harmoniously together; for their purpose of benefiting others to be fulfilled; and for all their necessities to be supplied. Finally, he aspires that the monastic sangha always keep their vows. As one who lives in a monastery myself, I know how important all these things are to the daily well-being of a monk or nun.

10.46

May the wise and learned be revered
And always be sustained by offerings.
With minds suffused with purity,
May their renown spread far and wide.

10.47

May beings never languish in the lower realms;
May pain and hardship be unknown to them.
Enjoying more than godlike strength and beauty,
May buddhahood for them be swiftly gained.

10.48

Again and yet again may sentient beings
Make offerings to all the buddhas.
And with Buddha's unimagined bliss
May they enjoy undimmed and constant
    happiness.

10.49

May all the bodhisattvas now fulfill
Their high intention for the sake of beings,
And sentient beings likewise now receive
The good the buddhas have in store for them.

10.50

And may the arhats and pratyekabuddhas
At length attain their perfect happiness.

Our greatest suffering is sometimes caused by rejecting kindness and support. We may perceive this help as negative or suspicious and, because of our paranoia, be unable to benefit from it. This is almost a definition of being in a lower realm. Shantideva wishes that sentient beings be open enough to receive all blessings and good fortune.

10.51

And may I also, through Manjushri's kindness,
Reach the ground of Perfect Joy,
And throughout the stream of all my lives
Embrace monastic ordination.

10.52

Thus may I abide, sustained
By simple, ordinary fare.
And in every life obtain
A dwelling place in perfect solitude.

10.53

Whenever I desire to gaze on him
Or put to him the slightest question,
May I behold the unobstructed vision
Of Manjughosha, my protector.

10.54

To satisfy the needs of beings
Dwelling in the ten directions, to the margins
    of the sky,
May I reflect in every deed
The perfect exploits of Manjushri.

Our own happiness is sometimes the hardest thing to wish for. But in these verses, Shantideva dedicates the merit for his own well-being. In verse 51, he aspires to have a direct experience of emptiness. This is traditionally called the realization of the first bhumi, *the ground of Perfect Joy.*

10.55

And now as long as space endures,
As long as there are beings to be found,
May I continue likewise to remain
To drive away the sorrows of the world.

10.56

The pains and sorrows of all wandering beings—
May they ripen wholly on myself.
And may the virtuous company of bodhisattvas
Bring about the happiness of beings.

Verse 55 is said to be a favorite of the Dalai Lama. It summarizes better than any other stanza the longing and spirit of the bodhisattva path.

An example of the kind of thinking expressed in verse 56 is the practice of *tonglen*.

10.57

May the Doctrine, only remedy for suffering,
The source of every bliss and happiness,
Be nurtured and upheld with reverence,
And throughout a vast continuance of time, endure!

The Buddhist teachings have endured for over twenty-five hundred years. They lasted until the eighth century, so Shantideva could benefit from them; and they lasted from the eighth century until now, maybe because of aspirations like this. The Buddha taught, however, that everything is impermanent and that even his teachings will be lost. Hearing this makes me think we'd be wise to make good use of them while they last.

10.58

And now to Manjughosha I prostrate,
Whose kindness is the wellspring of my good intent.
And to my virtuous friends I also bow,
Whose inspiration gave me strength to grow.

This last verse is a recollection of the kindness of the bodhisattvas and spiritual friends who've helped us on the path—a final expression of gratitude and veneration. According to tradition, it is said three times.

• • •

This concludes chapter 10 and brings us to the end of Shantideva's teachings. May you find these teachings as inspiring and supportive as I have and use them to inform your life.

Although composed long ago, these instructions could make a significant difference in how each of us works with the challenges of these times. They could help us realize our full potential and support us in becoming peacemakers: effective, responsible, and compassionate citizens in a turbulent world.

We can consider Shantideva's words as pith instructions for working with difficulties still to come. If learning to not make matters worse isn't a skill we all need to develop rapidly, I don't know what is. And Shantideva doesn't stop there. He gives us precise teachings on how to develop compassion for even our "enemies" and how to foster love instead of hatred.

Trungpa Rinpoche devoted the last years of his life to giving teachings for creating an enlightened society, calling these "Shambhala Vision." This lineage of teachings is still being presented today by his son, Sakyong Mipham Rinpoche. The message is simple yet profound. We all have the inborn wisdom to create a wholesome, uplifted existence for ourselves and others. Shantideva's words further support this message. We can think beyond our own little cocoon and try to help this troubled world. Not only will our friends and family benefit, but even our "enemies" will reap the blessings of peace.

If these teachings make sense to us, can we commit to them? In these times, do we really have a choice? Do we have the option of living in unconscious self-absorption? When the stakes are so high, do we have the luxury of dragging our feet? In the spirit of friendship, as members of the same family and passengers on the same boat, I share these concerns with you. May these teachings help each of us to make a difference. Following the example of my teachers and Shantideva himself, I wish us all good fortune—and good luck!

> May bodhichitta, precious and sublime,
> Arise where it has not yet come to be;
> And where it has arisen may it not decline,
> But grow and flourish ever more and more.

Acknowledgments

MY PRIMARY INSPIRATION comes as always from my teachers: the Vidyadhara Chögyam Trungpa Rinpoche; His Holiness the Sixteenth Karmapa; the Seventeenth Karmapa, His Holiness Ogyen Trinley Dorje; His Holiness Dilgo Khyentse Rinpoche; Venerable Thrangu Rinpoche; Sakyong Mipham Rinpoche; and my principal teacher at this time, Venerable Dzigar Kongtrul Rinpoche.

The writings of His Holiness the Dalai Lama have done more to familiarize the general public with Shantideva than any other teachings. I am indebted to his commentaries and especially to his book *Healing Anger,* which gives line-by-line instruction on the sixth chapter of *The Way of the Bodhisattva.* The oral teachings of Venerable Dzongsar Khyentse Rinpoche on chapters 1 through 7 were a primary source of information and inspiration. I also relied heavily for chapter 1 on the commentaries of Khenpo Kunpal and Khenpo Choga, translated by Andreas Kretschmar.

In my studies, I have referred repeatedly to the various translations of this text and would like to especially thank the Padmakara Translation Group. The introduction to the Padmakara translation was particularly helpful. I have also consulted transcripts of teachings given by Venerable Ponlop Rinpoche at Gampo Abbey. I would also like to express gratitude to Kokai Roberts, whose teachings on chapter 6 were a major influence, and to Tim Olmsted, for his excellent teachings on chapter 8.

Finally, my heartfelt appreciation to all the good people who worked so hard to bring this book to fruition: Gigi Sims, who transcribed my oral teachings; Sue Keeley, who typed, researched, traveled, and encouraged; Warner Keeley, who compiled the glossary; Clare Ming, Glenna Olmsted, and Margaret Jones Callahan, who typed the manuscript; Helen Tworkov, whose valuable insights considerably improved the manuscript; Eden Steinberg of Shambhala Publications for her suggestions and support; and finally, my editor, Helen Berliner, who did the heroic job of creating a finished book from the original transcripts.

Appendix

STUDY GUIDELINES

HERE ARE SOME SUGGESTIONS for studying *The Way of the Bodhisattva* alone or in a group.

Reading Out Loud

Traditionally *The Way of the Bodhisattva* is read out loud. This is done so that it can be heard by as many sentient beings as possible, including children going off to school, the squirrels and dogs, and all the little bugs. They may not truly hear it now, but it may seep into their pores and somehow affect them in a positive way.

Patrul Rinpoche frequently taught outside, and the text would be read so that all the birds and animals and anyone passing by could hear and benefit from it. That's the general idea. It's the attitude of opening your doors to all sentient beings.

Memorizing

As you read each chapter, try to memorize at least one stanza. You can write it down on an index card and put it up where you can see it. Say it over and over until you remember it. This will definitely be of benefit.

Journaling

Whether you're in a group or individual study situation, it is helpful to keep a notebook where you can record your experience of a particular stanza. For example, after reading or memorizing a verse, just walk around with it for awhile. See what it means to you and write that down, even if it's brief. Later, after you've gone to a class or discussion group, or just lived with it a bit longer, you might want to write more. The life experience of just a day or two can be significant.

Dedicating the Merit

If you wish to, when you finish a session of reading, you can conclude by dedicating the merit of your study. One way to do this is to chant one or more verses of dedication from Shantideva's tenth chapter. The verses of dedication can then be followed by the visualization practice below.

A Visualization for Ending a Session of Study

After dedicating the merit, you could end with the following visualization. With eyes closed, visualize in front of you the text of Shantideva's *The Way of the Bodhisattva*. It can be in the form of this book or a traditional text wrapped in cloth. You can regard this as an embodiment of compassion, loving-kindness, and wisdom. The text also represents your longing to alleviate your own suffering, so that you can do your part to alleviate the suffering of the world.

Seeing this in front of you, visualize that the book turns into light. You can imagine this any way you wish. The light radiates out and then dissolves into you. You can imagine that it fills your body and makes you feel very happy, which is to say, you actually feel the bodhichitta qualities of love, compassion, and an open, unfettered heart and mind. End by radiating this light out to everybody in your immediate space and then to all beings in your town, state, country, and the whole world.

Glossary

ALL CROSS-REFERENCES appear in small capitals. The abbreviation "Skt." stands for Sanskrit and "Tib." stands for Tibetan.

ARHAT (Skt.) A practitioner at the highest stage of spiritual attainment on the foundation *yana* (or hinayana) path. *See also* YANAS, THREE.

BHUMIS, TEN (Skt.) Each of the ten stages that the bodhisattva must go through to attain Buddhahood: perfect joy, stainless, luminous, radiant, difficult to conquer, face-to-face, far-reaching, immovable, having good intellect, and cloud of dharma.

BODHICHITTA (Skt.) Awakened heart or mind. Relative bodhichitta is our aspiration and perseverance to become awakened so we can be of benefit to all suffering beings. Absolute bodhichitta is our awakened mind, free from concepts, that sees the emptiness of all phenomena.

CHARNEL GROUND Historically, charnel grounds were places in ancient India where dead bodies were left to be devoured by wild animals. In contemporary society, a charnel ground could be anywhere that does not hide the truth of suffering and therefore has a desperate, hopeless, or terrifying quality. Bodhisattvas are not afraid of these situations and are inspired to work with such chaos.

DHARMA (Skt.) Generally speaking, dharma is any truth, norm, or law. From the Buddhist point of view, Dharma refers to the teachings of the historical Buddha, Shakyamuni. Also referred to as buddhadharma.

KLESHAS (Skt.) Sometimes translated as "neurosis," "afflictions," or "defiled emotions." Strong emotions that reliably lead to suffering: aggression, craving, ignorance, jealousy, arrogance, pride, and all their offspring.

MAHAYANA BUDDHISM The "great vehicle" of bodhisattvas. This path emphasizes the practice of compassion and cultivation of the wisdom of emptiness, the ultimate nature of self and all phenomena. With the motivation to deliver all beings from the suffering of the unenlightened state, it leads to the attainment of buddhahood for the sake of others. Mahayana Buddhism flourished in the northern Asian countries of China, Korea, Japan, Mongolia, and Tibet. *See also* YANAS, THREE.

NIDANA(S) (Skt.) The twelve links that form the chain of conditioned arising: (1) ignorance, (2) formations or impulses, (3) consciousness, (4) name and form, (5) the six realms of the senses, (6) contact, (7) sensation, (8) craving, (9) clinging, (10) becoming, (11) birth, and (12) old age and death.

PARAMITA(S) (Skt.) The six practices of the mahayana path: generosity, discipline, patience, exertion or enthusiasm, meditation, and wisdom. They are called "transcendent" because they carry us across the river of confused existence to "the other shore" of enlightenment.

RINPOCHE (Tib.) An honorific meaning "precious one"; a title given to revered teachers of Tibetan Buddhism.

SAMSARA (Skt.) The vicious cycle of suffering caused by a constant search for security.

SANGHA (Skt.) The community of the followers of the Buddhist path.

SHAMATHA (Skt.) "Calm abiding" meditation. One of the two main Buddhist meditation practices, *shamatha* focuses on calming the mind and developing mindfulness.

SHENPA (Tib.) Usually translated as "attachment" or "fixation," it is the nonconceptual feeling of being hooked; it is the charge behind emotions, and more fundamentally, the charge behind the sense of "me."

SHRAVAKA(S) (Skt.) Literally, "hearers." Those who hear the Buddha's first-turning (hinayana) teachings and apply them to their lives, with a focus on individual liberation. *See also* YANAS, THREE.

SIX REALMS According to Buddhist teachings, these are six broad categories of experience into which samsaric beings are born as a result of past karma, or actions. In the three "lower realms" of animals, hungry ghosts, and hells, suffering predominates. In the three "higher realms" of the mundane gods, *asuras* or demigods, and human beings, suffering is mitigated by temporal pleasures.

SUTRA(S) (Skt.) Buddhist sutras refer to the teachings attributed to Shakyamuni Buddha. These took the form of discourses and dialogues with students.

TONGLEN (Tib.) Sending and taking practice. A meditation practice that develops equanimity and compassion by taking in the suffering of others, and giving away all that is positive and good.

YANAS, THREE (Skt.) The three developmental stages, or "vehicles," for traveling the road to enlightenment, known in Tibetan Buddhism as "hinayana," or foundation *yana*, "mahayana," and "vajrayana." Each has a specific view of the journey and a specific body of knowledge and practice.

Bibliography

Translations & Commentaries

Batchelor, Stephen, trans. *A Guide to the Bodhisattva's Way of Life.* Dharamsala: Library of Tibetan Works and Archives, 1979. Few notes; but elegant, poetic language and an extensive analysis of chapter 9, the "wisdom chapter."

Crosby, Kate, and Andrew Skilton, trans. *The Bodhicharyavatara: The Guide to the Buddhist Path to Awakening.* Birmingham, England: Windhorse, 2002. This is a reprint of the acclaimed 1995 Oxford University Press edition. Extensive scholarly notes.

Dalai Lama. *A Flash of Lightning in the Dark of Night.* Boston: Shambhala Publications, 1994. An abbreviated commentary on the entire text.

———. *Healing Anger.* Ithaca: Snow Lion Publications, 1997. This is a commentary on the sixth (patience) chapter only.

———. *Transcendent Wisdom: A Commentary on the Ninth Chapter of Shantideva's Guide to the Bodhisattva Way of Life.* Trans. B. Alan Wallace. Ithaca: Snow Lion Publications, 1988.

Elliott, Neil, trans. *Guide to the Bodhisattva's Way of Life: A Buddhist Poem for Today.* Ulverston and Glen Spey: Tharpa Publications, 2002. A clear translation with an excellent glossary and few buzzwords.

Padmakara Translation Group, trans. *The Way of the Bodhisattva.* Boston: Shambhala Publications, 1997. A beautiful, authoritative translation, with extensive explanatory notes and background material. (This is the translation of the text used in this book.)

Wallace, Vesna A., and B. Alan Wallace, trans. *A Guide to the Bodhisattva Way of Life.* Ithaca: Snow Lion Publications, 1997. A prose translation with a brief introduction and translators' notes.

Related Readings

Chögyam Trungpa Rinpoche. *Cutting Through Spiritual Materialism.* Berkeley: Shambhala Publications, 1973. See particularly the section called "Styles of Imprisonment" for a description of hell as a psychological state.

———. *Training the Mind and Cultivating Loving-Kindness.* Boston: Shambhala Publications, 2003. An excellent companion to *The Way of the Bodhisattva.*

Dzigar Kongtrul Rinpoche. *It's Up to You.* Boston: Shambhala Publications, 2005.

Pema Chödrön. *The Places That Scare You.* Boston: Shambhala Publications, 1997. Gives pertinent practices that complement *The Way of the Bodhisattva.*

Sakyong Mipham Rinpoche. *Turning the Mind into an Ally.* New York: Riverhead Books, 2003. Clear teachings on how to meditate; a helpful companion to chapter 5 of *The Way of the Bodhisattva.*

Audiotapes

Chögyam Trungpa Rinpoche, with Ösel Tendzin. *The Way of the Bodhisattva.* A nine-talk seminar on Shantideva's text, Naropa Institute, Boulder, Colo., June 1980. Covers such topics as the bodhisattva vow and mahayana practices. Available from Shambhala Shop. Website: *www.shambhalashop.com.*

Dzongsar Khyentse Rinpoche. *The Way of the Bodhisattva.* A thirty-one-audiotape commentary on Shantideva's text. From Siddhartha's

Intent, 486 West 26th Avenue, Vancouver, B.C., Canada, V5Y 2K2. Website: *www.siddharthasintent.org.* E-mail: Siddhartha@sprynet.com.

Pema Chödrön. *The Way of the Bodhisattva.* A twelve-talk commentary (sixteen audiotapes) on the first eight chapters, given at Gampo Abbey, 2001. (Also available in transcript form.) Great Path Tapes and Books, 330 E. Van Hoesen, Portage, MI 49002. (269) 384-4167.Website: *www.pemachodrontapes.org.* E-mail: gptapes@aol.com.

―――. *The Excellence of Bodhichitta,* a weekend program at Karmê Chöling, Vermont, May 2002. An in-depth teaching on the first chapter of *The Way of the Bodhisattva,* and an excellent introduction to the practice of *tonglen.* Also available in transcript form. Great Path Tapes and Books, 330 E. Van Hoesen, Portage, MI 49002. (269) 384-4167. Website: *www.pemachodrontapes.org.* E-mail: gptapes@aol.com.

―――. *City Retreat II: Transforming Confusion into Wisdom,* Berkeley, Cal., 1999. Covers the *lojong* ("mind training") slogans, plus *tonglen,* equality practice, transforming painful circumstances into the path, and extending *lojong* to one's whole life. These practices complement Shantideva's text. Great Path Tapes and Books, 330 E. Van Hoesen, Portage, MI 49002. (269) 384-4167. Website: *www.pemachodrontapes.org.* E-mail: gptapes@aol.com.

―――. *City Retreat III: The Four Limitless Qualities,* Berkeley, Cal., 2001. Highly recommended overview of the four limitless qualities of loving kindness, compassion, joy, and equanimity. Guided loving kindness meditation, bodhichitta and compassion, the power of attention, three methods for dissolving stuckness, working with upheavals and the practice of equanimity, and continuing practice in everyday life. These practices complement Shantideva's text. Great Path Tapes and Books, 330 E. Van Hoesen, Portage, MI 49002. (269) 384-4167. Website: *www.pemachodrontapes.org.* E-mail: gptapes@aol.com.

―――. *The Bodhisattva's Way of Life,* Berkeley, Cal., 2002–2004. Pema Chödrön's oral commentary on Shantideva's *Bodhicharyavatara, the Way of the Bodhisattva.* Also available in transcript form. Great Path Tapes and Books, 330 E. Van Hoesen, Portage, MI 49002. (269) 384-4167. Website: *www.pemachodrontapes.org.* E-mail: gptapes@aol.com.

Other Transcripts

Andreas Kretschmar, trans. *Bodhisattva-charyavatara, Entering the Conduct of the Bodhisattvas,* accompanied by a translation of *Drops of Nectar.* This is a translation of an important commentary on Shantideva's text by Khenpo Kunpal (a direct student of Patrul Rinpoche), with further elaboration by Khenpo Choga's oral commentary. All texts and commentaries have been presented by the translator as a gift of dharma. English text is edited by Judith S. Amtzis. Website: *www.kunpal.com.*

Index

Resources

For information about meditation instruction or to find a practice center near you, please contact one of the following:

SHAMBHALA MEDITATION CENTERS
1084 Tower Road
Halifax, NS b3h 2y5
Canada
www.shambhala.org

SHAMBHALA EUROPE
Kartäuserwall 20
50678 Köln
Germany
www.shambhala-europe.org

KARMÊ CHÖLING
369 Patneaude Lane
Barnet, VT 05821
www.karmecholing.org

SHAMBHALA MOUNTAIN CENTER
151 Shambhala Way
Red Feather Lakes, CO 80545
www.shambhalamountain.org

GAMPO ABBEY
Pleasant Bay
Cape Breton, NS boe 2p0
Canada
www.gampoabbey.org

Naropa University is the only accredited, Buddhist-inspired university in North America. For more information, contact:

NAROPA UNIVERSITY
2130 Arapahoe Avenue
Boulder, CO 80302
www.naropa.edu

Audio and video recordings of talks and seminars by Pema Chödrön are available from:

THE PEMA CHÖDRÖN FOUNDATION
PO Box 770630
Steamboat Springs, CO 80477
www.pemachodronfoundation.com

KALAPA RECORDINGS
1084 Tower Road
Halifax, NS b3h 2y5
Canada
www.shambhalamedia.org

Heart Advice: Weekly Quotes from Pema Chödrön

Visit shambhala.com/pemaheartadvice to sign up for Heart Advice and receive weekly words of wisdom from Pema Chödrön.